Separation of Powers, the Judiciary and the Politics of Constitutional Adjudication

Over the last 25 years, the doctrine of separation of powers has been established as both a foundational value and a structural principle applied by the courts in interpreting the relationship between South Africa's constitutional structures. Jurisprudentially, the practicalities and contours of how, when and by whom the separation of powers should be determined has proven to be controversial. Therefore, the past decade has been characterised by heightened political contestation, often resulting in extensive litigation posing thorny political issues. This has had profound implications for the judiciary and raised difficult questions on the very nature of South African constitutionalism.

These political contestations gathered even greater momentum and urgency during the early days of COVID-19 in 2020, when the first iteration of this book was produced as a special issue of the *South African Journal on Human Rights*. This timely volume brings together critical reflections on developments in South Africa's separation of powers jurisprudence and theory, the role and function of the judiciary in shaping the landscape of constitutional politics through its judgments, as well the implications of this for the consolidation of South Africa's democratic constitutional project. It makes an important contribution to the debate on the politics of constitutional adjudication in light of the doctrine of separation of powers. This book will be of interest to researchers and advanced students of politics, history, law and legal theory, human rights, and African studies.

Sanele Sibanda is a senior lecturer in the Department of Jurisprudence, Faculty of Law, University of Pretoria, South Africa. He is a critical scholar who teaches and researches in the areas of constitutionalism, jurisprudence, constitutional law and theory, and Indigenous law. He is an editor of the *South African Journal of Human Rights*. He holds a PhD degree from the University of the Witwatersrand.

Separation of Powers, the Judiciary and the Politics of Constitutional Adjudication

Edited by
Sanele Sibanda

Routledge
Taylor & Francis Group
LONDON AND NEW YORK

First published 2023
by Routledge
4 Park Square, Milton Park, Abingdon, Oxon OX14 4RN

and by Routledge
605 Third Avenue, New York, NY 10158

Routledge is an imprint of the Taylor & Francis Group, an informa business

British Library Cataloguing in Publication Data
A catalogue record for this book is available from the British Library

ISBN13: 978-1-032-32975-8 (hbk)
ISBN13: 978-1-032-32976-5 (pbk)
ISBN13: 978-1-003-31758-6 (ebk)

DOI: 10.4324/9781003317586

Typeset in Minion Pro
by Newgen Publishing UK

Publisher's Note
The publisher accepts responsibility for any inconsistencies that may have arisen during the conversion of this book from journal articles to book chapters, namely the inclusion of journal terminology.

Contents

Citation Information vi
Notes on Contributors viii

1 Introduction 1
Sanele Sibanda

2 Separation of powers and the institutional supremacy of the Constitutional Court over Parliament and the executive 7
Felix Dube

3 The judicialisation of politics in South Africa: A critique of the emerging trend 33
Hoolo Nyane

4 Esoteric decision-making: Judicial responses to the judicialisation of politics, the Constitutional Court and *EFF II* 52
Lauren Gildenhuys

5 Are judicial monitoring institutions a legitimate remedy for addressing systemic socioeconomic rights violations? 76
Ropafadzo Maphosa

6 Designing remedies for a recalcitrant administration 100
Gaurav Mukherjee and Juha Tuovinen

Index 124

Citation Information

The chapters in this book were originally published in the *South African Journal on Human Rights*, volume 36, issue 4 (2020). When citing this material, please use the original page numbering for each article, as follows:

Chapter 1

Introduction to special issue: Separation of powers, the judiciary and the politics of constitutional adjudication
Sanele Sibanda
South African Journal on Human Rights, volume 36, issue 4 (2020), pp. 287–292

Chapter 2

Separation of powers and the institutional supremacy of the Constitutional Court over Parliament and the executive
Felix Dube
South African Journal on Human Rights, volume 36, issue 4 (2020), pp. 293–318

Chapter 3

The judicialisation of politics in South Africa: A critique of the emerging trend
Hoolo Nyane
South African Journal on Human Rights, volume 36, issue 4 (2020), pp. 319–337

Chapter 4

Esoteric decision-making: Judicial responses to the judicialisation of politics, the Constitutional Court and EFF II
Lauren Gildenhuys
South African Journal on Human Rights, volume 36, issue 4 (2020), pp. 338–361

Chapter 5

Are judicial monitoring institutions a legitimate remedy for addressing systemic socioeconomic rights violations?
Ropafadzo Maphosa
South African Journal on Human Rights, volume 36, issue 4 (2020), pp. 362–385

Chapter 6

Designing remedies for a recalcitrant administration
Gaurav Mukherjee and Juha Tuovinen
South African Journal on Human Rights, volume 36, issue 4 (2020), pp. 386–409

Notes on Contributors

Felix Dube, is a postdoctoral fellow attached to the South African Research Chair in Cities, Law and Environmental Sustainability (CLES), Faculty of Law, North-West University, South Africa.

Lauren Gildenhuys, is a practising attorney with an interest in constitutional law and judicial politics.

Ropafadzo Maphosa, is a researcher at the South African Institute for Advanced Constitutional, Public, Human Rights and International Law, a centre of the University of Johannesburg.

Gaurav Mukherjee, is an SJD candidate in comparative constitutional law at Central European University, Budapest/Vienna.

Hoolo Nyane, is an associate professor of public law and head of the Public and Environmental Law Department at University of Limpopo, South Africa.

Sanele Sibanda, is a senior lecturer in the Department of Jurisprudence at the Faculty of Law, University of Pretoria, South Africa.

Juha Tuovinen, is a Postdoctoral Researcher at Aarhus University, Denmark.

Introduction

Sanele Sibanda

This special issue of the *South African Journal on Human Rights* arises from a general call for papers that was issued in October 2019. The special issue has come to fruition in circumstances that none of us could ever have imagined at the time of its conceptualisation. No one imagined that within six months from that date a health pandemic would sweep across the world, plunging humanity into crisis and bringing life to a virtual standstill while simultaneously redefining the norms of human movement, interaction and exchange. Indeed, the impact of Covid-19 and the regulations taken in order to protect public health were felt everywhere, including our editorial processes.

While the pandemic brought death, despair and upheaval and disrupted the order of social, political, cultural, economic and religious life as we know it, questions around the involvement of the courts and the judiciary in the nation's political contestations became more pronounced. Rather than abating, in line with the slowness induced by the pandemic, these political contestations gathered greater momentum and urgency. For example, as I write this introduction, the number of politically charged matters being litigated or headed towards litigation continues to accumulate, further heightening the inter- and intra-branch tensions between constitutional structures. At the time the special issue was being conceptualised, our collective frame of reference was informed by the Jacob Zuma presidency and characterised by an increase in civil society and political actors involved in disputes turning to the courts to resolve what were clearly political controversies.

Little has changed in that the accumulation of politically charged cases involving former president Zuma, persons thought to be associated with him and, more generally, the governing African National Congress (ANC) continues. The pinnacle point in this respect, at the time of writing, is the Constitutional Court case emanating from the Zondo Commission on State Capture in which the former president has been found guilty of the crime of contempt of court and sentenced to an effective 15-month term of imprisonment.[1]

There are, of course, other matters not involving Zuma that have been equally mired in political controversy. Profound questions have been raised concerning the separation of powers doctrine and where the lines should be drawn under our system of constitutional

---

[1] *Secretary of the Judicial Commission of Inquiry into Allegations of State Capture, Corruption and Fraud in the Public Sector including Organs of State v Zuma* (CCT 52/21) [2021] ZACC 18.

supremacy, especially with respect to the court's remedial powers.[2] Whether one believes it was the Zuma presidency that fuelled the pace at which the judicialisation of politics occurred in South Africa or whether it is a natural consequence of a strong model of judicial review under a regime of constitutional supremacy, the arrival of this special issue makes an important contribution to the debate on the politics of constitutional adjudication in light of the doctrine of separation of powers.

Much literature in South African constitutional scholarship has considered the doctrine of separation of powers; it is accepted as axiomatic within our constitutional system. Over the last 25 years, the South African courts have expounded on the doctrine on numerous occasions, making decisions and crafting remedies primarily in terms of its logics. Thus, much like the rule of law, the separation of powers has emerged as a constitutional doctrine, foundational value and justiciable legal principle that is potentially implicated in every case where the courts interpret relations between constitutional structures and how they exercise their powers. Arguably, this reflects how many understand the nature of separation of powers within the South African constitutional system. However, this common understanding has not obviated the doctrine being subject to ever-increasing contestation. Its operation has placed the courts at the epicentre of settling political disputes and, naturally, having the last word on the meaning of the South African Constitution.

Jurisprudentially, the practicalities and contours of how, when and by whom the separation of powers should be determined have proven to be challenging. This has had profound implications for the judiciary: first, in terms of its relations with other constitutional structures, and second – and most important – how it determines the parameters of when and where courts *should* themselves intervene. In short, where and when it is appropriate and necessary for courts to assert their constitutional jurisdiction over a matter while being mindful of the fact that they themselves are subject to the Constitution is an important terrain of scholarly discussion, as Felix Dube reminds us in his contribution to this special issue.[3]

Dube's contribution sets the pace of the issue, as he boldly proposes that to make institutional sense of the nature of the Constitutional Court in terms of its positioning and powers under the Constitution, it is best to regard it not simply as a court, but as a *sui generis* constitutional structure occupying the apex position of both the 'legal and political order'. In short, Dube argues that South Africa's is a system of judicial supremacy.[4] On a cursory reading, Dube's proposition and argument are highly

---

[2] A small sample of the types of matters either recently decided by or before the courts are (1) the matter in which the Public Protector is challenging the impeachment procedure against her by the National Assembly (*Public Protector v Speaker of the National Assembly* [2020] 4 All SA 776 (WCC) (9 October 2020); (2) the successful challenge of the findings and holdings of the Seriti Commission on arms procurement (*Corruption Watch v Arms Procurement Commission* 2020 (2) SA 165 (GP)); (3) a recently instituted challenge by the Council for the Advancement of the South African Constitution (CASAC) against recommendations for judicial appointment made by the Judicial Service Commission to the President (K Maugham 'Casac takes JSC to court for its "unconstitutional" interviews of ConCourt justice nominees' *News24.com* (3 June 2021) <https://www.news24.com/news24/southafrica/news/just-in-casac-takes-jsc-to-court-for-its-unconstitutional-interviews-of-concourt-justice-nominees-20210603>); and (4) the finding of illegality with respect to the Ingonyama Trust in KwaZulu-Natal <https://www.groundup.org.za/media/uploads/documents/itb_judgment_11_june_2021.pdf>

[3] F Dube 'Separation of powers and the institutional supremacy of the Constitutional Court over Parliament and the executive' (2020) 36 *South African Journal on Human Rights* 293.

[4] Ibid.

provocative, especially when considered against a background of separation of powers literature premised on an orthodox doctrinal conception of three co-equal branches theoretically derived from the period of the European Enlightenment. However, to merely focus on Dube's conclusion without closely considering his argument is to avoid an uncomfortable question. Dube asks how we are able to reconcile the Constitutional Court's powers and status with the ordinary/orthodox separation of powers doctrine when, in his view of the evidence, the prevailing doctrine fails to account for the Constitutional Court's elevated role in matters of law and politics, relative to the legislative and executive branches. Dube suggests that making this shift in how we imagine the Constitutional Court is critical for the purposes of formulating theory about the Court's powers, especially in light of what he argues are its clearly discernible democratic, political and law-making (legislative) mandates. Implicit in Dube's provocation is a question to other interlocutors: what would happen to our theory and understanding of separation of powers if it were premised on a more accurate description of the institutional positioning of the Court that takes into account its multiple mandates, rather than on the basis of an antiquated theoretical account of co-equality between the branches? Understood within the context of his contribution, Dube can be understood to be calling for better, more contextual and grounded theory of the South African separation of powers doctrine.

Ultimately, Dube's contribution suggests that we should embrace the Court's superior position within our constitutional system and accept that its part in the nation's politics is inevitable once parties to a dispute turn to it for a remedy. In this respect, Dube introduces a key factor in navigating the politics of constitutional adjudication, namely the Court's remedial powers, which he describes as 'far-reaching (if not nearly infinite)' and bordering on 'textually unlimited'.[5] This concern with the Court's remedial powers is a common theme across the contributions in this special issue, with remedies widely seen as representing that imaginary line that is argued to either have been respected or breached when determining whether a court has acted legitimately within its proper constitutional limits or engaged in judicial overreach.

If Dube's view suggests that we must, as a matter of theoretical integrity, accept judicial supremacy as real, and that we must embrace it as a product of design rather than happenstance, then Hoolo Nyane's contribution, which follows Dube's, cautions against the normalisation of the Constitutional Court as a 'super-branch'.[6] Read in conversation with Dube's contribution, Nyane's is the caution of a more orthodox or traditionalist doctrinal scholar who regards the judicialisation of politics as posing a serious danger to democracy.

Nyane's contribution encapsulates a deep-seated and widely shared concern for the need to determine 'the proper place that must be occupied by the judiciary' in post-apartheid South Africa in the face of the judicialisation of politics, which he identifies as an emerging trend. According to Nyane, while still somewhat unsettled, the judicialisation of politics as a 'notion connotes "the reliance on courts and judicial means for

[5] Ibid 304.

[6] H Nyane 'The judicialisation of politics in South Africa: A critique of the emerging trend' (2020) 36 *South African Journal on Human Rights* 319.

addressing core moral predicaments, public policy questions and political controversy"'.[7] In Nyane's view, these are ordinarily matters outside of the court's purview. Therefore, by assuming jurisdiction on plainly political matters and failing to apply what he calls 'time-honoured principle[s]' such as the 'political question doctrine', courts have been 'over-enthusiastic' in interpreting their remedial powers. Such has been their enthusiasm, according to Nyane, that they have taken their powers to 'mean literally anything, including overreach into the functions of the political branches of government'.[8] Nyane provides a robust critical appraisal that usefully tracks the frequency and deepening nature of 'overreach'. In so doing, he argues that the impetus towards the judicialisation of politics can be associated with certain identifiable factors, including 'the realisation of transformative constitutionalism theory'.[9] Ultimately, Nyane's anxiety seems to stem from what he conceives of as an unmanageable blurring of the lines between law and politics that has (mis)placed law as being *the* central driver of social transformation to the exclusion of the two political branches, among other considerations. In spite of this evident anxiety, Nyane, like the rest of the contributors, accedes to the notion that courts have a role to play in politics under a supreme constitution. However, he differs from the others with respect to how expansive or intrusive that role should be, especially where certain remedies necessarily encroach on the domain of the other branches.

Less reticent about the important and decisive role played by the judiciary in resolving constitutional disputes that have 'macro-political' ramifications, Lauren Gildenhuys accepts as inevitable the notion that courts adjudicating within a constitutional law framework will make decisions, the political implication or consequences of which will in all likelihood have an impact on inter-branch relations.[10] For Gildenhuys, the question is manifestly not *whether* the judiciary can or should involve itself in matters that immerse the judiciary in politics, but rather *what* is the 'proper response' for the court when faced with such cases. Rather than avoiding the political issues, Gildenhuys suggests that the proper response for courts is a strategic one that entails deciding matters in line with the imperatives of esoteric decision-making techniques. According to Gildenhuys, esoteric decision-making occurs when courts rely on 'apolitical, technical and legal justifications to substantiate a judicial outcome that is preferred for political reasons, which remain unexpressed'.[11] Through an examination of some politically contentious cases, she argues that there already exists a judicial repertoire of esoteric decision-making techniques primed to 'downplay' the role of politics in adjudication in order to safeguard the courts' legitimacy and institutional security.

In this special issue, the *Economic Freedom Fighters (Democratic Alliance as Intervening Party) v Speaker of the National Assembly*[12] (*EFF II*, also known as the impeachment decision) case can be read as representing the high-water mark as far as

---

[7] Ibid 323.
[8] Ibid 337.
[9] Ibid 333.
[10] L Gildenhuys 'Esoteric decision-making: Judicial responses to the judicialisation of politics, the Constitutional Court and *EFF II*' (2020) 36 *South African Journal on Human Rights* 338.
[11] Ibid 339.
[12] *Economic Freedom Fighters (Democratic Alliance as Intervening Party) v Speaker of the National Assembly* 2018 (2) SA 571 (CC).

cases reflecting the judicialisation of politics in South Africa is concerned. All five submissions constituting this special issue expressly referring to this case also suggest as much. It is, therefore, unsurprising that Gildenhuys subjects this case to close scrutiny, as she seeks to elaborate on the value of esoteric decision-making in shielding the courts from political controversy when deployed carefully, as compared to the dangers it poses when done ineptly. That said, Gildenhuys' focus on strategy and techniques begs a few questions about the normative measures or standards to be applied in determining the success or failure of a particular instance of esoteric decision-making. Therefore, while esoteric decision-making justifies the court's right to act in politically charged matters, less clear is whether – or even how – this kind of decision-making informs the substance of decisions, in particular the types of remedies handed down.

The issue of remedial powers and the types of remedies the courts hand down, in particular the level of their intrusiveness in what is usually understood as the 'pre-eminent domain' of the other branches, represents the sharpest line of tension between courts paying due deference to other branches and the courts straying into the thorny terrain of judicial overreach. Ropafadzo Maphosa's contribution most directly addresses the question of remedies, in particular structural interdicts.[13] Maphosa responds to commentary questioning the legitimacy of intrusive orders the courts make in socio-economic rights adjudication while focussing on a particular structural interdict, namely what she terms the 'expert remedial formulation model' as deployed in *The Black Sash Trust v Minister of Social Development*[14] and *Mwelase v Director-General for the Department of Rural Development and Land Reform.*[15] Clearly connecting the intrusiveness of the remedies in these cases with a choice the Constitutional Court made to embrace a strong – as opposed to weak – judicial review model, Maphosa argues that these decisions are not only in keeping with the Court's earlier jurisprudence, but are also, in essence, a natural progression of the Court legitimately exercising its supervisory authority over its orders. In other words, Maphosa suggests that the expert remedial formulation model is an extension of the Constitutional Court's jurisprudence and demonstrates this by providing a detailed taxonomical account of the different models of structural interdicts through the cases. Beyond providing a thoughtful account of how the courts' remedies jurisprudence has evolved, Maphosa's submission also provides useful context for the last contribution in the special issue, which examines in greater depth the question of intrusive remedies.

The final special issue contribution comes from Gaurav Mukherjee and Juha Tuovinen.[16] It is a thought-provoking article that reflects on the courts' powers to design intrusive remedies. Working from the premise that there is little or no room for courts to avoid the judicialisation of politics, the authors identify the specific factors that explain *why* in *Mwelase,*[17] which concerns a 'recalcitrant administration', it was justifiable for the Court to issue, under its supervisory jurisdiction, what is self-

[13] R Maposa 'Are judicial monitoring institutions a legitimate remedy for addressing systemic socioeconomic rights violations?' (2020) 36 *South African Journal on Human Rights* 362.
[14] *The Black Sash Trust v Minister of Social Development* 2018 (12) BCLR 1472 (CC).
[15] *Mwelase v Director-General for the Department of Rural Development and Land Reform* 2019 (6) SA 597 (CC).
[16] G Mukherjee & J Tuovinen 'Designing remedies for a recalcitrant administration' (2020) 36 *South African Journal on Human Rights* 386.
[17] Note 15 above.

evidently an invasive order that gave a court-appointed 'Special Master' an executive function. The authors are critical of the thinly reasoned majority judgment, particularly its failure to clarify the logics and reasons underlying the choice of remedy; this fact is what leads to Mukherjee and Tuovinen to closely examine the case history, the role of government and the implications of a failure to act before settling on eight crucial factors that explain the choice of remedy. These factors, the authors suggest, may be useful points of reference for providing 'normative and doctrinal guidance' in identifying the types of cases where intrusive orders may be warranted in future.

As a means to test the utility of these factors against a different set of facts and in another setting, the authors apply them to the well-known Indian *Right to Food* case.[18] Whether *Right to Food* is an apt comparator is open to debate, yet it presents an opportunity to test Mukherjee and Tuovinen's factors against a well-known example where post-colonial administrative malaise has drawn the courts into the adjudication of politically charged disputes concerning socio-economic distribution. Mukherjee and Tuovinen's contribution is important, going beyond general questions of the legitimacy of courts to act in politicised matters to a consideration of specifics to be taken into account as courts design effective, if invasive, remedies while striving not to engage in judicial overreach.

In conclusion, there is as much within this special issue to give one cause for reflection as there is with which one can disagree. Either way, the contributors must be commended for producing a stimulating and engaged set of papers on the judicialisation of politics in South Africa from different perspectives. It is our hope at the *South African Journal on Human Rights* that this special issue serves to stimulate and enrich the debate on the important questions that it traverses. Furthermore, it is our hope that other researchers with strong views on the matters raised will take up the challenge to make their views known by further engaging what is clearly a phenomenon that we will be grappling with for the foreseeable future.

Disclosure statement

No potential conflict of interest was reported by the author(s).

[18] *People's Union for Civil Liberties v Union of India* Petition (Civil) No. 196/2001 (Indian Supreme Court case).

Separation of powers and the institutional supremacy of the Constitutional Court over Parliament and the executive

Felix Dube

ABSTRACT
South African judges often caution against judicial encroachment into what they perceive as the exclusive domains of the legislature and the executive. Their caveats stem from the doctrine of separation of powers, which classically divides state authority between the three branches of government. However, the classification of the courts, particularly the Constitutional Court, as a branch of the government potentially misconstrues the division of state authority in the Constitution of the Republic of South Africa, 1996. The powers and authority of the Constitutional Court place it at the apex of the legal and political order such that from a conceptual and practical view, the Court is constitutionally superior to Parliament and the executive. As such, a traditional understanding of the doctrine of separation of powers does not properly reflect the South African constitutional arrangement. This contribution re-evaluates the relevance and application of the doctrine of separation of powers in contemporary jurisprudence. It recognises the superiority of the Constitutional Court over Parliament and the executive and shows that the time has come to consider the institutional supremacy of the Constitutional Court as a possible doctrine of constitutional law in South Africa.

Legal scholars treat the South African judiciary as a branch of the government within the context of the doctrine of separation of powers, which they view as a core feature of the Constitution of the Republic of South Africa, 1996. The classification of the courts as one of the three branches of the government flows from many court judgments in which judges alluded to a constitutional arrangement in which the branches of government exercise equal but distinct powers. In numerous judgments and extra-curial writings discussed in this contribution, judges often caution against judicial encroachment into what they perceive as the exclusive domains of Parliament and the executive. However, the classification of the judiciary, particularly the Constitutional

Court, as a branch of the government misconstrues the division of state authority in the Constitution.

In this contribution, I argue that the Constitutional Court is institutionally supreme to Parliament and the executive owing to its establishment as a *sui generis* institution with a legal and political mandate in post-apartheid South Africa. The powers and authority of the Constitutional Court place it at the apex of law and politics. Conceptually and practically, the Court is constitutionally superior to Parliament and the executive. As such, the doctrine of separation of powers, in its original understanding as propounded by the philosophers of the Enlightenment, does not properly reflect the South African constitutional arrangement. The time has come to recognise the institutional supremacy of the Constitutional Court as a doctrine in the discourse on separation of powers.

Five arguments justify the consideration and recognition of the superiority of the Constitutional Court over Parliament and the executive. First, the Constitution endows the Constitutional Court with functions and authority that, for all practical purposes, give the Court more powers than the legislature and the executive. Second, the Constitutional Court is the guardian of the Constitution. Since the Constitution is the supreme *law*, one can only imagine the magnitude of the powers of its institutional guardian. Third, the Constitutional Court is a *sui generis* institution whose functions include democratic representation. Whereas Parliament and the executive represent the majority will (and to a limited extent, the minorities), the Constitutional Court represents the values that underlie the Constitution and safeguards the founding values against encroachment by the legislative and executive representatives. Fourth, the Constitutional Court has a superior role in constitutional politics. Its judgments have settled some of the most contentious political disputes. Lastly, the Constitutional Court has law-making powers that, on closer examination, exceed the combined law-making powers of Parliament and the executive.

1. Contextualising the supremacy of the Constitutional Court as a possible doctrine of constitutional law in South Africa

This contribution is built on the premise that the Constitutional Court is institutionally supreme to Parliament and the executive. In other terms, this contribution is about the superiority of the Constitutional Court over Parliament and the executive. It is not about the supremacy of the Constitution – which is above all *laws* in South Africa, per s 2 of the Constitution. The Constitutional Court is an *institution* that, like all institutions, is not above the law but is under the law and is limited by the Constitution. Thus, there should be no confusion on the fundamental difference between, on the one hand, the supremacy of the Constitution as *law*, and on the other hand, the institutional supremacy of the Constitutional Court over Parliament and the executive in relation to its final say on the constitutionality of the actions of these two branches.

This contribution shows that as a *sui generis institution* that is subject to the Constitution but that exercises superior authority vis-à-vis Parliament and the executive, the Constitutional Court has powers to say what the Constitution means, to invalidate Acts of Parliament, to legislate through reading-in and reading-out words from statutes, and to order Parliament to make particular laws. These powers point to superiority over Parliament and cannot be reconciled with the classical doctrine of separation of powers. Also, the Constitutional Court's judicial supervision of some aspects of executive action by instructing members of the executive what to do, how to do it and when to do it is inconsistent with the traditional understanding of the doctrine of separation of powers.

From a theoretical standpoint, the institutional supremacy of the Constitutional Court flows from the doctrine of judicial supremacy, which has been mooted in other jurisdictions since the 18th century.[1] Constitutional supremacy 'concerns the institutional structure of the organs of State [and] the *lower ranking* of the legislator'.[2] In this contribution, it is not difficult to imply a doctrine of Constitutional Court supremacy from the supremacy of the Constitution. As such, the supremacy of the Constitutional Court refers to its role as the highest constitutional interpreter, its capacity to make constitutional law, to legislate through its decisions, and to supervise the executive in its capacity as the guardian of the Constitution.

There is another reason to revaluate the place of the doctrine of separation of powers in contemporary South Africa with a view to reshaping the discourse to reflect constitutional reality along the lines of what could be tentatively termed the doctrine of the institutional supremacy of the Constitutional Court. The doctrine of separation of powers is a remnant of the Enlightenment. Arguably, viewing the South African constitutional arrangement from the lenses of 18th century European philosophers – who put forward their theories on the separation of powers at a time when humanity knew no supreme constitution, no justiciable Bill of Rights and no Constitutional Court – not only disempowers attempts to free the legal system from the clutches of colonial concepts but also defies constitutional realities brought by the emerging jurisprudence of the Constitutional Court on the distribution of constitutional power. This should be understood in the context that the time to build constitutional jurisprudence on the foundation of local theoretical interventions, values, principles and systems, which could be the ideal premises upon which to enhance constitutionalism, is long overdue.[3]

2. The origins and application of the doctrine of separation of powers

The genesis of the doctrine of separation of powers is credited to John Locke and Baron de Montesquieu, who argued that state power is prone to abuse when

---

[1] See CG Haines, who argued that the 'precedents and principles which resulted in the American doctrine of judicial supremacy were formulated and announced on the continent of Europe and in England prior to the time of the [18th century] American Revolution'; CG Haines *American Doctrine of Judicial Supremacy* (1914) 63. In 1931, HE Willis analysed the meaning of the doctrine of the supremacy of the United States Supreme Court; HE Willis 'The doctrine of the supremacy of the supreme court' (1931) 6 *Industrial Law Journal* 223–259. The doctrine continued to develop throughout the world, although Gardbaum argues that it is 'a concept frequently employed in both domestic and comparative constitutional theory but rarely carefully defined and systematically analysed'; S Gardbaum 'What is judicial supremacy?' in GJ Jacobsohn & M Schor (eds) *Comparative Constitutional Theory* (2018).

[2] J Limbach 'The concept of the supremacy of the constitution' (2001) 64 *Modern Law Review* 1 (original emphasis retained).

[3] See the remarks in *S V Makwanyane* 1995 (3) SA 391 (CC) para 304.

the lawmaker also interprets and enforces the law.[4] In contemporary constitutional theory, this doctrine is an element of constitutionalism that divides and constrains public power through distinctive constitutional institutions.[5] Theoretically, the doctrine seeks to prevent branches of government from accumulating excessive powers, deters the arbitrary exercise of power, permits government branches to exercise only those functions prescribed by law, and proscribes them from usurping powers from one another.[6] Ultimately, the separation of powers purports to prevent authoritarianism.[7] Essential to the separation of powers is the prohibition of the branches from delegating plenary powers to one another.[8] This prohibition ensures that the legislature does not abdicate its functions[9] and prevents the accumulation of excessive powers in the executive, thereby providing a mechanism for the collective and individual accountability of public office-bearers.[10] Separation of powers protects the rule of law and correlates with government legitimacy, democracy and economic development.[11] A glance into history reveals that the doctrine originated from the principle that in a state, the legislature, the executive, and the judiciary must be functionally independent.[12]

The Constitutional Court said that South Africa adopted its model of separation of powers in direct response to the abuses of power occasioned by the system of parliamentary sovereignty under colonial and apartheid rule.[13] The doctrine found its way into South Africa when Constitutional Principle VI of the Interim Constitution required the drafters of the Constitution to incorporate 'separation of powers between the legislature, executive and judiciary, with appropriate checks and balances to ensure accountability, responsiveness and openness.'[14] However, the text of the current Constitution does not mention the separation of powers at all, although, during the constitutional certification process, the Constitutional Court was satisfied that the Constitution complies with all the requirements for a separation of powers and that the drafters incorporated a separation of powers

---

4 However, scholars do not agree on who, between Montesquieu and John Locke, originated the doctrine of separation of powers. For the contrasting opinions, see CM Fombad 'An overview of separation of powers under modern African constitutions' in CM Fombad (ed) *Separation of Powers in African Constitutionalism* (2016) 59–60; D Landau 'The evolution of the separation of powers in the Global South and Global North' in D Bilchitz & D Landau (eds) *The Evolution of the Separation of Powers: Between the Global North and the Global South* (2018) 1–2; and S Ratnapala 'John Locke's Doctrine of the Separation of Powers: Re-Evaluation' (1993) 38 *The American Journal of Jurisprudence* 189, 190.

5 M Loughlin & N Walker 'Introduction' in M Loughlin & N Walker (eds) *The Paradox of Constitutionalism: Constituent Power and Constitutional Form* (2007) 1.

6 See A Kavanagh 'The constitutional separation of powers' in D Dyzenhaus & M Thorburn (eds) *Philosophical Foundations of Constitutional Law* (2016) 234.

7 M Vile Constitutionalism and the Separation of Powers 2 ed (1998) 16–17.

8 See, generally, Executive Council of the Western Cape Legislature v President of the Republic of South Africa 1995 (4) SA 877 (CC).

9 See C Möllers 'Separation of powers' in R Masterman & R Schütze (eds) *The Cambridge Companion to Comparative Constitutional Law* (2019) 248. Möllers further points out that the delegation of the powers of one branch to another is in itself a 'classical problem' with the doctrine of separation of powers.

10 *De Lange v Smuts* 1998 (3) SA 785 (CC) para 60.

11 See P Langa '"A delicate balance": The place of the judiciary in a constitutional democracy – the separation of powers in the South African Constitution' (2006) *South African Journal on Human Rights* 2, 9.

12 See W Bondy The separation of government powers in history, in *Theory, and in the Constitution* (2004) (Part I).

13 South African Association of Personal Injury Lawyers v Heath 2001 (1) SA 883 (CC) para 24.

14 See Constitutional Principle VI in Schedule 4 of the Constitution of the Republic of South Africa Act 200 of 1993 (Interim Constitution). The Interim Constitution has been repealed.

into the text.[15] The Constitutional Court further declared that it is self-evident that the doctrine of separation of powers is part of the constitutional design.[16] Whether this interpretation is correct is subject to debate. Sebastian Seedorf and Sanele Sibanda agree with the judicial approach and argue that the 'doctrine is to be found in the provisions outlining the functions and structure of various organs of state and their respective independence and interdependence'.[17]

In a contemporary critique of the place of the doctrine of separation of powers, such as this contribution, and in view of the recent case law, it is debateable whether it was not enough for the Constitutional Court to merely declare that the Constitution incorporates the doctrine of separation of powers when the constitutional text does not expressly mention the doctrine. One may argue that the fact that Constitutional Principle VI in the Interim Constitution mandated the separation of powers does not automatically mean that the current Constitution encompasses the doctrine. This doctrine is not the only one implied by the Constitutional Court from the 'spirit' of the Constitution, as the Court has infused certain doctrines, principles and values (such as transformative constitutionalism and *ubuntu*) into the core of the Constitution, although the Constitution does not expressly mention the same.[18]

The Constitutional Court has not only declared that the doctrine of separation of powers is part of the Constitution but it has also assumed exclusive powers to determine the nature of the doctrine. Consequently, the doctrine of separation of powers is pliable and vulnerable to constant modification by the Constitutional Court. In *De Lange v Smuts*, the Constitutional Court first hinted how it intended to mould the doctrine of separation of powers.[19] The Constitutional Court said that it would reflect on South Africa's history in developing a model of separation of powers to ensure that under the current constitutional dispensation, government power is restrained and not abused. This declaration effectively means that the determination of the boundaries of state authority is a matter of final determination by the Constitutional Court and that the Court will develop the doctrine on its terms, guided by the supremacy of the Constitution.

The pliability of the doctrine of separation of powers became evident in the first constitutional certification judgment when the Constitutional Court said that there is no universal model for separation of powers and that it would develop a distinct model of separation of powers for South Africa.[20] In *De Lange*, the Constitutional Court recognised the need to restrain government power and to

---

[15] See Ex parte Chairperson of the Constitutional Assembly: In re Certification of the Constitution of the Republic of South Africa, 1996 1996 (4) SA 744 (CC) paras 106–112. See also Certification of the Amended Text of the Constitution of the Republic of South Africa, 1996 1997 (2) SA 97 (CC) paras 52, 63.

[16] Glenister v President of the Republic of South Africa 2011 (3) SA 347 (CC) para 29.

[17] S Seedorf & S Sibanda 'Separation of powers' in S Woolman & M Bishop (eds) *Constitutional Law of South Africa* (2014) 20.

[18] F Dube 'The South African Constitution as an instrument of doing what is just, rights and fair' (2020) 54 *In Die Skriflig* a2601 5.

[19] *De Lange* (note 10 above) para 60.

[20] *Certification of the Constitution I* (note 15 above) para 108. However, Möllers (note 9 above) finds it problematic and against the classical separation of powers 'that one organ can finally decide all questions of constitutional law, including the meaning of separation of powers'.

ensure that public power is not so diluted that the government cannot make timely decisions in the interest of the public.[21] Consequently, it is up to the courts, in general, and the Constitutional Court, in particular, to determine – on a case-by-case basis – the proper application of separation of powers. Furthermore, it is up to the courts to infer the proper application of checks and balances from the text of the Constitution.[22] Whereas the doctrine of separation of powers recognises the functional division and independence of the law-making, judicial and executive institutions,[23] checks and balances prevent government branches from 'usurping power from one another'[24] and also preclude government institutions and personnel from overstepping constitutional boundaries.

However, it is unavoidable for the branches of government to impose restraints on one another.[25] Checks and balances also operate when different government institutions work together to produce a legally binding decision.[26] In addition, checks and balances are intended to halt the implementation of decisions that violate the law. Judgments in which the courts invalidate decisions of the executive are examples of checks and balances working to prevent constitutional and legislative violations.[27] The implied separation of powers and checks and balances mean that, ultimately, the courts determine how to enforce the rule of law through the separation of powers and checks and balances. The consequence is that the apex Court has the final say on the correct division of government power and how to enforce checks and balances. Naturally, the Constitutional Court would not adopt an interpretation model that diminishes its powers within the broad scope of separation of powers. The Constitutional Court's history shows that it is prepared to assert its authority to the highest level and that its interpretative approach would inevitably strive to increase its powers.[28]

3. Establishing the Constitutional Court as a *sui generis* institution

This section analyses the establishment of the Constitutional Court to show that the Constitutional Assembly, which drafted the Constitution, deliberately gave the Constitutional Court enormous powers by granting it a constitution-making role and conceivably unlimited powers of judicial review. Like its counterparts in Europe, the Constitutional Court was created as a quasi-political and *sui generis* institution with

---

[21] See the remarks in *De Lange* (note 10 above) para 60.
[22] See *Certification of the Constitution I* (note 15 above) para 112.
[23] Ibid para 109.
[24] Ibid.
[25] Ibid para 108.
[26] R Grant & R Keohane 'Accountability and abuses of power in world politics' (2005) *American Political Science Review* 29, 30.
[27] See Democratic Alliance v Minister: International Relations and Cooperation 2017 (3) SA 212 (GP); Law Society of South Africa v President of the Republic of South Africa 2019 (3) SA 30 (CC); Corruption Watch NPC v President of the Republic of South Africa; Nxasana v Corruption Watch NPC 2018 (2) SACR 442 (CC); Democratic Alliance v President of the Republic of South Africa; Economic Freedom Fighters v State Attorney 2019 (1) All SA 681 (GP).
[28] The application of the doctrine of separation of powers by the Constitutional Court is contested in legal scholarship. See, for instance, N Raboshakga 'The doctrine of separation of powers and interim interdict cases involving the state: *National Treasury v. Opposition to Urban Tolling Alliance: Note*' (2014) *South African Law Journal* 740. The author criticises the way the Constitutional Court applied the doctrine of separation of powers in the case.

a decisive say on both judicial and political affairs.[29] This argument does not intend to imply extrajudicial involvement in politics but to show that the adjudication of political matters is part and parcel of the Constitutional Court's jurisdiction. To understand the quasi-political powers of the Constitutional Court, it is important to note that the Constitutional Court was created as a vehicle for a political transition and as a guarantee of constitutionalism in post-apartheid South Africa. To appreciate this argument, it is imperative to note that the Constitutional Court exercises different roles that revolve around law and politics in tackling the legacy of the past and charting a path for the future. Heinz Klug notes that the 'Court's image as well as its judicial authority are the product of a very particular set of conditions and politics and cannot be taken for granted now or in the future. Implicit in this argument is the idea that the Constitutional Court plays a number of different roles that vary over time'.[30]

Klug's argument enables us to understand and appreciate the importance of the historical circumstances that led to the establishment of the Constitutional Court. The first consideration is that one of the fundamental questions that arose during the negotiations and transition from apartheid to constitutional democracy was how to balance majoritarian aspirations with constitutionalism. The government of the National Party was concerned about the possibility that the democratic government would deviate from the 34 Constitutional Principles enshrined in schedule 4 of the Interim Constitution. Hence, the negotiating parties agreed to establish a quasi-political institution that is *sui generis*, in the form of the Constitutional Court, to certify the compliance of the final constitutional text with the 34 Constitutional Principles and to test the constitutional validity of legislation and executive conduct going forward into the new era and beyond.[31] The parties agreed that once certified by the Constitutional Court, the Constitution would not be challenged in any court of law.[32] The move was unprecedented in the history of constitution-making.[33] Nowhere in the history of humanity has a court been created to certify the constitutionality and compliance of a constitution with pre-agreed legal and political principles.[34]

Although there were concerns that a justiciable Bill of Rights would entrench the 'privileges' of the minority,[35] there was wide acceptance of the need to create the Constitutional Court. The African National Congress (ANC) was apprehensive at the prospect that the Appellate Division of the Supreme Court, which was untransformed and possibly reactionary at the time, would review and set aside the decisions of the

[29] See, K Kelemen *Judicial Dissent in European Constitutional Courts: A Comparative and Legal Perspective* (2018) 10–11 on the sui generis nature of constitutional courts.

[30] H Klug 'Constitutional authority and judicial pragmatism politics and law in the evolution of South Africa's Constitutional Court' in D Kapiszewski, G Silverstein & RA Kagan (eds) *Consequential Court: Judicial Roles in Global Perspective* (2013) 93.

[31] See s 71(2) of the Interim Constitution.

[32] See s 71(3) of the Interim Constitution and D Robertson *The Judge as Political Theorist: Contemporary Constitutional Review* (2010) 228.

[33] H Botha 'Instituting public freedom or extinguishing constituent power? Reflections on South Africa's constitution-making experiment' (2010) 26 *South African Journal on Human Rights* 66, 69.

[34] R Hirschl 'The new constitutionalism and the judicialization of pure politics worldwide' (2006) 75 *Fordham Law Review* 721, 732. E Cameron *Justice: A Personal Account* (2014) 134–135 argues that the certification role played by the Constitutional Court in the adoption of the final Constitution was an innovative procedure devised by the Constitutional Assembly to protect the legitimacy of the Constitution.

[35] See S Issacharoff *Fragile Democracies: Contested Power in the Era of Constitutional Courts* (2015) 173.

democratic government.[36] Whereas the negotiating parties agreed on the need for the judiciary to constrain government excesses, the ANC refused to entrust that obligation to the judges of the Appellate Division because the judges were politically contaminated by their service to the apartheid regime and had enabled and legitimised rule by law under apartheid.[37] Hence, the parties settled on the introduction of the Constitutional Court as one of the institutional mechanisms for the protection of the rights and interests of minorities. Since the establishment of the Constitutional Court was not enough to safeguard and guarantee against majoritarian encroachment,[38] the Interim Constitution mandated the limitation of legislative and executive powers, in line with the prescripts of constitutionalism, and created other institutions to support constitutional democracy.

There is an important aspect to note about the readiness of the last apartheid government to embrace human rights and constitutional review during the transitional period. Reflectively, it is ironic that the National Party government, which had excluded judicial review,[39] advocated for the establishment of an apex court armed with extensive powers of review to insulate the new political minorities against majoritarian encroachment.[40] In this context, Francois Venter argues that the entrenchment of rights and the establishment of strong institutions was not a result of the genuine intents of the constitutional drafters but an 'unintended consequence of constitution-writing propelled by the winds of globalisation'.[41]

Nevertheless, the creation of the Constitutional Court and the adoption of a justiciable Bill of Rights affirmed the desirability of constitutionalism to the fledgeling democracy. When they entrusted the certification of the text of the final Constitution on the Constitutional Court, the negotiating parties embraced constitutional review and set the tone for the judiciary in the new South Africa. The negotiators succeeded in creating a delicate balance between the extremes of outright majoritarianism with constitutionalism. The balance helped to ease the anxiety and concerns of the new political minority.[42] Judicial review further served as a political guarantee and a bridge of the transition from apartheid to constitutional democracy. Gerhard van der Schyff notes that:

> The judicial review of legislation as one of the cornerstones of the new order has come to reflect a principled preference for its perceived benefits over and above the idea that the political process was by itself the answer in having rights permeate society. On the

[36] P Langa & E Cameron 'The Constitutional Court and the Supreme Court of Appeal after 1994' (2010) *Advocate* 28, 32.

[37] For a discussion of how apartheid judges legitimised harsh apartheid injustices, see D Dyzenhaus *The Constitution of Law: Legality in a Time of Emergency* (2006) 20–23 and H Graver *Judges Against Justice: On Judges When the Rule of Law is Under Attack* (2015) 36.

[38] Issacharoff (note 35 above) 171.

[39] Section 59(2) of the Republic of South Africa Constitution Act 32 of 1961 and s 34(3) of the Republic of South Africa Constitution Act 110 of 1983 outlawed judicial review in apartheid South Africa.

[40] See R Hirschl 'The political origins of judicial empowerment through constitutionalization: Lessons from four constitutional revolutions' (2000) *Law & Social Inquiry* 91, 134. Political minorities often resort to the constitutionalisation of rights and judicial review to protect their interests during constitutional transitions – see SA Lemieux & DJ Watkins *Judicial Review and Contemporary Democratic Theory: Power, Domination and the Courts* (2018) 24.

[41] F Venter 'Liberal democracy: The unintended consequence – South African Constitution-writing propelled by the winds of globalisation' (2010) 26 *South African Journal on Human Rights* 45. See also H Klug *Constituting Democracy: Law Globalism, and South Africa's Political Reconstruction* (2000) 1–2.

[42] D Moseneke *My Own Liberator: A Memoir* (2016) 301.

other hand, the introduction of judicial review has also served as a political device to address the fears of the white minority that they might be sidelined by a new parliament which they could no longer dominate numerically. This is because expanding the vote has meant changing the composition of political organs, which could in turn drown out the voice of the previously advantaged classes. Combined, these two reasons imply that judicial review was chosen not only because it presented a new substantive model for the country's future, but also because it served as a bridge to securing that new future.[43]

The negotiating parties accepted in 1994 that the Constitutional Court would become a very influential political body.[44] President Mandela admonished the first bench of the Constitutional Court not to be another rubber stamp of the executive and the legislature and implored the justices to be creative and independent on the bench.[45] The apparent juridification of politics and the politicisation of the role of the Constitutional Court in the constitution-making process made the Constitutional Court a decisive political player beyond the certification process. The decisive powers of the Constitutional Court did not mean that it set out to compete with politicians. The powers of the Constitutional Court in the certification process gave it a comfortable footing to express its position on purely political questions.[46] Although some of the issues in the constitutional certification cases dealt with strictly constitutional and human rights matters, some were mostly political (albeit with traces of legal and constitutional substance), such as provincial autonomy and questions on proportional representation and democracy. Constitutional Principle XVIII, which protected the powers and functions of provinces, was mainly a political requirement.[47] Since it was a product of political compromise, the Constitutional Court was not at liberty to frustrate the will of the majority who made its creation possible.[48] Frustrating 'the people' would have meant a stillbirth for the Constitutional Court.

However, the Constitutional Court found the first text of the final Constitution deficient in fully complying with some of the Constitutional Principles.[49] From a political standpoint, Samuel Issacharoff argues that when the Constitutional Court refused to certify the first text, it was merely enforcing pre-agreed political guarantees espoused in the 34 Constitutional Principles.[50] The political role of the Constitutional Court was amplified by the fact that some of its first justices were political appointees and ANC cadres. For instance, Sachs J was a member of the first ANC delegation to the second round of negotiations.[51] His activism started early in his student life before he attended the Congress of the People, which adopted the Freedom Charter in 1955.[52] Sachs J admitted that his historical circumstances and political consciousness influenced his

[43] G van der Schyff Judicial Review of Legislation: A Comparative Study of the United Kingdom, the Netherlands and South Africa (2010) 45.
[44] K O'Malley 'South Africa: Designing new political institutions' in M Faure & J-E Lane (eds) *South Africa: Designing New Political Institutions* (1996) 75.
[45] <https://www.sahistory.org.za/archive/speech-president-nelson-mandela-inauguration-constitutional-court-johannesburg-14-february-1>.
[46] See, for instance, the Constitutional Court's contentious view on proportional representation in *Certification of the Constitution I* (note 15 above) para 186.
[47] Robertson (note 32 above) 229.
[48] See Klug (note 41 above) 116 for a discussion.
[49] See *Certification of the Constitution I* (note 15 above).
[50] Issacharoff (note 35 above) 181.
[51] Robertson (note 32 above) 226.
[52] <https://www.sahistory.org.za/people/judge-albert-louis-albie-sachs>.

thinking on the bench.[53] The following section analyses the powers and authority that make the Constitutional Court immensely powerful and constitutionally superior to the other branches of government.

4. The institutional supremacy of the Constitutional Court over Parliament and the executive

4.1 Superior constitutional functions, powers and authority

When the Constitutional Court exercises its powers to safeguard the supremacy of the Constitution, the rule of law and the founding values, it enjoys pre-eminence as the highest court in South Africa.[54] Hence, the contribution of the Constitutional Court to contentious matters, such as politics, is vast.[55] The Constitutional Court may decide not only constitutional matters[56] but also appeals in other matters of general public importance that are relevant for its consideration.[57] This provision is critical because it expands the jurisdiction of the Constitutional Court from constitutional matters to all matters the Constitutional Court deems fit to consider in the public interest. One of the implications is that when it comes to the Constitutional Court, nothing is seemingly off the table. The Constitutional Court can adjudicate any matter if it deems the matter to be generally important for the public.

Thus, s 167(3)(b)(ii) of the Constitution gives the Constitutional Court unlimited jurisdiction, which trumps the traditional understanding of the doctrine of separation of powers. It means, for example, that if litigants present the Constitutional Court with a matter that ordinarily falls within the purview of legislative or executive competence or is highly political in nature, the Constitutional Court will hear and decide the matter if the matter raises an arguable point of law that is generally important for the public. The Constitutional Court has jurisdiction to decide whether a matter is generally important to the public to warrant its intervention. In *Economic Freedom Fighters v Public Protector v Gordhan*, the Constitutional Court decided 'a matter which has a political bite to it [because it is] understandable why the public would have an interest in it'.[58] The wording of this extract suggests that political matters are covered in s 167(3) of the Constitution as matters that are generally important to the public for consideration by the Constitutional Court.

Prior to the Constitution Seventeenth Amendment Act of 2012, the Constitution gave the Constitutional Court jurisdiction only on constitutional matters, although that did not stop the Constitutional Court from adjudicating political questions.[59] As such, the jurisprudence on separation of powers developed by

---

[53] A Sachs *We, the People: Insights of an Activist Judge* (2016) 211.

[54] Section 167(3)(a) of the Constitution.

[55] See Robertson (note 32 above) 226. See also Klug (note 41 above) 95.

[56] Section 167(7) of the Constitution defines a constitutional matter as one that includes 'any issue involving the interpretation, protection or enforcement of the Constitution'.

[57] Section 167(3) of the Constitution, inserted by s 3(a) of the Constitution Seventeenth Amendment Act of 2012.

[58] Economic Freedom Fighters v Gordhan; Public Protector v Gordhan 2020 (8) BCLR 916 (CC) para 97.

[59] Examples include *Glenister* (note 16 above) para 67; and *S v Lawrence; S Negal; S v Solberg* 1997 (4) SA 1176 (CC) para 42.

the Constitutional Court prior to the 2012 constitutional amendment should be viewed in the light that the Constitutional Court did not have express jurisdiction to decide all kinds of matters, as it was expressly limited to constitutional matters. However, the Constitutional Court continues to apply its jurisprudence on separation of powers developed prior to the 2012 constitutional amendment.[60] Although the Constitutional Court continues to do so because of its allegiance to the doctrine of judicial precedent (it being common cause that it is bound by its previous decisions unless such decisions are manifestly incorrect such that they cannot stand in a free and democratic society based on human dignity, equality and freedom), the approach cannot be reconciled with s 167(3) of the Constitution.[61]

The powers of the Constitutional Court are further entrenched in s 167(3)(c) of the Constitution, which stipulates that only the Constitutional Court may make a final determination on whether it has jurisdiction and whether the matter is admissible and justiciable. Section 167(4) of the Constitution gives the Constitutional Court a monopoly to decide:

a. disputes between organs of state in the national or provincial sphere concerning the constitutional status, powers or functions of any of those organs of state;
b. on the constitutionality of any parliamentary or provincial Bill, but may do so only in the circumstances anticipated in section 79 or 121;
c. applications envisaged in section 80 or 122;
d. on the constitutionality of any amendment to the Constitution;
e. that Parliament or the President has failed to fulfil a constitutional obligation; or to
f. certify a provincial constitution in terms of section 144.[62]

The exclusive jurisdiction of the Constitutional Court is augmented by its powers to review and confirm declarations of invalidity of Acts of Parliament, provincial Acts and the actions of the President made by the High Court and the Supreme Court of Appeal.[63] The requirement ensures that the Constitutional Court has a final determination on the constitutionality of parliamentary legislation enacted by the supposedly elected representatives and the head of state. Together with other superior courts, the Constitutional Court has powers to issue explanatory and corrective orders for the legislature and the executive to undertake specific duties in specific ways, to make

[60] See, for example, *Economic Freedom Fighters v Speaker of the National Assembly* 2018 (2) SA 571 (CC) para 223–278, in which Mogoeng CJ dissented solely on the basis of the doctrine of separation of powers. For a context to the dissent, see *Economic Freedom Fighters v Speaker of the National Assembly* 2016 (3) SA 580 (CC) para 43.

[61] Notwithstanding its fidelity to the doctrine of judicial precedent, the Constitutional Court has overruled some of its decisions. See, for example, *Minister of Justice and Constitutional Development v Prince; National Director of Public Prosecutions v Rubin; National Director of Public Prosecutions v Acton* 2018 (6) SA 393 (CC), in which the Constitutional Court overruled *Prince v President Cape Law Society* 2002 (2) SA 794 (CC).

[62] Section 167(4) of the Constitution.

[63] Section 167(5) of the Constitution.

information available to the public and interdict them from undertaking unconstitutional actions.[64] When the conduct of a public office-bearer threatens constitutional values on the need to respect the rule of law and to ensure accountable, responsive and open governance, the Constitutional Court will utilise its powers to craft an extraordinary remedy, such as ordering the executive to report to the Constitutional Court periodically on its progress towards solving an issue.[65]

The Constitutional Court can coin new remedies to meet the peculiar circumstances of each case. As a result, mandatory and structural interdicts – which subject the executive, Parliament and organs of state to supervision by the Constitutional Court – ensure compliance with both the Constitution and the Constitutional Court's order.[66] Together with the High Court and the Supreme Court of Appeal, the Constitutional Court has considerable leeway to grant appropriate, just and equitable remedies.[67] These wide powers can be interpreted as far-reaching (if not nearly infinite), although the Constitutional Court has attempted to downplay its powers for strategic reasons.[68] When it comes to the Bill of Rights, the Constitutional Court may give any order that it considers appropriate.[69] Constitutional remedies are both open-ended and contextually flexible since 'there is no constitutional straightjacket'[70] for the tailoring of remedies. The yardstick is that a constitutional remedy should vindicate and entrench the rule of law.[71] In the last two decades, the Constitutional Court used its powers in many cases and declared many statutes and the conduct of both Parliament and the President inconsistent with the Constitution and invalid.

In contemporary times, the Constitutional Court has asserted its superior position within the constitutional dispensation by granting prospective relief to litigants to prevent impending violations of the Constitution, halting continuing violations with interdicts and granting restorative relief for violations already committed.[72] The constitutional remedies give effect to the founding values, the Bill of Rights and specific constitutional provisions. Constitutional damages include monetary awards. Monetary compensation ensures that citizens whose representatives violated rights compensate affected persons. However, the Constitutional Court does not award constitutional damages when there are alternative remedies.[73] The exercise of judicial discretion in granting just and equitable remedies implies textually unlimited powers since the determination of what is just and equitable solely depends on the Constitutional Court.

[64] M Flinders The Politics of Accountability in Modern States (2018) 132–133.
[65] See, for instance, the order of the court in *Black Sash Trust v Minister of Social Development* 2017 (5) BCLR 543 (CC) para 76.
[66] Van der Schyff (note 43 above) 192.
[67] Section 172(1)(b) of the Constitution.
[68] See *Glenister* (note 16 above) para 33 and *Doctors for Life International v Speaker of the National Assembly* 2006 (6) SA 416 (CC) paras 37–38.
[69] See *Fose v Minister of Safety and Security* 1997 (3) SA 786 (CC) paras 18–19.
[70] Bel Porto School Governing Body v Premier Western Cape 2002 (3) SA 265 (CC) para 180. See Sanderson v Attorney-General, Eastern Cape 1998 (2) SA 38 (CC) para 27; Bengwenyama Minerals (Pty) Ltd v Genorah Resources (Pty) Ltd 2011 (4) SA 113 (CC) para 85.
[71] *Nxasana* (note 27 above) para 82. See also *Steenkamp v Provincial Tender Board of the Eastern Cape* 2007 (3) SA 121 (CC) para 29. See also s 172 on certain powers of the Constitutional Court in constitutional matters.
[72] See, for instance, *Black Sash Trust I* (note 65 above).
[73] Rail Commuters Action v Transnet Ltd t/a Metrorail 2005 (2) SA 359 (CC) paras 77–78. See also Minister of Safety and Security v Van Duivenboden 2002 (3) All SA 741 (SCA) para 21.

Since the Constitutional Court is the guardian of the Constitution – the instrument from which rights and duties stem – one might want to consider that it has unfettered discretion to determine the nature of remedies in the process of vindicating the violation of rights. However, unfettered discretion to determine remedies does not mean that the Constitutional Court can do what it wants whenever its judges so desire. No. That would be contrary to the spirit of s 2 of the Constitution, which provides that the Constitution is supreme. No matter how far the Constitutional Court goes to craft remedies, it may not transgress the Constitution, for doing so would be violating its jurisdiction.

4.2 Guardianship of the Constitution

The Constitutional Court is the sole guardian of the Constitution.[74] O'Malley argues that Chapter 7 of the Interim Constitution, whose terms Chapter 8 of the Constitution incorporates, established the Constitutional Court as a guardian of the Constitution.[75] In this context, the term 'guardian of the constitution' refers to an institution with a constitutional mandate to protect the constitution against infringement.[76] The role of a constitutional guardian is to limit and constrain the legislature and the executive from undermining a constitution. The Constitutional Court guarantees constitutionalism and has a mammoth task to ensure that the legislature, the executive, other organs of state and the people do not violate the founding values of the Constitution. In several decisions, the Constitutional Court has proclaimed its role as the guardian of the Constitution.[77] However, the Constitution does not expressly stipulate that the Constitutional Court is the guardian of the Constitution but merely gives the Constitutional Court powers to determine constitutional matters.[78] This argument is not meant to project the impression that the Constitutional Court violates the Constitution by proclaiming itself as the upper guardian of the Constitution but serves to illustrate that the Constitutional Court has no doubt about its constitutional obligation to protect the Constitution. In this regard, one might view the entrenchment of constitutional review as a form of mistrust of Parliament and the executive, and the Constitutional Court as a *sui generis* institution designed to express the drafters' mistrust and constitutional vigilance.[79] Consequently, the role of the Constitutional Court is not to enforce the will of the legislature and the executive but to ensure that their conduct meets constitutional muster.

[74] Klug (note 41 above) 101.
[75] O'Malley (note 45 above) 75.
[76] L Vinx The Guardian of the Constitution: Hans Kelsen and Carl Schmitt on the Limits of Constitutional Law (2015) 174.
[77] See *Glenister* (note 16 above) para 33; *Mazibuko v Sisulu* 2013 (6) SA 249 (CC) para 135; *International Trade Administration Commission v Scaw South Africa (Pty) Ltd* 2012 (4) SA 618 (CC) para 92; *S v Mamabolo* 2001 (3) SA 409 (CC) para 63. See also Cameron (note 34 above) 107, 109.
[78] See s 167(7) of the Constitution.
[79] See Sachs (note 53 above) 4 on the institutions of mistrust established by the Constitution.

The most crucial role of the Constitutional Court's guardianship of the Constitution is to block unconstitutional amendments to the Constitution. The supremacy of the Constitution is crucial in this context because a constitution contains the law of making other laws.[80] When they established the Constitution, the constitutional drafters tacitly gave the Constitutional Court powers to test the substantive and procedural constitutionality of amendments to the Constitution.[81] Whereas the Constitution is both a legal and a political instrument, and since the Constitutional Court is at the apex of the legal system, the question arises whether the Constitutional Court is also at the apex of the political order in South Africa. The answer to this question is crucial to the main argument in this contribution since the traditional understanding of the doctrine of separation of powers implies that courts should solely concern themselves with the adjudication of disputes through legal interpretation. To answer the question, one needs to consider the interplay of the role of the Constitutional Court with democracy, politics and law-making, as is done in the following subsections.

4.3 The democratic mandate

Judiciaries have been criticised as 'unelected, unrepresentative and largely unaccountable elites'.[82] In South Africa, judges have been accused of pushing for a 'judicial dictatorship' and for undermining the will of the people.[83] Unfortunately, the criticisms flow from a constitutionally insupportable and outdated traditional conceptualisation of the doctrine of separation of powers, which views the courts as no more than mere arbiters of disputes. In contemporary South Africa, the courts do not govern but serve the people in an equal but different manner from the legislature and the executive. Mogoeng CJ argues that judges are 'unelected servants of the people'[84] bestowed with the mandate to ensure constitutional vigilance in the exercise of public power. The Constitutional Court is one of several institutions that enforce the democratic commands in the Constitution. As such, the Constitutional Court plays a prominent role in directing the democratic process.[85] It is common cause that the Constitution does not oblige the Constitutional Court to accede to unlawful and unconstitutional majoritarian preferences. Instead, the Constitution requires the judiciary to test majoritarian preferences against the standard of reasonableness and other constitutional prescripts.[86] When the legislature and the executive violate the Constitution, the Constitutional Court has no discretion but a duty to intervene.[87]

---

[80] C Möllers The *Three Branches: A Comparative Model of Separation of Powers* (2013) 126.

[81] By reason, an amendment of the Constitution is a constitutional matter because s 167(7) of the Constitution stipulates that a 'constitutional matter includes any issue involving the interpretation, protection or enforcement of the Constitution'.

[82] Flinders (note 64 above) 141. See also Van der Schyff (note 43 above) 55–56.

[83] See S Pityana, 'Constitutional Challenges Facing South Africa' <http://www.wolpetrust.org.za/conferences/conf2012/smpityana.pdf> 20.

[84] *United Democratic Movement v Speaker of the National Assembly* 2017 (5) SA 300 (CC) para 4.

[85] Issacharoff (note 35 above) 9.

[86] See Grant & Keohane (note 26 above) 32.

[87] *Scaw* (note 77 above) para 92; *Glenister* (note 16 above) para 33.

In South Africa, the argument that judicial officers are unelected and therefore have no democratic mandate to make a final determination on the choices of democratically elected public office-bearers overlooks several issues. First, members of the National Assembly, in their totality, do not derive a direct mandate from citizens because of the proportional representation system that makes citizens vote for political parties as opposed to specific persons aspiring for legislative office. Since the National Assembly elects the President, who appoints other members of the national executive, one cannot say that constitutional review trumps the legislative preferences of the majority of citizens.[88] Second, members of the executive exercise their powers not because of their democratic role as members of the National Assembly but by virtue of their single-handed appointment by the President.

Third, the President can choose two members of Cabinet outside the National Assembly. The two members may be ordinary citizens with expertise in complex areas. The option available to the President to choose two members of Cabinet outside the National Assembly reinforces the view that the executive has no direct and uncontested mandate from the people.[89] Fourth, most legislation is delegated legislation made by members of the executive who, as argued, are not directly elected by citizens. Lastly, civil servants in state departments develop government policies for approval by Cabinet members. One cannot say civil servants exercise power on behalf of the people because civil servants are unelected but appointed to perform functions at the direction of politicians in the executive. Whereas most civil servants enjoy formal protection from executive interference, they are most responsive and responsible to their political bosses.

Constitutional review affirms the Constitutional Court as a limitation on majoritarian powers because there are no guarantees that executive members will conform to the Constitution and observe all the laws all the time. The recent history of South Africa is replete with examples of the propensity of the executive to engage in constitutional misdemeanours, to misbehave, to act unlawfully and prejudicially, and with reckless disregard of legal procedures. Constitutional review enables the Constitutional Court to step in as the last line of defence for the Constitution and for the people against the arbitrary exercise of public power. The overriding powers of the Constitutional Court make it a crucial *sui generis* institution for the maintenance of political morality and the protection of the rights of vulnerable groups in society.[90] The justices of the Constitutional Court have the constitutional authority to speak for everyone as they form part of a *sui generis* institution whose obligation is to ensure that the values and principles chosen by the people of South Africa, as espoused in the Constitution, prevail. Therefore, the Constitutional Court is a protective *sui generis* institution that safeguards the broader interests of society. It is not surprising that the Constitutional Court has the authority to make final determinations on moral and political issues, even if the issues are controversial and seemingly unsuitable for judicial consideration. When the Constitutional Court overrules unconstitutional legislation or

---

[88] Van der Schyff (note 43 above) 54.
[89] Section 91(2)(c) of the Constitution.
[90] Sachs (note 53 above) 13; *Makwanyane* (note 3 above) para 88.

executive conduct, the justices act on behalf of all the people in rejecting encroachment on founding constitutional values. As such, when the Constitutional Court invalidates unconstitutional conduct – such as an unconstitutional amendment – the Constitutional Court does not undermine popular sovereignty but upholds it.

Although the foregoing analysis affirms the democratic nature of constitutional review, it is necessary to consider the democratic legitimacy of constitutional review in this contribution. In general, constitutional democracies considerably support constitutional review and judicial oversight because deficiencies in accountability lead to popular consciousness against legislatures and executive branches.[91] In a contemporary constitutional democracy such as South Africa, the Constitutional Court operates within a legal framework in which citizens combat the inadequacies of electoral accountability and parliamentary oversight through constitutional review. Inadvertently, constitutional review slowly shifts the role of the Constitutional Court from the adjudication of disputes to oversight of core executive functions, making the Court a powerful institution on accountability. Constitutional review is vital to accountability because a constitutional democracy cannot sustain its legitimacy without an independent institution – the Constitutional Court in the case of South Africa – which checks the exercise of public power.[92]

Scholars often present constitutional review as a necessary add-on to democracy[93] and an auxiliary precaution that prevents the abuse of power and ameliorates deficiencies in the accountability of public office-bearers.[94] Constitutional review also enjoys independence from political influences because judicial processes are not adulterated by partisan politics. The justices of the Constitutional Court claim their legitimacy as 'neutral servants of "the law"'.[95] However, the democratic legitimacy of the courts ultimately rests on the moral standing of the judiciary[96] and the democratic theory advocated by the courts.[97] Judicial review of democratic decisions, such as statutory enactments, is necessary because a majority decision does not necessarily mean that the decision is lawful, just, right or even democratic.[98] In a contemporary populist era, there is a greater need to guard against majoritarian decisions to prevent 'the tyranny of the majority'.[99] Generally:

> Even a legislature that is scrupulously faithful to electoral majorities may nevertheless represent the people poorly, for electoral majorities are themselves unsatisfactory substitutes for the people as a whole. That is so for two reasons: first, the majority is not the same thing as the whole, and, second, the electorate is not the same thing as the people [...] a majority is by definition merely a fraction of the people. In order to speak on behalf of the people, a government must take into account the interests and

91 Flinders (note 64 above) 131.
92 See N Dimitrijević 'Always above the law? Justification of constitutional review revisited' in M Jovanović (ed) *Constitutional Review and Democracy* (2015) 39.
93 See R Bellamy *Political Constitutionalism: A Republican Defence of the Constitutionality of Democracy* (2007) i.
94 S Weir & D Beetham *Political Power and Democratic Control in Britain* (1999) 429.
95 M Shapiro & A Sweet *On Law, Politics & Judicialization* (2002) 3.
96 C Eisgruber *Constitutional Self-Government* (2001) 57.
97 Lemieux & Watkins (note 40 above) 11.
98 See Weir & Beetham (note 94 above) 429.
99 See *Daniels v Scribante* 2017 (4) SA 341 (CC) para 153 on contemporary angry rhetoric and intransigent attitudes, whose perils exceed those of history and the frailties of its telling.

opinions of all the people, rather than merely those of a majority or some other fraction of the people.[100]

Although majority rule is evidently more democratic than minority rule, the people still need protection from the controllers of the levers of power. The Constitution endows the Constitutional Court with the power to test the lawfulness, rationality, proportionality and other aspects of government conduct and to use the Constitution as a benchmark for the validity of government conduct. Parliament, for its part, has no power to alter Court decisions. When enactments have been set aside for constitutional invalidity, the legislature is pushed to consider its conduct in more serious and principled terms.[101] However, the Constitutional Court should guard against majoritarian influences, such as public opinion, because the Constitution commits the Constitutional Court to fulfil its obligations as an independent arbiter of the Constitution, even if Court decisions may contradict a national consensus. The Constitutional Court should not concern itself with popular opinion because popular opinions are only relevant to Parliament.[102] Also, the Constitutional Court is not a politically responsible institution and is not accountable to public opinion.[103] The constitutional obligation of the Constitutional Court is to decide issues without fear, favour or prejudice.[104] The following section advances the idea that the Constitutional Court enjoys institutional supremacy also because of its democratic mandate, which is deep-rooted in politics.

4.4 The political mandate

The Constitutional Court has decided many political questions.[105] The judicialisation of politics in South Africa, which manifests in the use of the courts – particularly the Constitutional Court – by political actors to advance their interests and to gain legitimacy on their contribution to the rule of law, makes the Constitutional Court a major contributor and influencer of political discourse.[106] However, it is not clear how the Constitutional Court should react when invited by litigants to decide political questions. The justices of the Constitutional Court often frown on politically laden matters.

---

100 Eisgruber (note 96 above) 49–50.

101 S Gardbaum The New Commonwealth Model of Constitutionalism (2013) 74.

102 *Makwanyane* (note 3 above) paras 88–89.

103 Ibid para 305. See also Eisgruber (note 96 above) 60.

104 Section 165(2) of the Constitution.

105 In *Economic Freedom Fighters v Gordhan* (note 58 above) para 97, the Constitutional Court defined a political matter as 'a matter which has a political bite to it'. In several prior cases, the Constitutional Court acknowledged the political nature of cases which it has decided. See, for example, *Economic Freedom Fighters I* (note 60 above) para 43; *Glenister* (note 16 above) para 67 and *Negal* (note 59 above) para 42.

106 B Dressel 'The judicialization of politics in Asia: Towards a framework of analysis' in B Dressel (ed) *The Judicialization of Politics in Asia* (2012) 4. For an alternative definition, see R Hirschl, who defines the judicialisation of politics as 'the reliance on courts and judicial means for addressing core moral predicaments, public policy questions, and political controversies'; R Hirschl 'The judicialization of politics' in RE Goodin (ed) *The Oxford Handbook of Political Science* (2013) 253. The politicisation of apex courts is not peculiar to South Africa but is prevalent in most states that have adopted constitutional supremacy. For a synopsis, see R Hirschl 'The Judicialization of Mega-Politics and the Rise of Political Courts' (2008) *Annual Review of Political Science* 93.

Jafta J admonished political actors to find political solutions to political problems[107] and further referred to Davis J, who issued the following warning against the juridification of political disputes:

> There is a danger in South Africa, however, of the politicisation of the judiciary, drawing the judiciary into every and all political disputes as if there is no other forum to deal with a political impasse relating to policy or disputes which clearly carry polycentric consequences beyond the scope of adjudication. In the context of this dispute, judges cannot be expected to dictate to Parliament when and how it should arrange its precise order of business matters. What courts can do, however, is to say to Parliament: 'you must operate within a constitutionally compatible framework; you must give content to section 102 of the Constitution; you cannot subvert this expressly formulated idea of a motion of no confidence. However, how you allow that right to be vindicated is for you to do, not for the courts to so determine'.[108]

Davis J objected to what he perceived as an invitation to the judiciary to intrude into the political arena and to what he viewed as an invitation to create a juristocracy in South Africa.[109] In Davis J's view, judicial intrusion into the legislative terrain invites unwarranted criticism and imperils constitutional democracy.[110] In the past, Mogoeng CJ lamented the undesirability of political attacks (flowing from Court judgments perceived as political) on the judiciary and urgently met with President Jacob Zuma to discuss harsh criticism of the courts.[111] In October 2017, Mogoeng CJ said that it was undesirable for political parties to resolve their internal disputes in the courts and warned that '[if] we push our courts [sic] to the point where it literally becomes a raw political player, we are exposing it to criticism that could have been avoided'.[112] To protect the courts against accusations of overreach, the Chief Justice reasoned, political parties must resolve disputes internally.[113] Arguably, the justices of the Constitutional Court should not object to decide politically flavoured disputes because it has been seen at the beginning of this contribution that the justices preside over a *sui generis* and quasi-political institution that was designed by politicians for the achievement of political objectives.

Since the Constitution is a political instrument designed to regulate the legal order, it follows that individuals assigned to decide political disputes at a judicial level should be politically conscious enough to give effect to the intentions of the constitutional drafters. Some of the justices of the Constitutional Court have demonstrated political consciousness by continually referring to South Africa's emotive and contested political history in judgments.[114] Some of the justices have

---

107 *Mazibuko II* (note 77 above) para 83.

108 *Mazibuko II* (ibid), quoting *Mazibuko, Leader of the Opposition in the National Assembly v Sisulu MP Speaker of the National Assembly* 2013 (4) SA 243 (WCC) 256E-G.

109 Ibid 256H.

110 Ibid.

111 <https://www.enca.com/south-africa/ten-key-points-agreed-zuma-and-mogoeng>.

112 <http://www.huffingtonpost.co.za/2017/10/26/mogoeng-political-parties-must-resolve-issues-inside-the-family-first_a_23256319/>.

113 Ibid.

114 In *Doctors for Life* (note 68 above) para 62, the Constitutional Court said that the 'nature of our democracy must be understood in the context of our history'. See also *Makwanyane* (note 3 above) paras 156, 220, 262–266, 302, 322; *Certification of the Constitution I* (note 15 above) para 10; *Azapo v President of the Republic of South Africa* 1996 (4) SA 672 (CC) paras 2–3; *Merafong Demarcation Forum v President of the Republic of South Africa* 2008 (5)

deliberately framed their judgments in strong political language as an illustration of their political consciousness.[115] In so doing, the justices have shown that they are not mere legal robots exercising a fundamental constitutional duty but that they are politically conscious public office-bearers with a political role in a quasi-political institution. Thus, one appreciates that the constitutional duty of the Constitutional Court extends far beyond the traditional understanding of the role of a court. It must be noted that political consciousness on the bench of the Constitutional Court does not necessarily mean partisanship or prejudice, although both are inevitable when judicial ethics are compromised. The Constitutional Court, like all constitutional courts, needs to be impartial and must avoid appearances of partisanship and prejudice to protect its legitimacy.[116]

4.5 The law-making mandate

Section 82 of the Constitution entrusts the custody of all official records of Acts of Parliament to the Constitutional Court. In this section, I argue that the Constitutional Court has an inherent law-making role that is far more potent than that of Parliament. By necessity, the Constitutional Court is a lawmaker.[117] The judicio-legislative role arises from s 39 of the Constitution, the justiciability of the Bill of Rights and the Constitutional Court's guardianship of the Constitution, taken together with the power to grant extensive remedies. The Constitutional Court has a constitutional duty to develop the common law to 'promote the spirit, purport and objects of the Bill of Rights'.[118] The Constitutional Court also has the authority to order the enactment of legislation (which it has done on so many occasions and which is seen in this contribution as a form of initiating legislation) with specific instructions on what to include and not to include in the legislation. The Constitutional Court can also strike down aspects of the common law that are inconsistent with the Constitution and mould it in a manner it sees fit.[119] Undoubtedly, these are law-making powers meant to safeguard the Constitution as a cornerstone of the legal order and a guarantee of democracy and rights.

In many instances, the Constitutional Court has proven that it has the ability and the will to rewrite the law. In *S v Makwanyane*, it essentially amended the Criminal Procedure Act 51 of 1977 when it struck down capital punishment in s 277(1)(a) of the Act. The section mandated the capital sentence for some persons convicted of murder. When Parliament has omitted or failed to use legislation to protect constitutional rights, the Constitutional Court may exercise its law-making powers by directing

SA 171 (CC) para 208; *City of Tshwane Metropolitan Municipality v AfriForum* 2016 (6) SA 279 (CC) paras 1–2; and *Economic Freedom Fighters I* (note 60 above) para 1; and *AfriForum v University of the Free State* 2018 (2) SA 185 (CC) paras 1–6.

115 See, for example, *Du Plessis v De Klerk* 1996 (3) SA 850 (CC) para 119; *Daniels* (note 99 above) paras 152–155.

116 For a discussion, see Möllers (note 80 above) 128.

117 See Van der Schyff (note 43 above) 59.

118 Section 39(2) of the Constitution.

119 See, for instance, *Tshabalala v S; Ntuli v S* 2020 (5) SA 1 (CC) (extension of the common law doctrine of common purpose to encompass rape cases).

Parliament to amend an offending statute or enact a statute to cure a constitutional defect.[120] The Constitutional Court often reads in and reads out provisions from the enactments between the date of the order and the amendment or enactment of legislation.[121]

When the Constitutional Court has found part of legislation constitutionally inconsistent, it has often given Parliament grace periods, typically of two years, to amend offending parts of legislation. However, the grace periods have been accompanied with ultimatums that in the event of Parliament's failure to amend the statutes within the specified periods, reading words into and out of the impugned statutes would become automatic and permanent.[122] While it is indisputable that court directives to Parliament to amend or enact legislation within specified periods give Parliament greater latitude on how to regulate a complex issue that cannot be properly 'regulated' with court orders due to limited institutional expertise in the judiciary, they have the unintended effect of railroading Parliament and the executive into making laws these two political branches would not have been eager to make. Such directives cannot be reconciled with the classical separation of powers. The same could be said when the Constitutional Court monitors the implementation of its decisions by ordering the executive to submit periodic reports to it on the implementation of its decisions.

5. Some thoughts on the implications of the institutional supremacy of the Constitutional Court

This section revisits the separation of powers and applies the doctrine in the context of the powers and authority of the Constitutional Court discussed above. The foregoing analysis shows that the Constitutional Court enhances democracy by ensuring that the legislature and the executive abide by the Constitution. It also shows that the Constitutional Court does not have the discretion to pronounce on alleged constitutional violations but that it has an obligation to intervene when the Constitution is breached.[123] Thus, Frank Michelman correctly observes that no part of South African law 'can remain outside the Constitution's gaze'.[124] The separation of powers does not impede the Constitutional Court (upon application by litigants) from pronouncing on the constitutional validity of legislative or executive conduct because the Constitutional

120 Parliament enacted the Civil Union Act 17 of 2006 in compliance with a court order in *Minister of Home Affairs v Fourie* 2006 (1) SA 524 (CC) to enact legislation to provide for same-sex marriages. In a controversial decision in *Minister of Justice and Constitutional Development v Prince; National Director of Public Prosecutions v Rubin; National Director of Public Prosecutions v Acton* 2018 (6) SA 393 (CC), the Constitutional Court ordered Parliament to amend the Drugs and Drugs Trafficking Act 140 of 1992 and the Medicines and Related Substances Control Act 101 of 1965 to allow the possession and use of cannabis in private dwellings.

121 See the order in *New Nation Movement NPC v President of the Republic of South Africa* 2020 (8) BCLR 950 (CC).

122 See, for instance, *Minister of Home Affairs v Fourie* 2006 (1) SA 524 (CC) para 161, in which the Court said that 'if Parliament fails to cure the defect within twelve months, the words "or spouse" will automatically be read into section 30(1) of the Marriage Act'.

123 Section 172(1)(a) of the Constitution provides that the courts, when deciding on constitutional matters, '*must* declare that any law or conduct that is inconsistent with the Constitution is invalid to the extent of its inconsistency' (emphasis added).

124 FI Michelman 'The rule of law, legality and the supremacy of the Constitution' in S Woolman & M Bishop (eds) *Constitutional Law of South Africa* (2008) 46.

Court must ensure scrupulous compliance with the Constitution by all.[125] If the Constitutional Court does not do so, simply because of actual or anticipated political criticism, the Constitutional Court will be in breach of its constitutional obligation and would thus be acting unlawfully.

However, it is not always clear how, and to what extent, the Constitutional Court should intervene in a dispute, particularly in instances in which the applicants invite the Constitutional Court to decide matters that, since its establishment, have naturally fallen within parliamentary and executive domains. Although it is common cause that government conduct inconsistent with constitutional provisions is invalid and could be set aside by the Constitutional Court,[126] it is not immediately apparent to what extent the Constitutional Court can restrain the wishes of the majority of South Africans, supposedly expressed unequivocally through democratic processes that democratic representatives undertake. Since constitutional democracy places constitutional values and fundamental rights beyond the whims and caprices of unchecked majoritarian power, citizens affected by constitutionally inconsistent legislative or executive conduct have a right to constitutional review.[127] The source of public power (citizens, in the case of Parliament) is an irrelevant consideration when it comes to the test of constitutionality which the Constitutional Court applies when deciding disputes. In this light, constitutional review does not make the reviewing authority – the Constitutional Court – an opposition of the legislature or the executive.[128]

The Constitution does not have answers to all issues arising every day. It merely sets the framework for the government of the state. As such, Parliament, the executive, organs of state and the people should seek the interpretation, wisdom and guidance of the Constitutional Court on their duties and obligations. Thus, constitutional review is a handy mechanism for the determination of the nature and extent of public powers and authority. Bearing in mind that the Constitution is also a political document that was adopted by politicians to realise a political objective, it is only necessary that there be an institution, in the form of the Constitutional Court, to decide on the meaning of the Constitution, particularly when the 'real' political players do not agree on its meaning.[129]

However, the classical majoritarian dilemma emerges. Alexander Bickel coined the notion of counter-majoritarianism and said that when the 'Court declares unconstitutional a legislative act or the action of an elected executive, it thwarts the will of representatives of the actual people of the here and now; it exercises control, not [on] behalf

---

125 See *Heath* (note 13 above) para 25.

126 See ss 2 and 172(1)(a) of the Constitution.

127 Speaker of the National Assembly v De Lille MP [1999] 4 All SA 241 (A) para 14.

128 Sachs (note 53 above) 182.

129 Some of the cases in which the Constitutional Court was called upon the decide on the meaning of the Constitution when the 'real' political players could not agree on its meaning were *Economic Freedom Fighters I* (note 60 above) (whether the remedial action of the Public Protector binds Parliament when not set aside on review); *UDM v Speaker* (note 84 above) (whether the Speaker of the National Assembly has authority to order a secret ballot in a motion of no confidence in the President) and *Economic Freedom Fighters II* (note 60 above) (the relevant procedure between impeachment and motions of no confidence when the President has violated the Constitution).

of the prevailing majority, but against it […] [I]t is the reason the charge can be made that judicial review is undemocratic'.[130]

Like Bickel, other critics of constitutional review also assume that judicial review is counter-majoritarian and therefore presumptively at odds with democracy.[131] Scott Lemieux and David Watkins criticise Bickel's assumption of a counter-majoritarian difficulty from two angles. First, they argue that his theory is flawed because it is an inaccurate description of what judicial power entails and because the theory assumes that the legislative and executive branches represent popular majorities. Second, they argue that even if the counter-majoritarian difficulty were correct, it does not present all the normative challenges that Bickel and his disciples advance. The scholars proceed to argue that, in principle, counter-majoritarianism is good because minorities and other less politically powerful individuals need the protection of their rights against encroachment by wielders of the levers of state power.[132] Their argument echoes the sentiments in *Makwanyane*[133] that judicial review protects minorities and marginalised groups who cannot adequately protect their rights through the democratic process. Lemieux and Watkins' most potent argument in favour of constitutional review is that the preferences of the majority people in a state are 'inherently unknowable and irrational',[134] hence the need to subject legislative action to review to protect the public good. The argument is a restatement of the dangers of the whims and caprices of unchecked majoritarian power.

In the seminal 78th Federalist Paper, Alexander Hamilton made a pivotal case for judicial review,[135] arguing that the confusion around judicial review emerged from the argument that when a court sets aside a constitutionally inconsistent enactment adopted by a democratically representative and properly constituted legislature, the court in effect places itself superior to the legislature. Hamilton said that a legislature operates on delegated authority, whose terms of reference is the constitution. Hence, the legislature must act consistently with the instrument delegating its authority – the constitution. A failure of the judiciary to review and set aside constitutionally offensive statutes would mean that the legislature – the delegatee – is superior to the people from whom the delegated power derives. In his final analysis, Hamilton was unconvinced by the argument that courts substitute their opinions for the intentions of the legislature.[136] Based on this argument alone, pessimistic perceptions and fears of constitutional review as an instrument of the tyranny of the minority fall away.[137]

From a South African constitutional view, the counter-majoritarian argument fails to consider that South Africa is a constitutional democracy in which democratic governance depends on a supreme law – the Constitution – and also that the Constitutional Court wields significant power that cannot be fully reconciled with Bickel's description of 'the least dangerous branch'.[138] Constitutional democracy does

---

[130] AM Bickel The Least Dangerous Branch: The Supreme Court at the Bar of Politics 2 ed (1986) 16–17.
[131] Lemieux & Watkins (note 40 above) 9–10.
[132] Ibid.
[133] *Makwanyane* (note 3 above) para 88.
[134] Lemieux & Watkins (note 40 above) 132.
[135] See A Seagrave The Accessible Federalist: A Modern English Translation of 16 Key Federalist Papers (2017) 71.
[136] Ibid 72.
[137] See Eisgruber (note 96 above) 60.
[138] See Klug (note 41 above) 95.

not merely benefit from parliamentary democracy but depends on essential institutions and organs of state such as the Constitutional Court. The Constitutional Court exercises the delegated power of citizens to hold the legislature and executive accountable[139] because the Constitution is the source of all power in the state and the principal instrument through which power is delegated to the branches of government and organs of state. When ensuring that Parliament and the executive act consistent with the Constitution, constitutional review barricades and fortifies public power from abuse.[140] The proper functioning of constitutional democracy, in which the exercise of the powers bestowed by representative democracy must comply with constitutional prescripts, requires constitutional review to ensure constitutional compliance.[141]

However, constitutional review is a form of checks and balances which, in the strictest sense, is incompatible with a Montesquieu and Lockean form of separation of powers.[142] In modern times, it is difficult to adequately understand constitutional review through the lenses of the traditional model of separation of powers.[143] One accepts that the separation of powers is blurred due to the diffusion of constituted power between Parliament, the executive and the judiciary.[144] Pursuant to its promise in *De Lange*,[145] in which it said that it would develop a distinctive model of separation of powers, the Constitutional Court constantly remodels the separation of powers to enable the judiciary to effectively keep the exercise of legislative and executive power in check.[146] The model of separation of powers developed by the Constitutional Court enables the judiciary to devise new approaches to difficult questions and to put its massive constitutional powers into use to hold the legislature accountable and to prevent executive dominance.

The nature and extent of the Constitutional Court's powers to review legislative and executive conduct presents unique questions for the judiciary and calls for a careful balancing of several factors, including representative democracy, to ensure that the Constitutional Court does not unnecessarily invade legislative and executive domains.[147] As such, the Constitutional Court should adopt an approach that shows great judicial deference and restraint towards the political arms of government while at the same time ensuring that these approaches do not grant a free pass to Parliament and the executive to violate the Constitution. Institutional comity demands the Constitutional Court to avoid substituting parliamentary and executive decisions for its will.[148] The Constitutional Court must consider the implications of its decisions on the doctrine of separation of powers, as traditionally understood and constitutionally

---

139 A Goetz & R Jenkins Reinventing Accountability: Making Democracy Work for Human Development (2005) 1.
140 See M Beloff 'Neither cloistered nor virtuous? Judges and their Independence in the New millennium' (1999) *Denning Law Journal* 153, 166.
141 See *UDM v Speaker* (note 84 above) para 1.
142 H Napel, J Luiten & W Voermans 'Introduction' in H-M Napel & W Voermans (eds) *The Powers That Be: Rethinking the Separation of Powers: A Leiden Response to Möllers* (2015) 10.
143 Robertson (note 32 above) 1.
144 Napel et al (note 142 above) 7.
145 *De Lange* (note 10 above) para 60.
146 Van der Schyff (note 44 above) 47.
147 See *Economic Freedom Fighters I* (note 60 above) para 93.
148 See *Bato Star Fishing v Minister of Environmental Affairs* 2004 (4) SA 490 (CC) para 46; *National Treasury v Opposition to Urban Tolling Alliance* 2012 (6) SA 223 (CC) para 65; and *Makwanyane* (note 3 above) para 107.

ordained, while at the same time ensuring that it exercises effective checks and balances to promote and protect the Constitution. The Constitutional Court must guard against judicial activism and at the same time avoid timidity that may expose the constitutional order to violations.[149]

In extreme circumstances, the Constitutional Court may exercise oversight over executive functions that ordinarily fall within the jurisdiction of the President and the national executive. When one examines the extraordinary order of the Constitutional Court in *Black Sash Trust v Minister of Social Development*,[150] questions arise. Why, and to what extent, should the Constitutional Court supervise its counterparts in this manner? What is the impact thereof on the separation of powers? The questions arise mostly because Cabinet members are responsible to the President, their appointing authority, and accountable to the National Assembly.[151] Therefore, structural interdicts with a supervisory element are controversial. They blur the lines between, on the one hand, ensuring the implementation of a Court order by a complacent executive, and on the other hand, judicial supervision over the executive. If one subscribes to the concept of a separation of powers that places the judiciary at an equal level to the legislature and the executive, one can argue that the Constitutional Court can only grant supervisory orders in extreme cases in which the executive has demonstrated a lethargic or contemptuous unwillingness to implement a Court order on a vital constitutional issue. Nevertheless, the doctrine of separation of powers should not preclude the Constitutional Court from reaching out if convinced of the exigency to protect founding values.[152]

6. Conclusion

The Constitutional Court enjoys pre-eminence as an institutional guardian of the Constitution and a final arbiter of all legal and political disputes in South Africa. It stands above every institution and organ of state. It also stands above Parliament and the executive. Its institutional supremacy comes from two sources; namely, the Constitution (which gives it superior powers over Parliament and the executive) and from its jurisprudence through which the justices have effectively given the Constitutional Court more powers. Constitutional interpretation, which gives the Constitutional Court more powers, can be attributed to broad constitutional provisions that give it wide discretion on matters concerning its jurisdiction and remedies when the acts and omissions of Parliament and the executive are impugned. Consider, for example, the power of the Constitutional Court to order Parliament to make certain laws within certain timeframes. This power is not explicitly given by the Constitution or legislation. It is interpretatively derived from the wide powers to grant appropriate, just and equitable remedies.

The institutional supremacy of the Constitutional Court over the legislature and the executive does not properly fit into the traditional understanding of the doctrine of

[149] F Cachalia 'Separation of powers, active liberty and the allocation of public resources: The E-tolling case' (2015) 132 *South African Law Journal* 285, 312.

[150] *Black Sash Trust I* (note 65 above)

[151] See s 92 of the Constitution.

[152] See Robertson (note 32 above) 240.

separation of powers, which, ideally, places the legislature, the executive and the judiciary at the same level and assigns them distinct powers in the making, interpretation and enforcement of the law. In realisation of the institutional supremacy of the Constitutional Court, it is time to consider and recognise that the South African constitutional arrangement could be understood along the lines of judicial supremacy – in this case, Constitutional Court supremacy – than through the lenses of the doctrine of separation of powers. The Constitutional Court is not a mere court of law but a special institution, one of its own kind, with immense legal and political powers that loom larger than the doctrine of separation of powers. Inevitably, a continuous denial of the institutional supremacy of the Constitutional Court over the legislature and the executive on the pretext of the doctrine of separation of powers defies constitutional reality and could sustain the misconception of the role of the Constitutional Court in South Africa's constitutional democracy. That could be fatal for the development of jurisprudence in post-apartheid South Africa.

There is no denying that the Constitutional Court obtained its powers by deliberate design, not by oversight. Hence, the context and constitutional setting in which the Constitutional Court was established provide a more accurate vantage point of why the Constitutional Court has such superior powers. The context is also crucial for one to understand that when the Constitutional Court is confronted with political matters, it should not hide behind the doctrine of separation of powers. Instead, the Constitutional Court should confront such issues head-on with the comfortable assurance that it has legitimate constitutional authority (express or interpretatively derived) to decide any dispute and to make any order which it may deem necessary, even if such an order touches on the nerves of constitutional conservatives and politicians, and even if such an order offends the traditional understanding of the doctrine of separation of powers. The Constitutional Court should neither regret its powers in this regard, nor should it be ashamed to exercise the same. The only limit to its powers is the Constitution, in accordance with which it must always decide disputes.

The sustainability of constitutional democracy mainly depends on the vigilance of the Constitutional Court in enforcing the founding values of accountability, responsiveness and openness. Hence, the Constitutional Court should not hesitate to decide any dispute – even if it may be criticised on the grounds of the doctrine of separation of powers. It has been shown in this article that neither Parliament nor the executive has a greater democratic mandate than the Constitutional Court. As such, when the court exercises its powers and authority, it should not be guided solely by the doctrine of separation of powers but by a possible doctrine of its institutional supremacy over Parliament and the executive.

Acknowledgements

The author thanks Prof. Francois Venter and Dr Germarié Viljoen, who supervised the doctoral study from which this paper emanates. The author also extends gratitude to Prof. Anél du Plessis, Rosemary Mwanza, the anonymous reviewers and the editors for their comments that shaped the manuscript into publishable format.

Disclosure statement

No conflict of interest was reported by the author.

Funding

This paper is based in part on F Dube 'Enhancing democratic accountability through constitutionalism in South Africa' (2019) LLD thesis North-West University 178–192 and was completed in 2020 with the financial support of the National Research Foundation (grant number: 115581).

The judicialisation of politics in South Africa: A critique of the emerging trend

Hoolo Nyane

ABSTRACT
In apartheid South Africa, the judiciary was relegated to obscurity by a combination of executive dominance and legislative supremacy. The courts of law had a very narrow function, which was to search for, and implement, the 'intention of Parliament'. This paradigm shifted with the end of apartheid. In the new dispensation, the courts have consistently held that their role has changed markedly. They are now 'stronger' than they were under apartheid's constitutional edifice. This 'stronger' position of the judiciary is indisputably in keeping with the transformative nature of the new constitutional dispensation. However, the excessive power of the judiciary also has the potential to distort the desired balance between the three key branches of government; thereby judicialising the functions of the other two political branches. The untrammelled power of the judiciary is as dangerous as a parliament that operates in terms of the doctrine of parliamentary supremacy. The purpose of this article is to critique this arguably emergent pattern of judicialisation of politics in South Africa.

South African constitutional theory has undergone two fundamental phases in recent times – the apartheid phase and the democratic phase.[1] In both these phases, the role of the judiciary has remained at the centre of the discourse. In the apartheid era, the courts of law were overshadowed by the hegemony of the alliance between the executive and the legislature.[2] The courts and the law were sheer instruments of hegemony, rather than being countervailing forces against overzealousness.[3] In the broader scheme

---

[1] The theoretical differences of these phases are usually recapitulated in case law and scholarly writings. See, for instance, D van Wyk, J Dugard, B de Villiers & D Davis (eds) *Rights and Constitutionalism: The New South African Legal Order* (1994); *Ex parte Chairperson of the Constitutional Assembly: In re Certification of the Constitution of the Republic of South Africa, 1996* 1996 (4) SA 744 (CC); *S v Makwanyane* 1995 (3) SA 391 (CC); *Executive Council of the Western Cape Legislature v President of the Republic of South Africa* 1995 (4) SA 877 (CC); H Klug *The Constitution of South Africa: A Contextual Analysis* (2010); P de Vos & W Freedman (eds) *South African Constitutional Law in Context* (2014); I Currie & J de Waal *The New Constitutional Law and Administrative Law: Constitutional Law* (2001); IM Rautenbach & EFJ Malherbe *Constitutional Law* (2009).

[2] M Zvobgo 'The abuse of executive prerogative: A purposive difference between detention in black Africa and detention in white racist Africa' (1976) 6 *A Journal of Opinion* 38.

[3] J Dugard 'The judiciary in a state of national crisis with special reference to the South African experience' (1987) 44 *Washington & Lee Law Review* 477.

of things, the constitutional theory was also marshalled to justify this overbearing hegemony.[4] As John Dugard contends, 'judges […] adopted the sharp distinction between the legislative function and the judicial function inherent in the positivist, or command, theory of law, and regard it as their duty solely to analyse, interpret and give effect to the will of Parliament'.[5]

The two most important strands of constitutional theory that buttressed hegemony were the principles of parliamentary sovereignty[6] and executive prerogative.[7] Both these doctrines are rooted in British constitutional theory.[8] In its classical sense, the notion of parliamentary sovereignty entails three 'traits'. The first is the omnipotence of Parliament, which has 'the power […] to alter any law, fundamental or otherwise, as freely and in the same manner as other laws'.[9] The second trait is the existence of one corpus of law. The idea of distinguishing between constitutional law and other ordinary law, so that the former becomes the 'higher law', is alien to a classic English design. According to A.V. Dicey, there is 'under the English constitution no marked or clear distinction between laws which are not fundamental or constitutional and laws which are fundamental or constitutional'.[10] This classical British-based doctrine developed comfortably in South Africa during the apartheid era and morphed into a rationale for domination by both the legislature and the executive.[11] The judiciary was very quick to retreat and to assume the 'runner-boy' role of merely searching for the intention of Parliament and then implementing it without question.[12] In *Johannesburg Consolidated Investment Co v Johannesburg Town Council*,[13] the court held that the overriding justification for judicial intervention is the doctrine of *ultra vires* – the doctrine that power (*vires*) must be exercised within the confines of the law set out by

---

4 Ibid 497. See also AS Mathews 'The South African judiciary and the security system' (1985) 1 *South African Journal on Human Rights* 199, 203–5.

5 Dugard (note 3 above) 497.

6 Zvobgo (note 2 above).

7 I Currie *The Promotion of Administrative Justice Act in Context* (2007) 10; J Dugard *Human Rights and the South African Legal Order* (1978).

8 J Goldsworthy *Parliamentary Sovereignty: Contemporary Debates* (2010); E Delaney 'Judiciary rising: Constitutional change in the United Kingdom' (2013) 108 *North-western University Law Review* 543; N Barber 'The afterlife of parliamentary sovereignty' (2011) 9 *International Journal of Constitutional Law* 144; A Tucker 'Uncertainty in the rule of recognition and in the doctrine of parliamentary sovereignty' (2011) 31 *Oxford Journal of Legal Studies* 61.

9 AV Dicey *Introduction to the Study of the Law of the Constitution* (1885) 83.

10 Ibid 85.

11 See Dugard (note 3 above) who contends that 'From 1960 to 1982 the Appellate Division was presided over by Chief Justices who were politically sympathetic to the Government […] or jurisprudentially sympathetic to executive power […]. The majority of Judge Presidents of this period were likewise inclined. Although there was some questioning of judicial behaviour from academic quarters during this period, most judges seemed to be impervious to criticism and convinced that the policy of abstention or support for the executive was juridically sound'.

12 The position was stated in the English case of *British Railways Board v Pickin* [1974] 1 All ER 609, 622 (House of Lords of the United Kingdom) as follows: 'It must surely be for Parliament to lay down the procedures which are to be followed before a bill can become an Act. It must be for Parliament to decide whether its decreed procedures have in fact been followed. It must be for Parliament to lay down and to construe its standing orders and further to decide whether they have been obeyed; it must be for Parliament to decide whether in any particular case to dispense with compliance with such orders. It must be for Parliament to decide whether it is satisfied that an Act should be passed in the form and with the wording set out in the Act. It must be for Parliament to decide what documentary material or testimony it requires and the extent to which Parliamentary privilege should attach. It would be impracticable and undesirable for the High Court of Justice to embark on an enquiry concerning the effect or the effectiveness of the internal procedures in the High Court of Parliament or an enquiry whether in any particular case those procedures were effectively followed'.

13 *Johannesburg Consolidated Investment Company v Johannesburg Town Council* 1903 TS 111.

Parliament.[14] The height of this judicial deference was expressed in *Ndlwana v Hofmeyr*,[15] where the court confirmed that:

> Inasmuch as Parliament is now, since the passing of the Statute of Westminster, the supreme and sovereign law-making body in the Union, the Supreme Court has no power to pronounce upon the validity of an Act of Parliament duly promulgated and printed and published by proper authority.[16]

In a similar manner, the courts were excluded by the notion of executive prerogative, which originates from the royal prerogative in British constitutional theory.[17] In essence, it means that courts of law may not inquire into the exercise of powers that are pre-eminently in the executive sphere.[18] In South Africa the doctrine acquired a new, and unusually ugly, incarnation due to the apartheid context. The courts were generally loath to interfere with the powers of the executive in those circumstances where the statute invariably placed discretion in the hands of the minister concerned.[19]

The politico-legal transition that occurred in South Africa after apartheid changed the inter-branch balance of power.[20] The new constitutional dispensation rescued the judiciary from the doldrums. The jurisprudence of this transition has been ably described, both by the courts and scholars. The most apt explanation was made in *Baloro v University of Bophuthatswana*,[21] where the court stated that the courts in South Africa 'are now confronted by a rapid oscillation from the positivist jurisprudence founded on the sovereignty of Parliament to a jurisprudence based on the sovereignty of the law contained in the Constitution with a justiciable bill of rights'.[22]

This newfound role of the courts has effectively meant that the old frontiers of the judiciary have been pushed outwards significantly.[23] The political power of the judiciary has steadily increased hitherto; not only in South Africa but even at global level.[24] This expansion of judicial power has seen the courts encroaching into the functions of the other two political branches of government; hence the notion of judicialisation of

---

[14] See Dugard 'The judiciary and national security' (1982) 99 *South African Law Journal* 655, 657.

[15] *Ndlwana v Hofmeyr* 1937 AD 229. See also *Collins v Minister of the Interior* 1957 (1) SA 552 (A) 567, where Centilivres CJ specifically stated that 'If the provisions of a law are clear, we, as a court, are not concerned with the propriety of the legislation or policy of the legislature, our duty is to administer and interpret it as we find it'.

[16] Dugard (note 3 above) 229.

[17] *President of the Republic of South Africa v Hugo* 1997 (4) SA 1 (CC); H Wade 'Procedure and prerogative in public law' (1985) 1 *Law Quarterly Review* 180; *Laker Airways v Department of Trade* [1977] QB 643 (Court of Appeal of the United Kingdom); O Phillip & P Jackson *Constitutional and Administrative Law* (1987). At 269, the authors pointedly contend that 'the prerogatives that may be classed as executive, administrative or governmental are a relic of the powers which the King had when he really governed the country'. See also D Mitchell 'The royal prerogative in modern Scots law' (1957) *Public Law* 304; T Poole 'United Kingdom: The royal prerogative' (2010) 8 *International Journal of Constitutional Law* 146; *R (Bancoult) v Secretary of State for Foreign and Commonwealth Affairs or Bancoult (No. 2)* [2008] UKHL 61 (House of Lords of the United Kingdom).

[18] See *Chandler v DPP* [1964] AC 763 (House of Lords of the United Kingdom); *Council of Civil Service Unions v Minister for the Civil Service* [1985] AC 374 (House of Lords of the United Kingdom).

[19] *Donges v Dadoo* [1950] 2 All SA 357 (A).

[20] *Speaker of National Assembly v De Lille MP* [1999] 4 All SA 241 (A); E Mureinik 'A bridge to where? Introducing the interim Bill of Rights' (1994) 10 *South African Journal on Human Rights* 31; D Dyzenhaus 'The pasts and future of the rule of law in South Africa' (2007) 124 *South African Law Journal* 734.

[21] *Baloro v University of Bophuthatswana* 1995 (4) SA 197 (B).

[22] Ibid 243.

[23] C Hoexter 'The future of judicial review in South African administrative law' (2000) 117 *South African Law Journal* 484.

[24] R Hirschl 'The judicialization of mega-politics and the rise of political courts' (2008) 11 *Annual Review of Political Science* 93.

politics. In South Africa, judicialisation is inspired by several aspects of the new constitutional dispensation such as, but not limited to: the enforceability of socio-economic rights,[25] the emergence of the doctrine of legality,[26] the power of the judiciary to make structural interdicts[27] and – much more importantly – the theory of transformative constitutionalism. The latter theory has served to greatly legitimate the notion of empowered courts that have become active players in the dynamics of not only legal but also social transformation.[28] There is an emerging concern that the courts' power in South Africa is expanding dangerously into the provinces of other branches – the phenomenon that has been dubbed 'judicial overreach'.[29] For instance, in the case of *Economic Freedom Fighters v Speaker of the National Assembly,*[30] the Chief Justice criticised the majority judgment, which had allowed the court to inquire into the internal processes of Parliament, and called it 'a textbook case of judicial overreach – a constitutionally impermissible intrusion by the Judiciary into the exclusive domain of Parliament'.[31]

The purpose of this article is to critique this emerging pattern about the role of the judiciary in contemporary constitutional theory in South Africa. The article starts by re-visiting the whole notion of judicialisation of politics. The second part deals with decisions of the superior courts in South Africa, which arguably anchor this trend. In the end, the article argues that while the position of the courts under apartheid was clearly undesirable, today there is a genuine concern about judicialisation. Just as democracy suffers when the judiciary is in slumber, so too is there a huge danger to democracy when the judiciary is in overdrive.

1. Revisiting the notion of judicialisation of politics

1.1 The development of the notion of the judicialisation of politics

The judicialisation of politics is an emerging phenomenon, not only in South Africa but globally.[32] The notion is associated with the ascendancy of liberal constitutionalism – the notion that emphasises the limitation of powers of various government

[25] C Mbazira 'From ambivalence to certainty: Norms and principles for the structural interdict in socio-economic rights litigation in South Africa' (2008) 24 *South African Journal on Human Rights* 1; D Davis 'Adjudicating the Socio-economic rights in the South African Constitution: Towards "deference lite"' (2006) 22 *South African Journal on Human Rights* 300; *Government of the Republic of South Africa v Grootboom* 2001 (1) SA 46 (CC).

[26] *Fedsure Life Insurance Ltd v Greater Johannesburg Transitional Metropolitan Council* 1999 1 SA 374 (CC); *Pharmaceutical Manufacturers Association of South Africa and Another: In re Ex Parte President of the Republic of South Africa and Others* 2000 2 SA 674 (CC); C Hoexter 'The principle of legality in South African administrative law' (2004) 4 *Macquarie Law Journal* 165.

[27] See s 172(1) of the Constitution.

[28] D Moseneke 'The fourth Bram Fischer memorial lecture: Transformative adjudication' (2002) 18 *South African Journal on Human Rights* 309.

[29] M le Roux & D Davis *Lawfare: Judging Politics in South Africa* (2019).

[30] *Economic Freedom Fighters v Speaker of the National Assembly* 2018 (2) SA 571 (CC) (*EFF II*).

[31] Ibid para 223. The judges who wrote the majority judgment did not take kindly to the expression 'textbook case of judicial overreach'. At para 218 Jafta J retorted that 'what is unprecedented is the suggestion that the construction of the section embraced by the majority here constitutes "a textbook case of judicial overreach". The suggestion is misplaced and unfortunate'.

[32] A Sweet & T Brunell 'Trustee courts and the judicialization of international regimes: The politics of majoritarian activism in the ECTHR, the EU, and the WTO' (2013) 1 *Journal of Law and Courts* 61; C Tate & R Vallinder (eds) *The Global Expansion of Judicial Power* (1997); T Vallinder 'The judicialization of politics: A world-wide phenomenon: Introduction' (1994) 15 *International Political Science Review* 91; N Steytler 'The judicialization of

departments.[33] All facets of liberal constitutionalism – such as separation of powers, respect for human rights, the rule of law and judicial independence – have coalesced to limit the operational space of the political departments of government in favour of the judiciary.[34] In this coalition of liberal concepts, the (human) rights discourse has arguably emerged as most instrumental for the ascendancy of the judiciary.[35] Even when the criticism of judicialisation seems appealing, the judiciary normally derives its popular legitimacy from the rights discourse.[36]

As it is a newly emerging concept, clarity on the notion of judicialisation of politics is not yet settled.[37] Nevertheless, in its basic form, the notion connotes 'the reliance on courts and judicial means for addressing core moral predicaments, public policy questions, and political controversies'.[38] The concept has many incarnations, to wit: 'judicialism', 'judicial supremacy', 'government by judges', 'lawfare'[39] or 'juristocracy'.[40] All of them carry one central meaning – that the courts have expanded their province to deal with questions that they were prohibited from dealing with in the past. It is not limited to the courtroom only; it also has implications for the general management of public affairs. Everybody who is involved in the management of public affairs conducts him- or herself in a manner that anticipates what the courts will say on almost everything.[41] This is the phenomenon in terms of which politics is increasingly migrating from the branches of government and other institutions to the courts of law. As John and Jean Comaroff observe, politics itself 'is migrating to the courts […] conflicts once joined in parliaments, by means of street protests mass demonstrations, and media campaigns, through labour strikes, boycotts, blockades, and other instruments of assertions, tend more and more […] to find their ways to the judiciary'.[42]

Armed with the newfound devices of modern constitutionalism, the courts become emboldened to resolve these political questions to the extent that there is virtually no question under the new constitutional dispensation that the courts may not adjudicate. In that way, the notion of judicialisation of politics stands in sharp contrast with, and arguably replaces, the political question doctrine, which is a time-honoured principle

Namibian politics' (1993) 9 *South African Journal on Human Rights* 477; S Hunt 'The judicialization of politics in Canada and the United States' (2013) *Honors Projects* 39.

[33] A Amissah 'Constitutionalism and law in Africa' in D Ronen (ed) *Democracy and Pluralism in Africa* (1986) 14; C McIlwain *Constitutionalism: Ancient and Modern* (1947).

[34] M Vile *Constitutionalism and Separation of Powers* 2 ed (1998) 1.

[35] In *Fose v Minister of Safety and Security* 1997 (3) SA 786 (CC) para 69, the Constitutional Court noted that 'in a country where so few have the means to enforce their rights through the courts, it is essential that on those occasions when the legal process does establish that an infringement of an entrenched right has occurred, it be effectively vindicated. The courts have a particular responsibility in this regard and are obliged to "forge new tools" and shape innovative remedies, if needs be, to achieve this goal'.

[36] Ibid.

[37] R Hirschl 'Repositioning the judicialization of politics: *Bush v. Gore* as a global trend' (2002) 15 *Canadian Journal Law & Jurisprudence* 191; R Miller 'Lords of democracy: The judicialization of "pure politics" in the United States and Germany' (2004) 61 *Washington & Lee Law Review* 587; T Moustafa 'Law vs the state: The judicialization of politics in Egypt' (2003) 28 *Law and Society Inquiry* 883.

[38] R Hirschl 'The judicialization of politics' in RE Goodin (ed) *The Oxford Handbook of Political Science* (2009).

[39] H Corder & C Hoexter '"Lawfare" in South Africa and its effects on the judiciary' (2017) 10 (2–3) *African Journal of Legal Studies* 105.

[40] G Kanyeihamba 'The rule of law, judicialism, and development' (1984) 3 *Third World Legal Studies* 100; R Hirschl *Towards Juristocracy: The Origins and Consequences of the New Constitutionalism* (2009).

[41] R Kelemen 'Judicialisation, democracy and European integration' (2013) 49 *Representation* 295.

[42] J Comaroff & J Comaroff (eds) *Law and Disorder in the Postcolony* (2008) 17.

of constitutional law. It posits that courts will not adjudicate on questions that are purely political in nature; such questions are non-justiciable.[43] While the applicability of the doctrine under the new South African constitutional dispensation is a matter of considerable controversy,[44] allusions to it are observable from the *dicta* of some decisions of the Constitutional Court. As early as during the first certification case, the Court said:

> First and foremost, it must be emphasised that the Court has a judicial and not a political mandate […] Admittedly a constitution, by its very nature, deals with the extent, limitations and exercise of political power as also with the relationship between political entities and with the relationship between the state and persons. But this Court has no power, no mandate and no right to express any view on the political choices.[45]

Historically, the reasons for leaving these 'political questions' to branches of government other than the judiciary were many, but the main ones were the sovereignty of Parliament and executive prerogative. Parliament was regarded as supreme on legislative matters, while the executive was regarded as having the exclusive prerogative to decide on policy questions.[46] Indeed, in repressive political environments like apartheid South Africa, these constitutional devices quickly developed into instruments of repression.[47] Therefore, the legislature and executive, which were effectively in an alliance,[48] excluded the judiciary.[49]

When liberal constitutionalism triumphed against parliamentary supremacy globally,[50] courts became clothed with immense powers. South Africa's constitutional transition seems to epitomise this global movement. As Kelemen argues, there has been a global movement 'away from traditional notions of parliamentary supremacy towards models of democracy in which constitutional courts have the power of judicial review'.[51]

The justification for judicialisation occurs at both the political level and the legal level. At the political level, the upsurge of judicialisation is largely attributable to the

---

[43] M Mhango 'Separation of powers in Ghana: The evolution of the political question doctrine' (2014) 17 *Potchefstroom Electronic Law Journal* 2706.

[44] M Mhango 'Is it time for a coherent political question doctrine in South Africa? Lessons from the United States' (2014) 7 *African Journal of Legal Studies* 457.

[45] *In re: Certification of the Constitution of the Republic of South Africa* 1996 (4) SA 744 (CC) para 27.

[46] In the case of *Chandler v DPP* (note 18 above), the House of Lords held that: 'It is certainly true to say as a general rule that the courts will not review decisions of policy, whether made by the executive or by any other policymaking body'.

[47] Zvobgo (note 2 above); S Haynie *Judging in Black and White: Decision Making in the South African Appellate Division 1950–1990* (2003); *Sachs v Minister of Justice* 1934 AD 11.

[48] P Langa 'The separation of powers in the South African Constitution' (2006) 22 *South African Journal on Human Rights* 2; P Labuschagne 'The doctrine of separation of powers and its application in South Africa' (2004) 23 *Politeia* 84.

[49] C Forsyth *In Danger for their Talents* (1985). See also H Corder *Judges at Work* (1984) who captures the role of the judiciary in the apartheid era much more instructively as follows: 'It is well known, however, that by the mid-1960s at the latest, this judicial resistance to the undermining of the rule of law had been defeated, both by legislative intransigence as well as judicial acquiescence, and that the ensuing decades witnessed ever more abject abandonment by the courts of the basic tenets of justice in the face of legislated injustice and executive tyranny'.

[50] N Haysom 'Constitutionalism, majoritarian democracy and socio-economic rights' (1992) 8 *South African Journal on Human Rights* 451; D Law & M Versteeg 'The evolution and ideology of global constitutionalism' (2011) 99 *California Law Review* 1163; B Ackerman 'The rise of world constitutionalism' (1997) 83 *Virginia Law Review* 771.

[51] Kelemen (note 41 above) 295. See also J Ferejohn 'Judicializing politics, politicizing law' (2002) 65 *Law & Contemporary Problems* 41.

fall of parliamentary sovereignty and executive prerogative that had often mutated into instruments of political repression. Thus, it has become very easy to associate a strong judiciary with the gains of the transition from the 'past' to the 'new' constitutional dispensation.[52] Legally, the justification for 'stronger' judicial power is that it is an inevitable consequence of the new constitutional design, premised on strong judicial review, judicial independence, the rule of law and legality.[53] These principles have reinvigorated the judiciary to the extent that today virtually no aspect of government is immune from judicial scrutiny.[54]

1.2 The problematisation of judicialisation of politics

Like most politico-legal constructs, the notion of judicialisation of the judiciary has generated division amongst constitutional scholars and the judiciary alike. The most balanced assessment of this division of opinion on judicialisation is done by Michelle le Roux and Dennis Davis. The authors observe that judicialisation – which they call a 'lawfare' – is a double-edged sword. It can be both good and bad. They contend that it can be 'a good thing for adjudication to be political, in the sense that it advances the constitutional project and is undertaken by litigants and judges as an instrument to ensure that the constitutional vision is realised'.[55] The authors state that judicialisation 'is a bad thing when courts become the site of pure political contestation [...] [I]t draws the judiciary further into political arena than has traditionally been the case. It holds the promise of promoting more reasoned deliberation about key political and distributional claims but it can also turn the courts into juristocracy'.[56]

The arguments against judicialisation, on which this article is based, can be categorised under three heads, namely, deference-based, justiciability and judicial review arguments. First, the deference-based arguments posit that while the role of the judiciary is generally accepted, courts should accord respect to other branches since they were created to serve a legitimate purpose.[57] The basis of this set of arguments is the hallowed notion of separation of powers. Allowing the judiciary to have transcending powers is equally dangerous to the constitutional design. This view is best captured by the Constitutional Court in *National Coalition for Gay and Lesbian Equality v Minister of Home Affairs*,[58] where it warned that it must constantly keep in mind:

> the principle of the separation of powers and, flowing therefrom, the deference it owes to the legislature in devising a remedy [...] It is not possible to formulate in general terms what such deference must embrace, for this depends on the facts and

[52] Dyzenhaus (note 20 above).

[53] P Sewpersadh & J Mubangizi 'Judicial review of administrative and executive decisions: Overreach, activism or pragmatism?' (2017) 21 *Law, Democracy & Development* 201.

[54] In *EFF II* (note 30 above) Mogoeng CJ said: 'Courts ought not to blink at the thought of asserting their authority, whenever it is constitutionally permissible to do so, irrespective of the issues or who is involved'.

[55] Le Roux & Davis (note 29 above) 10.

[56] Ibid.

[57] L Steyn 'Deference: A tangled story' (2005) 2 *Public Law* 346; J Jowell 'Judicial deference and human rights: A question of competence' in P Craig & R Rawlings (eds) *Law and Administration in Europe: Essays in Honour of Carol Harlow* (2003) 67, 80; J Jowell 'Judicial deference: Servility, civility or institutional capacity?' (2003) 4 *Public Law* 592, 598.

[58] *National Coalition for Gay and Lesbian Equality v Minister of Home Affairs* 2000 (2) SA 1 (CC).

> circumstances of each case. In essence, however, it involves restraint by the courts in not trespassing onto that part of the legislative field which has been reserved by the Constitution, and for good reason, to the legislature.[59]

The notion of constitutional deference has taken root in South Africa, but the real challenge is to maintain the sensitive balance between deference and interference.[60] Mostly, the courts readily interfere and review the decisions of the other branches of government.

The second head of arguments against judicialisation are based on the notion of justiciability. This notion means that the judiciary should avoid or refrain from adjudicating 'those issues not properly suited for adjudication because such issues belong to the domain of the executive, the legislature or the political process'.[61] While justiciability is still an incidence of the separation of powers,[62] it differs from deference in that its main purpose is not necessarily to ensure that the court respects the terrains of other departments but, rather, to exclude the courts totally on certain questions that pre-eminently belong to other branches.[63] In US constitutional theory, justiciability is related to the political doctrine question.[64] The latter is specific about excluding the involvement of the courts on certain questions that are regarded as political. The doctrine holds that the existence of 'political questions – issues to be resolved and decisions to be made by the political branches of government and not by the courts – is axiomatic in a system of constitutional government built on the separation of powers'.[65] This doctrine identifies the legislature and the executive as the political branches of government that must handle 'political questions'. However, the line between a 'political question' and a 'non-political question' is always blurred.[66] In *Glenister v President of the Republic of South Africa*[67] the Constitutional Court attempted, albeit indirectly, to draw the line thus:

> Under our constitutional scheme it is the responsibility of the executive to develop and implement policy. It is also the responsibility of the executive to initiate legislation in order to implement policy. And it is the responsibility of Parliament to make laws. When making laws Parliament will exercise its judgment as to the appropriate policy to address the situation.[68]

---

[59] Ibid para 66. See also *United Democratic Movement v President of the Republic of South Africa* 2003 (1) SA 495 (CC).

[60] K Mclean 'Towards a framework for understanding constitutional deference' (2010) 25 *Southern African Public Law* 445.

[61] C Okpaluba & M Mhango 'Between separation of powers and justiciability: Rationalising the Constitutional Court's judgment in the Gauteng e-tolling litigation in South Africa' (2017) 21 *Law, Democracy & Development* 1.

[62] C Okpaluba 'Justiciability and standing to challenge legislation in the Commonwealth: A tale of the traditionalist and judicial activist approaches' (2003) 36 *Comparative and International Law Journal of Southern Africa* 25.

[63] See *Chandler* (note 18 above). See also *Ngxuza v Secretary, Department of Welfare, Eastern Cape Provincial Government* 2001 (2) SA 609 (E), where the court stated: 'The nature and extent of a Court's assessment of the justiciability of a constitutional issue is, I think, intimately related to the extent to which it judges that those issues can adequately and better be dealt with by other democratic means'.

[64] R Barkow 'More supreme than court: The fall of the political question doctrine and the rise of judicial supremacy' (2002) 102 *Columbia Law Review* 237.

[65] L Henkin 'Is there a "political question" doctrine?' (1976) 85 *Yale Law Journal* 597, 597; H Nyane 'A critique of proceduralism in the adjudication of electoral disputes in Lesotho' (2018) 17 *Journal of African Elections* 1; J Sarkin 'The political role of the South African Constitutional Court' (1997) 114 *South African Law Journal* 134.

[66] Mhango (note 44 above) 457.

[67] *Glenister v President of the Republic of South Africa* 2009 (1) SA 287 (CC).

[68] Ibid para 67.

Due largely to the ambiguity of the doctrine, some authors have suggested that it should not be accepted in South Africa.[69] In fact, it would be hard to invoke the doctrine in South Africa because the South African Constitutional Court 'has held in various judgments that the rule of law is a foundational value […] and that it requires that the exercise of all government power must be rationally related to a legitimate government purpose and that the judiciary exercises control in this regard'.[70]

The third head under which the arguments against judicialisation come is the hackneyed doctrine of judicial review. Judicial review is ordinarily the launchpad for judicialisation but a debate has been raging in the discourse of constitutional theory on whether the courts should continue to enjoy their privileged position of reviewing the decisions and actions of other departments.[71] As Alon Harel and Adam Shinar contend, '[t]he study of judicial review has to a large extent been a study of the constitutionalism–democracy debate'.[72] The executive and the legislature have sought to challenge the privileged position enjoyed by the judiciary because of the doctrine of judicial review. They claim that they have a more popular mandate than the judiciary does. Therefore, they are always frustrated by the constant overturning of their actions by a less popular branch. This view was expressed by former President Zuma when paying tribute to former Chief Justice Ngcobo:

> The executive, as elected officials, has the sole discretion to decide policies for government. The principle of separation of powers meant that the encroachment of one arm of the state on the terrain of another should be discouraged, and there should be no bias in this regard. We respect the powers and role conferred by our Constitution on the legislature and the judiciary. At the same time, we expect the same from these very important institutions of our democratic dispensation.[73]

This pushback is not only coming from political quarters; there is also an upsurge in scholarship to the effect that 'strong judicial review' is based on a flawed understanding of the inter-branch relationship.[74] This group of scholars is led by the US scholar Alexander Bickel, who argues that 'judicial review is a counter-majoritarian force in our system. […] when the Supreme Court declares unconstitutional a legislative act […] it thwarts the will of representatives of the actual people of the here and now'.[75] These scholars have pushed back against the ascendancy of judicialism to the extent that it is now doubted whether the courts should even continue to enjoy the status of being the final interpreters of the Constitution of the Republic of South Africa, 1996.[76] This view radically posits that each branch of government is best placed to interpret

---

[69] I Rautenbach 'Policy and judicial review – political questions, margins of appreciation and the South African Constitution' (2012) 1 *Journal of South African Law* 20.

[70] Ibid 26.

[71] J Fleming 'Judicial review without judicial supremacy: Taking the Constitution seriously outside the courts' (2005) 73 *Fordham Law Review* 1377, 1378–9 (giving examples of such theories).

[72] A Harel & A Shinar 'Between judicial and legislative supremacy: A cautious defense of constrained judicial review' (2012) 10 *International Journal of Constitutional Law* 950, 95s.

[73] Quoted in Rautenbach (note 69 above) 20–1.

[74] J Waldron 'The core of the case against judicial review' (2006) 115 *Yale Law Journal* 134s; Fleming (note 73 above); Harel & Shinar (note 74 above).

[75] A Bickel *The Least Dangerous Branch: The Supreme Court at the Bar of Politics* (1986) 16–17.

[76] E Gant 'Judicial supremacy and non-judicial interpretation of the constitution' (1997) 24 *Hastings Constitutional Law Quarterly* 359, 366–9.

constitutional values in relation to its functional area.[77] While these debates are mostly based on the US context, they have a direct relevance to the emergent pattern in South Africa.

2. Areas showing signs of judicialisation in South Africa

The changing role of the judiciary from the pre-democratic era, where it was limited by the political branches, to the new dispensation, where it plays its role as a co-equal branch of government, is a laudable development. The transition from parliamentary supremacy to constitutional supremacy saw the courts acquiring more power. In an early decision, *Executive Council of the Western Cape Legislature v The President of South Africa,*[78] the Constitutional Court noted that 'it is of crucial importance at this early stage of the development of our new constitutional order, to establish respect for the principle that the Constitution is supreme'.[79] The courts have consistently asserted their victory in subsequent cases.[80] In *S v Makwanyane*[81] the Constitutional Court explained how the new dispensation has accorded supremacy to the Constitution. It argued as follows:

> Now that constitutionalism has become central to the new emerging South African jurisprudence, legislative interpretation will be radically different from what it used to be in the past legal order. In that legal order, due to the sovereignty of parliament, the supremacy of legislation and the absence of judicial review of parliamentary statutes, courts engaged in simple statutory interpretation, giving effect to the clear and unambiguous language of the legislative text - no matter how unjust the legislative provision.[82]

A disturbing pattern emerges when the judiciary increasingly poses as a 'super-branch' in relation to the other two political branches. This pattern has manifested itself in some of the areas of the inter-branch relationship. Those areas are here-under discussed.

2.1 Holding the political branches accountable

Accountability is an integral part of the new model of constitutionalism in South Africa. The South African Constitution enshrines accountability in three distinct ways. First, unlike in the old dispensation, accountability is specifically enshrined as a foundational value of the new dispensation.[83] Secondly, it is also identified as a fundamental principle in many other aspects of the Constitution, such as 'public administration'.[84] Thirdly, and much more importantly, in terms of ss 55(2)*(a)* and *(b)*, the National Assembly has a distinct function to ensure that all executive structures of government

---

[77] M Tushnet *Taking the Constitution Away From the Courts* (2000).
[78] *Executive Council of the Western Cape Legislature v The President of South Africa* 1995 (4) SA 877 (CC).
[79] Ibid para 100.
[80] *Certification* (note 1 above).
[81] *Makwanyane* (note 1 above).
[82] Ibid para 301. In para 261, the court held further that the Constitution seeks to provide 'a transition from these grossly unacceptable features of the past to a conspicuously contrasting [...] future'.
[83] Section 1 of the Constitution.
[84] Section 195(1)*(f)* of the Constitution.

are held 'accountable'. Therefore, the Constitution places the responsibility to ensure accountability distinctively on the legislature, not the judiciary.

Nevertheless, this function has drifted to the judiciary in a pronounced manner in South Africa. Perhaps the justification is that there is a palpable inability on the side of the legislature to execute this function effectively. This dereliction is also common with the executive in South Africa. This deterioration in accountability and constitutionalism, on the side of political branches, has placed the courts in an unenviable position of being the 'last vintage'.

But that is not reason enough to judicialise the functions that the Constitution has specifically granted to the other branches. The most recent manifestations of this pattern were in the *Economic Freedom Fighters (EFF)* cases. In the first *EFF* case,[85] the facts were very intriguing because they dealt with Parliament's obligation to hold the President accountable.[86] What makes the facts even more intriguing for the purposes of this study is that all three branches of government were involved. In this case, the Public Protector, which is a Chapter 9 institution established by the Constitution,[87] had found that the President had violated his constitutional obligations by benefiting unduly from the non-security upgrades affected at his private residence. The Public Protector submitted her report to that effect to the National Assembly. The National Assembly, in turn, established two ad hoc committees to deal with the report. Both committees absolved the President. Therefore, the two opposition parties, the EFF and the Democratic Alliance approached the Constitutional Court for an order that by failing to act on the report of the Public Protector, particularly its remedial actions, the National Assembly had violated its constitutional obligation. The National Assembly was alleged to have violated its obligations in terms of ss 55(2) and 181(3) of the Constitution. The former provision obligates the National Assembly to provide for mechanisms 'to ensure that all executive organs of state in the national sphere of government are accountable to it; and (b) to maintain oversight of (i) the exercise of national executive authority, including the implementation of legislation; and (ii) any organ of state'.[88]

The gravamen of the case was that the National Assembly essentially failed in its duty to hold the President accountable. The National Assembly's defence was that there was no obligation on it to facilitate compliance with the report because the Public Protector has no powers to dictate to the National Assembly what to do. The Constitutional Court cautioned:

> It falls outside the parameters of judicial authority to prescribe to the National Assembly how to scrutinise executive action, what mechanisms to establish and which mandate to give them, for the purpose of holding the Executive accountable and fulfilling its oversight role of the Executive or organs of State in general. The mechanics of how to

---

85 *Economic Freedom Fighters v Speaker of the National Assembly; Democratic Alliance v Speaker of the National Assembly* 2016 (3) SA 580 (CC) (*EFF I*).

86 Parliament's obligation to hold the executive to account is embodied in s 55 of the Constitution.

87 Section 181 of the Constitution.

88 Section 181 establishes 'state institutions supporting democracy'. Section 181(3) provides that 'Other organs of state, through legislative and other measures, must assist and protect these institutions to ensure the independence, impartiality, dignity and effectiveness of these institutions'.

> go about fulfilling these constitutional obligations is a discretionary matter best left to the National Assembly. Ours is a much broader and less intrusive role.[89]

Despite this lofty statement of principle, the court went on to find that the National Assembly violated its constitutional obligation to hold the President accountable. The National Assembly had formed two ad hoc committees to deal with the Public Protector's report, but the court still found that the National Assembly did not do enough. It found that the National Assembly erred 'by passing a resolution that purported effectively to nullify the findings made and remedial action taken by the Public Protector and replacing them with its own findings and "remedial action"'.[90] Once again, the court imposed its sense of what is correct upon the National Assembly.

The approach continued in the *EFF II* case.[91] This case was related to *EFF I*, in that it still hinged on the Public Protector's findings and remedial actions. In the latter case the applicants sought, amongst other things, a declaratory order to the effect that failure by the National Assembly to put in place mechanisms for the removal of the President in terms of s 89(1) of the Constitution constitutes a violation of the Constitution. The majority judgment found that 'section 89(1) implicitly imposes an obligation on the Assembly to make rules specially tailored for an impeachment process contemplated in that section'.[92] The Constitutional Court, in turn, found that the National Assembly had violated this obligation, and the National Assembly was directed to make rules to facilitate the implementation of s 89 of the Constitution. This time the court was sharply divided,[93] unlike in the first case, when its decision was unanimous. The minority disagreed that the court had any role to play in directing the National Assembly on how to do its work, let alone to make rules. The Constitution states, without any equivocation, that the National Assembly shall regulate its own proceedings.[94] As mentioned previously, Mogoeng CJ, concurring in the minority judgment, called the majority judgment 'a textbook case of judicial overreach – a constitutionally impermissible intrusion by the Judiciary into the exclusive domain of Parliament'.[95] The minority judgment's central argument was that the principle of separation of powers prohibits the court from going so far as to tell Parliament 'to make rules'. In responding to this view, Jafta J, for the majority, stated that:

> The order proposed does not involve the exercise by this Court of the Assembly's powers. On the contrary, it requires the Assembly itself to exercise those powers and perform its constitutional functions without delay. This cannot be and is not a breach of

[89] *EFF II* (note 30 above) para 93. At para 43, the court had already admitted that 'to determine whether the National Assembly has fulfilled or breached its obligations will therefore entail a resolution of very crucial political issues. And it is an exercise that trenches sensitive areas of separation of powers. It could at times border on second-guessing the National Assembly's constitutional power or discretion'.

[90] Ibid para 98.

[91] *EFF II* (note 30 above).

[92] Ibid para 196.

[93] The majority of the court comprised seven judges; the minority comprised four judges.

[94] Section 57 of the Constitution provides that:
'(1) The National Assembly may—
(a) determine and control its internal arrangements, proceedings and procedures; and
(b) make rules and orders concerning its business, with due regard to representative and participatory democracy, accountability, transparency and public involvement'.

[95] *EFF II* (note 30 above) para 223.

the principle of separation of powers but consists in no more than the Court fulfilling its constitutionally assigned duty.[96]

Here the court is simply justifying why it has interfered with the work of the National Assembly. The National Assembly has considerable latitude to determine its own internal proceedings; it is not for the court to direct it to make rules 'without delay'.[97] As the minority judgment in the *EFF II* case suggests, it is apparent that although the Constitutional Court usually makes cursory comments about the need to respect the National Assembly and the executive,[98] it does not always seem to observe the boundaries between its work and the work of the other branches.

2.2 The enforcement of structural interdicts

Another area which has become the hotbed of judicialisation in South Africa is the enforcement of structural interdicts. This is a special kind of remedy that enables the courts to retain supervisory jurisdiction over the implementation of their orders. The Constitutional Court in *Pheko v Ekurhuleni Metropolitan Municipality*[99] justified the use of structural interdict in that it 'guarantees commitment to the constitutional values of accountability, responsiveness and openness by all concerned, in a system of democratic governance'.[100] The court went further to say that by 'granting the structural interdict a court secures a response in the form of reports and thereby prevents a failure to comply with the positive obligations imposed by its order'.[101] These are extraordinary remedial powers conferred on the courts by the Constitution.[102] The Constitution has not only granted the courts the power to invalidate laws and actions that violate the Constitution – which would be the basic powers of the courts – but has also granted the courts wide discretionary powers to supervise the implementation of their orders.[103] As the court stated in *Fose v Minister of Safety and Security*:[104]

---

[96] Ibid para 220.

[97] Ibid para 222, term 5 of the Court Order.

[98] *South African Association of Personal Injury Lawyers v Heath* 2001 (1) SA 883 (CC); *Van Rooyen v The State (General Council of the Bar of South Africa Intervening)* 2002 (5) SA 246 (CC); *Glenister* (note 67 above). In *Doctors for Life International v Speaker of the National Assembly* 2006 (6) SA 416 (CC) paras 37–8, the court made the following statement: 'The constitutional principle of separation of powers requires that other branches of government refrain from interfering in parliamentary proceedings [. . .] The principle has important consequences for the way in which and the institutions by which power can be exercised. Courts must be conscious of the vital limits on judicial authority and the Constitution's design to leave certain matters to other branches of government. They too must observe the constitutional limits of their authority. This means that the Judiciary should not interfere in the processes of other branches of government unless to do so is mandated by the Constitution'.

[99] *Pheko v Ekurhuleni Metropolitan Municipality* 2015 (5) SA 600 (CC).

[100] Ibid para 1.

[101] Ibid.

[102] Section 172(1) of the Constitution provides that:
When deciding a constitutional matter within its power, a court –
(a) must declare that any law or conduct that is inconsistent with the Constitution is invalid to the extent of its inconsistency; and
(b) may make any order that is just and equitable, including –
(i) an order limiting the retrospective effect of the declaration of invalidity; and
(ii) an order suspending the declaration of invalidity for any period and on any conditions, to allow the competent authority to correct the defect. See also C Okpaluba 'Extraordinary remedies for breach of fundamental rights: Recent developments' (2002) 17 *SA Public Law* 98.

[103] D Hirsch 'A defense of structural injunctive remedies in South African law' (2007) 9 *Oregon Review of International Law* 1.

[104] *Fose v Minister of Safety and Security* 1997 (3) SA 786 (CC).

> South African Courts have a wide range of powers at their disposal to ensure that the Constitution is upheld. These include mandatory and structured interdicts. How they should exercise those powers depends on the circumstances of each particular case. Here due regard must be paid to the roles of the Legislature and the Executive in a democracy. *What must be made clear, however, is that when it is appropriate to do so, Courts may – and, if need be, must – use their wide powers to make orders that affect policy as well as legislation.*[105]

These extraordinary remedial powers of the court have been the subject of intense judicial and scholarly analysis in South Africa.[106] By using these powers, courts attempt to fill the gap of non-compliance with their orders by other political branches of government. The duty to comply with the order of the court is the duty of every litigant; more so for the branch of government. If the court will invariably have to decide the disputes between the parties without finality, it means the matter is polycentric – that it was not justiciable in the first instance.[107] These kinds of cases have more often than not brought the courts into the province of other branches. As former Chief Justice Arthur Chaskalson potently contends, 'If there is not the political will, supervisory orders are not likely to be effective and may drag courts into long drawn battles that could more appropriately and more effectively be fought on the political terrain'.[108]

The most recent case in point at the Constitutional Court is *AllPay Consolidated Investment Holdings (Pty) Ltd v Chief Executive Officer, South African Social Security Agency*,[109] which concerned the provision of social grants by the South African Social Security Agency (SASSA).[110] This case ultimately entailed no less than five years of co-governance between the judiciary and the executive. In 2013, the Constitutional Court declared unconstitutional a contract between SASSA and Cash Paymaster Services, which was contracted by SASSA to manage grant distribution on its behalf.[111] The contract was invalidated but, due to the likely calamitous consequences of such

---

105 Ibid para 69 (emphasis added).

106 See Okpaluba (note 102 above); M Ebadolahi 'Using structural interdicts and the South African Human Rights Commission to achieve judicial enforcement of economic and social rights in South Africa' (2008) 83 *New York University Law Review* 1565. See also *Sanderson v Attorney-General, Eastern Cape* 1998 (2) SA 38. At para [38] the court said: 'It is appropriate at this juncture to make some brief observations about the remedy sought by the appellant. Even if the evidence he had placed before the Court had been more damning, the relief the appellant seeks is radical, both philosophically and socio-politically. Barring the prosecution before the trial begins – and consequently without any opportunity to ascertain the real effect of the delay on the outcome of the case – is far-reaching. Indeed it prevents the prosecution from presenting society's complaint against an alleged transgressor of society's rules of conduct. That will seldom be warranted in the absence of significant prejudice to the accused. An accused's entitlement to relief such as this is determined by section 7(4)(a) of the interim Constitution. In interpreting that provision in *Fose v Minister of Safety and Security* we adopted a flexible approach that is certainly inconsistent with the availability of a single remedy in North American jurisdictions. In our interpretation of section 7(4)(a) we understood "appropriateness" to require "suitability" which is measured by the extent to which a particular form of relief vindicates the Constitution and acts as a deterrent against further violations of rights enshrined in chapter 3'.

107 L Fuller 'The forms and limits of adjudication' (1978) 92 *Harvard Law Review* 353; JWF Allison 'Fuller's analysis of polycentric disputes and the limits of adjudication' (1994) 53 *Cambridge Law Journal* 367.

108 Former Chief Justice Arthur Chaskalson's speech 'Implementing socio-economic rights: The role of the courts', delivered as guest speaker at the Third Dullah Omar Memorial Lecture, organised by the Community Law Centre and the Faculty of Law at the University of the Western Cape (13 June 2006) 31.

109 *AllPay Consolidated Investment Holdings (Pty) Ltd v Chief Executive Officer, South African Social Security Agency* 2014 (1) SA 604 (CC) (*AllPay I*).

110 SASSA is a statutory agency established in terms of the South African Social Security Agency Act 9 of 2004 to administer social grants. See also the Social Assistance Act 13 of 2004.

111 See *AllPay I* (note 109 above).

a declaration of invalidity, the court suspended the invalidation on condition that either a new five-year tender would be awarded after a proper procurement process or SASSA itself would take over the payment of social grants when the suspended contract came to an end in March 2017. SASSA was ordered to report to the court on the progress made in respect of the new tender process and its outcome. In November 2015, SASSA reported that it had decided not to award a new tender. Instead, SASSA would no longer outsource the payment of grants; it would make the payments itself and the deadline of March 2017 would still be met. Despite this undertaking, SASSA failed to live up to the commitment made to the court that it would start the payment of grants by April 2017.[112] After this failure, another case, *Black Sash Trust v Minister of Social Development*,[113] was instituted in which the court was confronted with the situation where its orders in the previous cases had not been complied with. Still the matter could not be finalised. Hence, the court issued a very elaborate supervisory order in which, amongst other items, the declaration of invalidity of the contract was suspended for a further period of 12 months from April 2017. Judicialisation was embodied in the court order thus:

> The Minister and SASSA must file reports on affidavit with this Court every three months, commencing on the date of this order, setting out how they plan to ensure the payment of social grants after the expiry of the 12-month period, what steps they have taken in that regard, what further steps they will take, and when they will take each future step, so as to ensure that the payment of all social grants is made when they fall due after the expiry of the 12-month period.[114]

These *SASSA* cases are the epitome of the current inter-departmental relationship between the executive and judiciary, where the latter has taken on the function of virtually supervising the former. As Chuks Okpaluba and Mtendeweka Mhango pointedly contend, 'It is difficult to conceive an argument that the interdicts issued were non-intrusive, in fact, in respect of the executive function'.[115] This imbalance has huge potential to undermine the values of the Constitution.[116] The Constitutional Court became frustrated with the unending exercise of supervising the executive, and mulcted the Minister of Social Development with the order of costs to punish her for non-compliance with the supervisory orders of the courts. This was a clear case of a court asserting its supremacy over the executive.

2.3 The realisation of transformative constitutionalism theory

Another area where judicialisation is emerging as a cause for concern is in the realisation of the hallowed doctrine of transformative constitutionalism.[117] The postamble to

---

[112] See *AllPay I* (note 109 above).

[113] *Black Sash Trust v Minister of Social Development* 2017 (3) SA 335 (CC). For a review of the case, see B Nkrumah 'Averting looming tragedy: A review of *The Black Sash Trust v Minister of Social Development and Others*' (2018) 19 *Economic and Social Rights Review* 13.

[114] *Black Sash Trust* ibid para 76, term 7 of the Court Order.

[115] Okpaluba & Mhango (note 61 above) 13.

[116] *Black Sash Trust v Minister of Social Development and Others (Freedom Under Law Intervening)* 2018 (12) BCLR 1472 (CC).

[117] T Roux 'Transformative constitutionalism and the best interpretation of the South African Constitution: Distinction without a difference?' (2009) 20 *Stellenbosch Law Review* 258; KE Klare 'Legal culture and transformative constitutionalism' (1998) 14 *South African Journal on Human Rights* 146.

the Interim Constitution describes the Constitution as 'a historic bridge between the past of a deeply divided society characterised by strife, conflict, untold suffering and injustice, and a future founded on the recognition of human rights, democracy and peaceful co-existence'.[118] As a result, the Constitution and the law have firmly been located at the centre of broader societal transformation.[119] In turn, the courts have arrogated these kingpins of societal transformation as their trump cards to consolidate their power.[120] They have sought to use the theory of transformative constitutionalism to abandon the traditional methods of adjudication that were largely based on legal formalism – being restricted by the existing legal authority.[121] In the new dispensation the courts have sought to use the dictates of substantive justice to impose their own sense of transformation and egalitarianism.[122] This approach by the judiciary has been largely lauded for its ability to break the shackles of classical liberalism that would have clearly prohibited South Africa from shedding its past, which was based on extreme formalism.[123] Admittedly, the doctrine of transformative constitutionalism has helped the country escape the traditional confines of formal equality and moving towards substantive equality,[124] thereby placing 'less emphasis on technicalities and procedure so as to maximise the realisation of substantive rights'.[125] To that extent, the doctrine is laudable.

Nevertheless, the flip-side is that the doctrine has, arguably more than any other aspect of new South African constitutionalism, blurred the lines between politics and law.[126] It has created the impression that law is the single most important means of

---

118 Postamble of the Interim Constitution, Act 200 of 1993 (Interim Constitution). The Interim Constitution has been repealed.

119 P de Vos 'A bridge too far? History as context in the interpretation of the South African Constitution' (2001) 17 *South African Journal on Human Rights* 1.

120 D Moseneke 'The fourth Bram Fischer memorial lecture: Transformative adjudication' (2002) 18 *South African Journal on Human Rights* 309, 315.

121 *Du Plessis v De Klerk* 1996 (3) SA 850 (CC); *Bernstein v Bester* 1996 (4) BCLR 449 (CC); *Bato Star Fishing (Pty) Ltd v Minister of Environmental Affairs and Tourism* 2004 (4) SA 490 (CC); *Investigating Directorate: Serious Economic Offences v Hyundai Motor Distributors* 2001 (1) SA 545 (CC) para 21 where Langa CJ, as he then was, posited: 'The Constitution is located in a history which involves a transition from a society based on division, injustice and exclusion from the democratic process to one which respects the dignity of all citizens, and includes all in the process of governance. As such, the process of interpreting the Constitution must recognise the context in which we find ourselves, and the Constitution's goal of a society based on democratic values, social justice and fundamental human rights. This spirit of transition and transformation characterises the constitutional enterprise as a whole'.

122 M Kende 'The South African Constitutional Court's construction of socio-economic rights: A response to critics' (2003) 19 *Connecticut Journal of International Law* 617.

123 Klare (note 117 above) contends that the new South African Constitution is 'post-liberal'. Other countries in Africa have also started to identify their modern constitutions as 'post-liberal'. The Supreme Court of Kenya, in the case of *Speaker of the Senate v Attorney General 3* [2013] eKLR para 51, held that 'Kenya's Constitution of 2010 is a transformative charter. Unlike the conventional "liberal" Constitutions of the earlier decades which essentially sought the control and legitimisation of public power, the avowed goal of today's Constitution is to institute social change and reform, through values such as social justice, equality, devolution, human rights, rule of law, freedom and democracy'. See also L Hawthorne 'Legal tradition and the transformation of orthodox contract theory: The movement from formalism to realism' (2006) 12 *Fundamina* 71.

124 C Albertyn 'Substantive equality and transformation in South Africa' (2007) 23 *South African Journal on Human Rights* 253.

125 E Kibet & C Fombad 'Transformative constitutionalism and the adjudication of constitutional rights in Africa' (2017) 17 *African Human Rights Law Journal* 340, 353.

126 The contestation between law and politics has haunted the study of law since time immemorial. It created a protracted conflict between naturalists and positivists, amongst positivists themselves and, much more recently, between liberals and critical legal studies (including realists). See S Ratnapala *Jurisprudence* (2009).

societal transformation to the exclusion of all others.[127] If the project is to transform South African society, such an enterprise is and should be greater than law and the courts. If the law is promoted as the single most important driver of transformation, this will 'inevitably compel courts to engage in policy decision making or make orders that have significant budgetary implications such as in the enforcement of socio-economic rights'.[128] Hence, some scholars contend that the undue preoccupation with legal transformation is arguably responsible for the persistent legacies of apartheid – including abject poverty – in the country.[129] The undue emphasis on the role of law and the courts in the transformative project has, in some instances, been the basis for judicialisation of politics. In turn, other branches and sections of society play a peripheral role.

3. Conclusion

It seems that the courts in South Africa in general, and the Constitutional Court in particular, have joined the global upsurge in judicialisation of politics.[130] As demonstrated in the foregoing discussion, the justification for this phenomenon is the replacement, both in South Africa and globally, of the once-revered notion of parliamentary sovereignty with the confluence of constitutionalism and human rights discourse. The South African constitutional practice is particularly prone to judicialisation largely as a result of the country's apartheid history. The current activist role played by the judiciary in the transformative process is often justified by the historic injustices that were perpetrated by the alliance of the executive and legislature to the utter exclusion of the judiciary. The re-emergence of the judiciary from those depths is therefore justifiable.

However, the main task confronting constitutional jurisprudence in South Africa today is determining the proper place that must be occupied by the judiciary. In the early cases, the Constitutional Court properly emphasised that under the new order the privileges that were enjoyed by the executive and the legislature had been removed to the extent that they precluded the judiciary from inquiring into the legality of their actions. However, the later cases, such as the *SASSA* cases and the *EFF* cases, demonstrated that the court is judicialising the functions that would ordinarily fall into the province of the political branches.

In *EFF I*, the court took the function – to hold the executive to account – which is constitutionally vested in parliament. Admittedly, the National Assembly was crippled by political dynamics to implement the Public Protector's recommendation, which is

---

[127] Roux (note 117 above); R Teitel 'Transitional jurisprudence: The role of law in political transformation' (1997) 106 *Yale Law Journal* 2014; K van Marle 'Transformative constitutionalism as/and critique' (2009) 2 *Stellenbosch Law Review* 286; K van Marle 'Revisiting the politics of post-apartheid constitutional interpretation' (2003) 3 *Journal of South African Law* 549.

[128] Kibet & Fombad (note 125 above) 353.

[129] S Sibanda 'Not purpose-made! Transformative constitutionalism, post-independence constitutionalism and the struggle to eradicate poverty' (2011) 22 *Stellenbosch Law Review* 482. F Michelman 'Liberal constitutionalism, property rights, and the assault on poverty' (2011) 22 *Stellenbosch Law Review* 706 provides a more comprehensive rebuttal of Sibanda's criticism. Also see Sibanda's reply to Michelman: S Sibanda 'Not quite a rejoinder: Some thoughts and reflections on Michelman's liberal constitutionalism, property rights, and the assault on poverty' (2013) 24 *Stellenbosch Law Review* 329.

[130] C Guarneri & P Pederzoli *From Democracy to Juristocracy? The Power of Judges: A Comparative Study of Courts and Democracy* (2002); AS Sweet *Governing with Judges: Constitutional Politics in Europe* (2000).

effectively the function of accountability. But it is not for the court to unlock those political bottlenecks that stand in the way of accountability, for to do so is to whisk politics from its proper place and place it in the doorstep of the courtroom. The *EFF II* followed the same pattern, and even more as the court went as far as ordering the National Assembly to 'make rules without delay'.[131] Therein, the court was very clear about judicialisation. The nature of *EFF II* case was aptly captured by Zondo DCJ writing for the minority that the case was 'not about holding any President of the Republic accountable as such but about the National Assembly holding the current President […] accountable'.[132]

In the *SASSA* cases, and in other socio-economic rights cases,[133] the Constitutional Court inappropriately invoked structural interdicts to effectively co-govern with the executive. The *SASSA* cases spent no fewer than five years in the courts because the executive battled to implement the supervisory orders issued by the court. In the first instance, the matter was fairly straightforward: the court was simply required to invalidate the procurement process that led to the contracting of Cash Paymaster Services as the grants distributor on behalf of SASSA. Instead of only declaring the tender unconstitutional, the court invoked s 171 and wanted to supervise the consequences of the declaration of invalidity. This case illustrates the oft-cited saying that courts are better at telling the political branches 'you may not do that' than at telling legislatures or administrators 'here are the things you must do'.[134]

Judicialisation is further exacerbated by the manner in which the Constitutional Court has interpreted its remedial powers under the Constitution. The court seems to have become over-enthusiastic about both ss 38 and 172 of the Constitution, which empower the court to grant 'appropriate relief'[135] and 'make any order that is just and equitable'.[136] The courts, it has been argued, have interpreted these powers to mean literally anything, including overreach into the functions of the political branches of government.

---

[131] *EFF II* (note 30 above) para 2 of the Court Order.

[132] *EFF II* (note 30 above) para 1.

[133] D Brand 'Judicial deference and democracy in socio-economic rights cases in South Africa' (2011) 22 *Stellenbosch Law Review* 614.

[134] L Alexander 'Constitutionalism and democracy: Understanding the relation' in S Kautz et al (eds) *The Supreme Court and the Idea of Constitutionalism* (2009) 161.

[135] Section 38 of the Constitution. In the case of *Fose v Minister of Safety and Security* (note 32 above) para 66, the court defined 'appropriate relief' as follows: 'In our context an appropriate remedy must mean an effective remedy, for without effective remedies for breach, the values underlying and the rights entrenched in the Constitution cannot properly be upheld or enhanced'. See also *Olitzki Property Holdings v State Tender Board* 2001 (8) BCLR 779 (SCA), where the court concluded that that the lost profit in a procurement dispute would not be an appropriate constitutional remedy.

[136] Section 172(1)*(b)*. In *Komape v Minister of Basic Education* (1416/2015) [2018] ZALMPPHC 18 (23 April 2018) the court had to decide a case where a learner had died after falling into a pit latrine at school. At paras 56–7 the court remarked that: 'It has been acknowledged that courts are mandated, if a constitutional duty has been breached, to grant appropriate relief. To do so, courts may fashion new remedies, if necessary, depending on the nature of the case. Usual remedies may be held to be appropriate relief to protect and enforce the Constitution. Relief must also be just and equitable. An appropriate remedy may well be a structural interdict in terms whereof the defendants, as organs of state, are ordered to perform their constitutional obligations and in terms whereof the court may perform a supervisory function to ensure compliance with and proper implementation of the order'. The court went on to request the Ministry of Education to deliver a report within a designated time, detailing '[the] program developed by the relevant experts based for the installation of the toilets on an assessment made in respect of the suitable sanitation technology requirements of each school inclusive of a proposed date (and reasons for the proposed date) for the commencement of the work referred'.

Disclosure statement

No conflict of interest was reported by the author.

Esoteric decision-making: Judicial responses to the judicialisation of politics, the Constitutional Court and *EFF II*

Lauren Gildenhuys

ABSTRACT
Esoteric decision-making refers to the express reliance on apolitical, technical and legal justifications to substantiate a judicial outcome that is preferred for political reasons, which remain unexpressed. Historically, the Constitutional Court has, in the face of highly political cases, relied on a number of esoteric decision-making techniques. These include prevailing on narrow or apolitical sources of law; using technical, formalist modes of reasoning; and exploiting the indeterminism of the separation of powers. Esoteric decision-making may be a necessary and justified judicial response to instances of the judicialisation of politics in order to protect the institutional security, independence and legitimacy of courts. However, when used ineptly, it risks inviting the institutional vulnerability that its use seeks to avoid. To illustrate this point, this paper discusses the majority judgment in *EFF II* and contrasts it to previous instances in which the Court has applied esoteric decision-making more successfully. Given the prevalence of the judicialisation of politics in South Africa, the Constitutional Court's continued institutional legitimacy will depend on the careful and strategic application of esoteric decision-making in future cases.

1. Introduction

In December 2017, during Jafta J's delivery of the majority judgment in *Economic Freedom Fighters (Democratic Alliance as Intervening Party) v Speaker of the National Assembly*[1] (*EFF II*), Chief Justice Mogoeng Mogoeng made the unprecedented request that it be read into the Court record that he found the majority's decision to be a 'textbook case of judicial overreach'.[2] Mogoeng CJ's dissent went on to characterise the majority judgment as a 'constitutionally impermissible intrusion by the judiciary into the exclusive domain of Parliament'.[3]

---

[1] *Economic Freedom Fighters (Democratic Alliance as Intervening Party) v Speaker of the National Assembly* 2018 (2) SA 571 (CC).
[2] Ibid 223. The interruption can be viewed at <https://www.youtube.com/watch?v=sLUIWaJZIWc>
[3] Ibid 223.

Yet, as surprising as the Chief Justice's interruption might have been, his reference to judicial overreach was not novel. The years leading up to *EFF II* are replete with examples of politicians and members of the public criticising the South African judiciary for allegedly overstepping the bounds of its constitutional mandate. In May 2017, a public march against 'judicial overreach' was organised in KwaZulu-Natal.[4] Two months later, the then ANC secretary general, Gwede Mantashe, accused the judiciary of interfering in politics and 'playing into the political space'.[5] Two months after that, the ANC concluded at its 5th National Policy Conference that the use of the courts as a form of 'lawfare' to deal with political disputes should be 'resolved', and an end put to the attempts by 'privileged sectors of society to undermine the popular electoral mandate'.[6]

Given the nature of the cases the judiciary was called to decide during the Zuma presidency, these criticisms by the political elite were not unexpected. Some of the criticism also seems to stem from a general distrust of constitutional supremacy and judicial review itself, as Heinz Klug has noted.[7] However, underlying these criticisms is an important question: What is the proper response of the judiciary, and in particular the Constitutional Court, to high-profile cases that fall to be decided within the framework of constitutional law, but which may have significant macro-political consequences, and which will undoubtedly impact on relations between the branches of government, and the legitimacy[8] and institutional security of the judiciary itself?

It is against this background that I consider some recent examples of the Constitutional Court's response to the judicialisation of politics in South Africa, and the extent to which these attempts have been successful. Historically, the Constitutional Court has in the face of highly political cases relied on what I refer to as 'esoteric' decision-making, a concept first discussed in the South African context by Conrado Hübner Mendes.[9] Esoteric decision-making in the judicial context refers to the express reliance on apolitical, technical and legal justifications to substantiate a judicial outcome that is preferred for political reasons, which remain unexpressed. Esoteric decision-making techniques include, among others, prevailing on narrow or apolitical sources of law; using technical, formalist modes of reasoning; and exploiting the indeterminism of the separation of powers. Drawing on the works of Theunis Roux, Samuel Issacharoff and Mendes, it would appear that, as a strategic actor wary of jeopardising its long-term institutional security, the Constitutional Court has tended to

[4] Z Matiwane 'KZN ANC march against "frivolous" use of the judiciary' *The Mercury* 10 May 2017 <https://www.iol.co.za/news/politics/kzn-anc-march-against-frivolous-use-of-judiciary-9047910>.

[5] N Modjadji 'Judiciary playing into political space – Mantashe slams ruling' *SowetanLIVE* 10 May 2017 <https://www.sowetanlive.co.za/news/2017-05-10-judiciary-playing-into-political-space-mantashe-slams-ruling/>.

[6] African National Congress 'Strategy and Tactics of the African National Congress' 5th National Policy Conference Document (8 March 2017) para 206 <http://www.anc.org.za/sites/default/files/National%20Policy%20Conference%202017%20Stratey%20and%20Tactics.pdf>.

[7] H Klug 'Challenging constitutionalism in post-apartheid South Africa' (2016) 1 *Constitutional Studies* 41.

[8] I use the term 'institutional legitimacy' throughout this paper to refer to the level of broad public support for, and acceptance of, the Constitutional Court and its decisions. Institutional legitimacy 'feeds' the Court's power, as it is a 'precondition for the court's capacity to assert its veto role' in national politics (see T Roux *The Politics of Principle: The First South African Constitutional Court, 1995 – 2005* (2013) 31–32). Institutional security is a related concept that I use to refer to the degree to which the Court is insulated from political attack on its independence.

[9] CH Mendes 'Fighting for their place: Constitutional courts as political actors – A reply to Heinz Klug' (2010) 3 *Constitutional Court Review* 33.

use esoteric decision-making to downplay the political considerations underlying its judgments and avoid accusations that it has been 'playing politics'. However, given that esoteric decision-making presents a departure from the principles of political morality that generally guide judicial action, it is necessary to consider the particular risks that emerge when it is used ineptly. To illustrate this point, I discuss one of the most prominent examples of the judicialisation of politics[10] in recent history, namely, the Constitutional Court's decision in *EFF II*. In particular, I contrast the majority judgment in *EFF II* with previous instances in which the Court has applied esoteric decision-making more effectively.

I conclude that the Court needs to be more disciplined in its use of esoteric decision-making, to achieve the goal of preserving its legitimacy in the face of judicialisation. Esoteric decision-making may be a necessary and justified response to judicialisation, particularly when it is being used to protect the institutional security and legitimacy of the Court, and deliver outcomes required to protect the constitutional project as a whole. However, when it is applied ineptly, it risks inviting the very controversy that its use seeks to avoid. Ultimately, given the prevalence of judicialisation in South Africa, the Constitutional Court's continued institutional legitimacy will depend on the strategic and effective application of esoteric decision-making in future cases.

In Part 2, I briefly discuss the phenomenon of the judicialisation of politics, relying primarily on the framework developed by Hirschl and its applicability to the South African case. In Part 3, I draw on the works of Roux, Issacharoff and Mendes to consider previous strategic responses by the Constitutional Court to instances of judicialisation. In Part 4, I discuss the concept of esoteric decision-making, and demonstrate its role in key Constitutional Court cases, building on my analysis in Part 3. I then present a summary and critique of *EFF II* in Part 5, and in Parts 6 and 7 I develop my conclusions.

2. The courts, the ANC, and the 'judicialisation' of politics in South Africa

Before considering the Constitutional Court's historical responses to judicialisation, an understanding of the phenomenon is required. The 'judicialisation of politics' is a term that may be used to describe the high volumes of so-called 'political cases' that have been brought to the Constitutional Court for adjudication. One of the first proponents of the term was a political scientist, Ran Hirschl,[11] who argued that the judicialisation of politics was more likely to occur in democracies where certain institutional factors, judicial attitudes, and political determinants are present.[12] While an overview of Hirschl's theory is beyond the scope of this paper, it suffices to say that South Africa's politico-legal landscape is highly hospitable to the judicialisation of politics, for three key reasons. Firstly, in respect of institutional factors,[13] it has an independent judiciary with an active and well-respected apex court; supported by the institutionally insulated Office of the Chief Justice; and armed with wide-reaching judicial review mechanisms,

[10] For the remainder of the article, I use the shortened 'judicialisation' where brevity requires.
[11] R Hirschl 'The judicialization of politics' in R Goodin (ed) *The Oxford Handbook of Political Science* (2011) 253–274.
[12] Ibid 258–262.
[13] Ibid 263–267.

an expansive constitutional text, jurisdiction to hear any case of general public importance, an indeterminate concept of the separation of powers, and broad relief powers to make any order that is just and equitable.

Secondly, there is a high degree of judicial willingness[14] to adjudicate what are essentially political disputes, underpinned by the Court's early rejection of the political question doctrine and its view that even highly political decisions of other branches of government are justiciable.[15] Thirdly, the political environment[16] in which the Court operates has played a defining role in the process of judicialisation. The ANC's well-documented political dominance of the legislature and executive, together with its strict party discipline and the structure of the electoral system, has compromised the ability of traditional deliberative forums and oversight mechanisms to hold the executive, constituted as it is by the ruling party, to account.[17] This has meant that, increasingly, opposition and minority parties have turned to the courts, rather than traditional democratic forums, to challenge executive decisions.[18] Doing so also bolsters opposition parties' public profiles, which makes litigation an attractive political repertoire in its own right. Further, the political system has itself become dependent on the judicialisation of (party) politics, as political parties increasingly turn to the courts to adjudicate internal party disputes in the face of weakened intra-party dispute resolution mechanisms.[19]

There is, admittedly, some imprecision in the notion of the 'judicialisation of politics', as it assumes without explanation or justification that some political decisions are and should never be justiciable. This in turn leads to the age-old question of what is and isn't 'political'. I do not attempt to answer these questions here, but instead appeal to the instinct of legal and political science scholars alike that there are some questions that should be resolved in deliberative, participatory democratic forums, rather than by courts. The concept of the separation of powers necessarily entails that some matters

---

14 Ibid 266.

15 See O'Regan J's remarks in *Permanent Secretary of the Department of Education of the Government of the Eastern Cape Province v Ed-U-College (PE) (Section21)* 2001 (2) SA 1 (CC) paras 16–18; and Chaskalson CJ's comments in *President of RSA v South African Rugby Football Union* 2000 (1) SA 1 (CC) para 78. See also T Roux 'Principle and pragmatism on the Constitutional Court of South Africa' (2008) 7 *International Journal of Constitutional Law* 106, 126, especially footnote 82; and generally C Okpaluba 'Justiciability, constitutional adjudication and the political question in a nascent democracy: South Africa (part 1)' (2003) 18 *Southern African Public Law* 331 and C Okpaluba 'Justiciability, constitutional adjudication and the political question in a nascent democracy: South Africa (part 2)' (2004) 19 *Southern African Public Law* 114.

16 At the core of Hirschl's account of judicialisation is the notion that the judicialisation of politics can only take root if the political environment is receptive to it. See Hirschl (note 11 above) 267.

17 See generally S Issacharoff 'The democratic risk to democratic transitions' (2014) 5 *Constitutional Court Review* 1.

18 Some of the most noteworthy of these cases include *Justice Alliance of SA v President of the RSA* 2011 (5) SA 388 (CC); *Freedom under Law v Acting Chairperson, Judicial Service Commission* 2011 (3) SA 549 (SCA); *Southern Africa Litigation Centre v Minister of Justice and Constitutional Development* 2015 (5) SA 1 (GP); *Economic Freedom Fighters v Speaker of the National Assembly; Democratic Alliance v Speaker of the National Assembly (Corruption Watch (RF) NPC as amicus curiae)* 2016 (3) SA 580 (CC); *Democratic Alliance v Speaker of the National Assembly* [2016] JOL 35507 (CC); *Chairperson of the National Council of Provinces v Malema* 2016 (5) SA 335 (SCA); *Zuma v Democratic Alliance; Acting National Director of Public Prosecutions v Democratic Alliance* 2018 (1) SA 200 (SCA); *Black Sash Trust v Minister of Social Development (Freedom under Law NPC as Intervening Party and Corruption Watch (NPC) RF and another as amici curiae)* 2017 (3) SA 335 (CC); *Corruption Watch NPC v President of the Republic of South Africa; Nxasana v Corruption Watch NPC* 2018 (2) SACR 442 (CC).

19 Notable cases include *Ramakatsa v Magashule* 2013 (2) BCLR 202 (CC); *Dube v Zikalala* [2017] 4 All SA 365 (KZP); *Mgabadeli v African National Congress* [2017] ZAECGHC 131; *Mokoena v Magashule* [2017] ZAFSHC 224; *Ntozini v African National Congress* [2018] ZAGPJHC 415; *Ntamo v African National Congress Regional Executive Committee, OR Tambo Region* [2017] ZAECMHC 49; *Mabuza v Phosa* [2017] ZAGPPHC 139; *Fransman v Shabangu* [2016] ZAWCHC 189.

ought to fall beyond the ambit of judicial determination. Disputes that concern core legislative and executive prerogatives, the corroboration of regime change, questions of national identity, and restorative justice are most commonly associated with the judicialisation of politics.[20] Accordingly, where 'judicialisation of politics' is used in this paper, it refers to the judicialisation of those political dilemmas for which the constitutional text yields no clear or immediate answer, which are best suited to determination by representative political forums, where the decision-makers can, hypothetically, be held to account by the electorate. However, this definition makes no normative claim, in that it is not suggesting that South African courts should, in all circumstances, shy away from hearing such cases. If a populace hands over sovereignty to politically elected representatives, on condition that they comply with fundamental democratic rules once in power, then there must be some entity that is able to enforce those rules, and that entity is the judiciary. What this definition is acknowledging, though, is that ideally, courts should not be called to adjudicate certain intrinsically political cases, because in doing so their institutional security and integrity may become subject to attack. The invidious and unavoidable reality for the South African judiciary is that, owing to the combined impact of the institutional and political factors described above, it is legitimately positioned, indeed constitutionally called, to hear cases that are symptomatic of judicialisation.

Since South Africa's political context plays a significant role in fostering the judicialisation of politics, criticisms of the Constitutional Court as being 'interventionist' or 'activist' are revealed to be overly simplistic. However, the judiciary is ultimately a political actor in its own right, in that it is alive to external political threats to its power, and to political opportunities for strengthening its position vis-à-vis the other branches of government. This is neither problematic nor surprising: after all, it is in the interests of constitutional democracy that the courts retain their independence and institutional security; that their orders are complied with and respected, especially when those orders relate to other branches of the State; and that they retain the ability to enforce the social contract described above. The judiciary must nevertheless tread carefully, or risk the consequence that its power will be curtailed or its independence interfered with. This brings me to the core aim of this paper: to consider the nature of the Constitutional Court's previous responses to judicialisation, and specifically, how as an institutional actor it has sought to deliver legally defensible judgments while protecting its long-term institutional security in the face of judicialisation. The sections that follow will attempt to illustrate that much of the Court's response has to do with esoteric decision-making.

3. Judicialisation and the Constitutional Court

The Constitutional Court's track record in cases where it has been called to decide controversial political disputes that draw it directly into legislative or executive territory is well-documented. By surveying key examples from its record of decided cases, a trend in the Court's response to previous instances of judicialisation emerges.

---

[20] Hirschl (note 11 above) 257, and generally 258–262.

3.1 The Constitutional Court and nascent democracy

The judicial behaviour of the Constitutional Court during its early years (1995–2005) has been analysed by Roux (among others). Roux attempts to explain how the Court was able to cultivate a reputation for principled, legitimate decision-making while maintaining its institutional security in light of the ANC's political dominance by balancing 'principle' and 'pragmatism'.[21] In what would be a defining era of the Constitutional Court, it navigated a series of high-profile cases through careful political calibration. When support from ANC leaders, the wider political elite, or the public created a favourable political climate, the Court was able to follow principle. When it did not, the Court compromised on principle to ensure its institutional long-term survival and manage its relationship with the dominant party.[22] Roux's analysis, both in earlier and later work, recognises that the Constitutional Court does not act in a political vacuum, but is constantly having to manage the risk that its decisions will be ignored – an occurrence that signals the death of a court's power and relevance[23] – or that politicians will seek to interfere with its independence.

For example, in *Minister of Health v Treatment Action Campaign (No. 2)*[24] (*TAC*), the Court was able to overturn Thabo Mbeki's controversial AIDS policy, which limited the provision of antiretrovirals to pregnant women. In the face of staunch executive opposition, the Court was able to make a principled decision based on the right of access to healthcare due to the overwhelming public and media support for this outcome, support that was the product of the TAC's mass mobilisation efforts.[25] Another determinative factor was the manufacturer's offer to provide the antiretrovirals at no cost to the South African government for five years, allowing the Court to hand down

---

[21] T Roux 'Principle and pragmatism on the Constitutional Court of South Africa' (2008) 7 *International Journal of Constitutional Law* 106. In *The Politics of Principle* (note 8 above), Roux considerably develops the arguments published in his 2008 article. In the book, Roux appears to suggest that the concept of 'pragmatism' is insufficient to explain the Court's successes, noting that 'if all [the Court] ever did was make pragmatic compromises on principle, it would hardly have been the efficacious institution it was' (see 69–70). Further, Roux's argument shifts somewhat to take greater account of the Court's commitment to the ideal of adjudication according to law, and notes repeatedly that the Chaskalson Court would not have achieved the reputation it did in the comparative constitutional law community had it frequently abandoned principle in favour of 'pragmatism'. The book focuses on how the Court was able to remain committed to the ideal of adjudicating according to law, even in politically controversial cases, by positioning itself as a partner in the ANC's constitutional project as the enforcer of South Africa's highest moral aspirations, using the ANC's electoral dominance to shield it from decisions which went against public opinion, and adopting a context-sensitive review standard that allowed it to adjust its enforcement of the Constitution to the micro-politics of each case (see 47, 67, 257–260, 390–391). Crucially, however, Roux maintains the position that the Court compromised on principle in a particular class of cases – those in which the path of constitutional principle ran directly counter to the ANC's interests in maximising its electoral dominance (350, 363). In these cases, the Court was forced 'to compromise on constitutional principle to accommodate its institutional concerns' (363). Roux's later position, while conceptually more nuanced and reliant on a wider category of cases, does not mark a dramatic shift from his earlier work, at least to the extent that is relevant to this article.

[22] Ibid 106, 108. As explained in note 21, Roux moves away from the concept of 'pragmatism' in his later work. However, he maintains that in a small sample of cases, the Court sacrificed principled adjudication in the interests of maintaining its co-operative working relationship with the ANC and protecting its institutional independence (see Roux (note 8 above) 363–364).

[23] H Klug 'Finding the Constitutional Court's place in South Africa's democracy: The interaction of principle and institutional pragmatism in the Court's decision-making' (2010) 3 *Constitutional Court Review* 32.

[24] *Minister of Health v Treatment Action Campaign (No. 2)* 2002 (5) SA 721 (CC).

[25] Roux (note 21 above) 124–125. Roux notes that the Court dismissed separation of powers arguments, which formed the basis of the state's case, without much hesitation (see paras 96–106 of the judgment).

a principled decision while avoiding criticism for infringing on the executive prerogative of resource-allocation.[26]

However, in a small sample of cases, the Constitutional Court has departed from principle in order to protect its institutional security.[27] These cases demonstrate that, as a consequence of the absence of the political question doctrine in South African jurisprudence, the Court has had to rely on other technical arguments and devices to justify its retreat from bold, principled decision-making when political circumstances would not allow this.[28]

In *New National Party of South Africa v Government of the Republic of South Africa* (*NNP*)[29] for example, the Court avoided a principled reading of the constitutional right to vote, in order to adopt what was in effect a deferential approach to the legal dispute before it.[30] The NNP had challenged legislation that, although race-neutral at face value, would have the impact of rendering about 5 million predominantly white voters ineligible to vote due to the possession of the incorrect identity document.[31] Instead of developing meaningful jurisprudence on the significance of the right to vote (as the minority judgment did), the Court elected to apply the restricted rationality review[32] test to the legislation, instead of the more comprehensive reasonableness review standard that the minority applied and for which, arguably, the Constitution of the Republic of South Africa, 1996 provides.[33] Significantly, the Court relied on the separation of powers doctrine to justify its election to employ the more restricted review mechanism, emphasising the need to respect Parliament's choice of electoral scheme.[34] Roux posits that the Court would likely have taken into account the absence of a groundswell of public support for the principled outcome, and the fact that the NNP was the successor party of the National Party.[35] Further, the strong likelihood that the ANC was not in favour of a successful outcome for the NNP, given its interests in increasing its own electoral majority, indicates that the Court may well have relied on the separation of powers doctrine to avoid confrontation with the executive and legislative branches and protect its long-term institutional security.[36]

---

[26] Note 24 above 71.

[27] Roux (note 21 above) 131–132. Roux also discusses *Kaunda v President of the Republic of South Africa* 2005 (4) SALR 235 (CC), which 'concerned the executive's conduct of foreign relations'. The core issue was whether the South African government was under a duty to intervene to safeguard the (South African) applicants from the threatened violation of their rights in Zimbabwe. As Roux notes, 'denied the luxury of a political question doctrine, the majority used its literalist reading of section 7(1) to avoid the institutionally awkward consequences of the application of the Bill of Rights [...] Had the majority interpreted section 7(1) purposively to mean that the Bill of Rights binds the state in all its dealings with its citizens, wherever they happen to find themselves [physically], it would have had little option but to enforce the state's obligation to provide diplomatic protection of their human rights'.

[28] Ibid 125–126.

[29] *New National Party of South Africa v Government of the Republic of South Africa* 1999 (3) SALR 191 (CC).

[30] Roux (note 21 above) 126–127.

[31] Ibid 126; note 29 above 29–30.

[32] Rationality review only requires that there be a rational connection between the chosen legislative scheme and a legitimate government purpose that it seeks to achieve. See C Hoexter, *Administrative Law in South Africa* 2 ed (2012) 340–343.

[33] Roux (note 21 above) 127; note 29 above 15, 19, 21, 24.

[34] Ibid 126–127; note 29 above 24.

[35] Roux (note 21 above) 128.

[36] Ibid. See also Roux (note 8 above) 350, 363, wherein he notes that 'the path of constitutional principle ran directly counter to the ANC's pressing interest in maximising its share of the vote in the 1999 general election'.

3.2 The Constitutional Court and the Zuma presidency

In the late 90s and early 2000s, the Constitutional Court found itself deciding cases that were symptomatic of a young democracy navigating the teething problems of regime change, resource scarcity, and a new constitutional text. In the late 2000s, however, its most controversial cases were characteristic of a single-party democracy with an accountability deficit, and indeed were a direct product of the democratic malaise of the Zuma presidency. For this period of the Constitutional Court's record, the analysis of Issacharoff is particularly insightful.

Issacharoff argues that constitutional courts in strong-party democracies have three possible responses at their disposal: they can adopt a pragmatic approach that is thinly substantiated to limit further single-party dominance; or they can avoid confrontation with the political branch by using procedural and technical justifications for decisions that have the effect of limiting further political dominance; or they can provide a strong, principled response to power-grabbing attempts by the party in power that, although legally legitimate, may come at institutional cost.[37] Arguably, the Constitutional Court has adopted the second approach. Throughout the Zuma presidency, the Court was routinely called to decide politically controversial cases, most notable of which were judicial reviews of attempts by the executive and legislative branches to incapacitate and weaken accountability mechanisms.[38]

For example, in *Democratic Alliance v President of the Republic of South Africa*[39] (*Democratic Alliance*), the Court was asked to consider the validity of the appointment of the National Director of Public Prosecutions. This was a politically pertinent case, given the vast powers of the NPA to decide against whom to institute corruption charges. The Court applied the narrower standard of rationality review, finding that it had been procedurally irrational for the President to fail to consider evidence that suggested that the chosen candidate's integrity was compromised.[40] Expanding upon the principles that the Court had developed in its earlier decision in *Albutt v Centre for the Study of Violence & Reconciliation*,[41] the Court held that there was no reason to limit the principle that decisions should be rational both in process and final outcome to acts by the President in his capacity as Head of State.[42] Further, the Court found that a decision may be irrational if the decision-maker's failure to take a relevant factor into account 'colours the entire process with irrationality'.[43]

The fact that the Court avoided the reasonableness review standard, yet explicitly developed rationality review to require that each step of the process that led to the decision, as well as the decision itself, be rational, is indicative of its desire to achieve a certain outcome while still creating the impression that the case was decided on the

---

[37] S Issacharoff 'Constitutional courts and consolidated power' (2014) *NYU Public Law and Legal Theory Research Paper Series* Working Paper No.14–17 3–4; see also Issacharoff (note 17 above).
[38] Ibid 38.
[39] *Democratic Alliance v President of the Republic of South Africa* 2013 (1) SA 248 (CC).
[40] Issacharoff (note 37 above) 40; note 39 above 27–37.
[41] *Albutt v Centre for the Study of Violence & Reconciliation* 2010 (3) SA 293 (CC).
[42] Note 39 above 35.
[43] Ibid 39.

less intrusive of the two review standards.[44] In deciding the case on this basis, the Court was also able to avoid discussing the implications that such an appointment would have for one of the few remaining institutions capable of holding the ANC to account, a discussion that likely would have been necessitated if the reasonableness standard of review had been used.[45] Indeed, the Court explicitly held that it made no finding as to 'whether the President had an ulterior purpose in making the appointment'.[46] As a result, the Court was not only able to largely avoid public criticism from the ruling party, but it was also commended for its carefully reasoned and constitutionally legitimate development of the rationality test.[47]

Similarly, in *Glenister v President of the Republic of South Africa,*[48] the Court was faced with a challenge to the National Prosecuting Authority Amendment Act, which sought to dismantle a critical part of the NPA's anti-corruption unit. Although the Court's reasoning did rely to an extent on the s 7(2) duty of the State to respect and protect the rights in the Bill of Rights, the judgment turned, in the end, on an appeal to international and regional conventions and treaties to which South Africa is a party.[49] The majority judgment found that, given s 39(1)(b) of the Constitution requires courts to 'consider' international law when interpreting the Bill of Rights, 'international law, through the inter-locking grid of conventions, agreements and protocols […] unequivocally obliges South Africa to establish an anti-corruption entity with the necessary independence'.[50] Since South Africa's international law obligations required it to establish an anti-corruption unit free from political interference, the legislative enactment was unconstitutional.[51] As Issacharoff notes, 'placing responsibility for its decision on international law is an interesting judicial expedient'.[52] The Court deliberately avoided a confrontation with the 'constitutional underpinnings of democratic authority', instead turning to 'distant' international law principles.[53] Notably, the Court also dismissed the relevance of the ANC's dominance to the challenge.[54] This allowed the Court to deliver an outcome that protected accountability mechanisms from further erosion, while avoiding reasoning that could have earned it a reputation for stifling ANC power.[55]

The Court's judgment in *Glenister* has been positively received by some legal commentators for its innovative reliance on international law.[56] Others criticise the judgment for resorting to a strained interpretation of sections 39(1)(b) and 7(2) to justify the conclusion that non-binding international treaties required the Court to interfere with

---

[44] Issacharoff (note 37 above) 38–39.
[45] Ibid.
[46] Note 39 above 91.
[47] See, for example, A Price 'Evolution of the rule of law' (2013) 130 *South African Law Journal* 649.
[48] *Glenister v President of the Republic of South Africa* 2011 (3) SA 347 (CC).
[49] Ibid 183–186, 194.
[50] Ibid 192.
[51] Note 48 above 183–186, 194; Issacharoff (note 37 above) 41–42.
[52] Ibid 41.
[53] Ibid.
[54] Note 48 above 61, 62. Sujit Choudhry makes the same observation in relation to the court *a quo*'s judgment, see S Choudhry '"He had a mandate": The South African Constitutional Court and the African National Congress in a dominant party democracy' (2009) 2 *Constitutional Court Review* 5.
[55] Issacharoff (note 37 above) 41.
[56] See A Coutsoudis & M du Plessis 'We are all international lawyers now: The Constitution's international law trifecta comes of age' (2019) 136 *South African Law Journal* 440–442, 460; F Venter 'Containing the malady of corruption in South Africa: Can the courts stem the tide?' (2015) 132 *South African Law Journal* 748.

a clear policy choice falling within parliamentary prerogative.[57] Indeed, the minority judgment in *Glenister*, with which Mogoeng J (as he then was) concurred, went so far as to find that 'sections 39(1)(b) and 7(2) cannot be used to achieve the result contended for'.[58]

Glenister was less successful than *Democratic Alliance* in avoiding scrutiny from the political elite. While the Court sensibly avoided addressing the relevance of the ANC's dominance to the case, its unusual reliance on international law principles as the primary basis for its decision drew criticism from ANC corners. Foreshadowing his later remarks, Gwede Mantashe claimed that decisions like *Glenister* involved the Court in the 'political weighting of views', and implied such decisions indicated the Court might be seen to be 'seeking to arrest the functioning of Parliament'.[59] Criticism also came from academia. Prof. Ziyad Motala, for example, publicly criticised the judgment for '[lacking] cogency, depth of reasoning, or logic and fundamentally [ignoring] the text and separation of powers' and further opined that 'cherry-picking from international treaties […] might lead to the conclusion that the majority looked at this project through a strange lens […] some [might] conclude that this lens was ideological and political'.[60]

A common feature of the decisions in *Democratic Alliance* and *Glenister* is that the Court largely avoided developing a principled jurisprudential approach to challenging the ANC's increasing grip on power.[61] Echoing Issacharoff's observations, Choudhry notes that, during the Zuma presidency, the Court frequently 'rejected the relevance of the ANC's dominant status to the disposition of the appeals before it'.[62] In fact, Choudhry goes so far as to argue that the Court has an 'inadequate understanding of the concept of a dominant party democracy'.[63]

It is true that the Constitutional Court refrained from offering 'a substantive theorisation of the threat posed by the ANC's ongoing electoral dominance'.[64] But it is unfair to cast this reluctance as an 'inadequacy' on the part of the Court when one considers the political constraints under which it was operating, and the reality that South African legal culture[65] is largely intolerant of political considerations featuring in judicial reasoning.[66] The Court cannot afford to lose its reputation for handing down legally legitimate

---

57 See J Tuovinen 'The role of international law in Constitutional Adjudication: *Glenister v President of the Republic of South Africa*' (2013) 130 *South African Law Journal* 661; H Botha 'Representing the poor: Law, poverty and democracy' 2011 22(3) *Stellenbosch Law Review* 531 535.

58 Note 48 above 112.

59 See 'Mantashe's ConCourt Remarks Scandalous: DA' *News24* 18 August 2011 <https://www.news24.com/news24/mantashes-concourt-remarks-scandalous-da-20110818>. See also Botha (note 57 above).

60 Z Motala 'Divination through a strange lens' *TimesLive* 27 March 2011 <https://www.timeslive.co.za/ideas/2011-03-27-divination-through-a-strange-lens/>.

61 Issacharoff (note 37 above) 4, 39.

62 Choudhry (note 54 above) 33–34.

63 Ibid. Similarly, Issacharoff characterises the Court's approach as a failure to provide a substantive account of the notion of democracy (see note 17 above, 7–9).

64 T Roux 'Constitutional courts as democratic consolidators: Insights from South Africa after 20 years' (2016) 42(1) *Journal of Southern African Studies* 5.

65 'Legal culture' being the 'set of institutionalised, legal-professional norms and practices regulating permissible forms of judicial reasoning in a particular legal system' (Roux (note 8 above) 114). The legal culture of a jurisdiction determines the types of reasons that judges may give that the legal and broader political community will find persuasive. South African legal culture is generally described as 'formalist', in that courts are expected to rely on existing legal rules and principles in their reasoning to justify a particular outcome. Roux has described South African legal culture as one characterised by a strong attachment to the ideal of adjudication

decisions, as this is the core condition for it being handed its power. This may have been an even more serious consideration during the Zuma presidency, where the judiciary and the Office of the Public Protector were the few accountability mechanisms that remained uncaptured by political elites. Further, it is difficult to ignore the ANC's influence over the judicial appointments process when assessing the impact that a bold decision will have on the Court's long-term capacity to enforce the Constitution.[67] The threat of being labelled 'anti-democratic' or 'anti-ANC' may have been too real for the Court to openly undergird its decisions on the basis of the need to protect South Africa's democracy from the problems of single-party dominance and weak electoral competition, even if these considerations were key to the Court's decisions.[68]

As the next section intends to demonstrate, the Constitutional Court's strategic approach to politically controversial decisions, first developed in cases like *NNP*, and more recently deployed in the face of democratic erosion, relies on a particular approach to decision-making. This approach has become particularly important as a tool for responding to judicialisation, but it is not without risk.

4. Esoteric decision-making as a response to judicialisation

The above analysis of key cases symptomatic of the judicialisation of politics in South Africa reveals a trend in the Constitutional Court's approach. This trend is constituted by a range of strategic moves in the Court's decision-making arsenal, which include prevailing on narrow or distant sources of law; using technical, formalist modes of reasoning; deploying the apparently apolitical standards of rationality review; citing the indeterminacy of concepts such as 'democracy'; or exploiting the indeterminism of the separation of powers. These strategic moves are employed to retreat from politically controversial decisions in which the Constitution offers no immediately clear guidance; or to achieve constitutionally required outcomes without directly addressing the political nature of the cases before it, thereby avoiding the appearance of 'playing politics'.

It is important to note that in the cases in which these strategic moves are employed, the Court's public reasons for its decisions do not fully correlate with the considerations driving its reasoning. Considering the political morality underpinning adjudication, which requires judges to provide public reasons for their judgments, the question arises whether this strategic approach is defensible.[69] If the strategic approach detailed

according to law, that is, the belief that judges are constrained by law in their decision-making (Roux (note 8 above) 117–119).

[66] Roux (note 64 above) 12.

[67] Ibid 13. If one examines s 178(1) of the Constitution, which describes the composition of the Judicial Services Commission, it becomes clear that ANC-associated members are likely to be in the majority given the President and National Assembly's combined nomination powers.

[68] Roux (note 64 above) 13.

[69] Mendes (note 9 above) 39–40. Political morality consists in the principles that guide the use of power of political institutions (see J Raz *The Morality of Freedom* (1988) 3–4). The requirements of political morality in the judicial context are explained with reference to the rule of law. The rule of law requires 'principled adjudication', that is judicial decisions that are both 'reasoned and public', so as to create a shared understanding of that country's legal culture and 'feed expectations' of how judges may justify their decisions (see J Raz *Ethics in the Public Domain: Essays in the Morality of Law and Politics* (1994) 358–359; and for a useful discussion of Raz's views, Roux (note 8 above) 56). As Roux has noted, South African legal culture is strongly attached to the liberal ideal of adjudication according to law, which ideally requires reasoned and public decision-making (Roux (note 8 above)

above is not supported by the usual theories of political morality that explain adjudication, how can this approach be justified? The answer may lie in the concept of esoteric decision-making.

Esoteric decision-making describes a court's strategic nondisclosure of the political considerations underpinning its judgments.[70] These political considerations include the court's evaluation of the surrounding political constraints acting upon it; its anticipation of how its judgment will be received by other political actors; the potential impact of the decision on democratic stability or single-party hegemony; and whether the judgment is likely to render the court the subject of attacks on its independence.[71] According to Mendes, esoteric morality, manifested as esoteric decision-making in the judicial context, 'comprises considerations that cannot be publicly unveiled. Courts may play with several political cards, but political success largely depends on keeping these choices secret, under pain of being delegitimised or defeated'.[72] Mendes' interpretation of the concept is derived from Peter Singer and Katrzyna Lazari-Radek's original statement of the moral proposition of esoteric morality as 'it may be right to do and privately recommend, under certain circumstances, what it would not be right to advocate openly'.[73]

Esoteric morality in the adjudicative context recognises that the biggest risk to a court's power is that its decisions will be ignored.[74] This risk is especially present when courts render bold, interventionist judgments that are at odds with the interests of the political elite.[75] Managing this risk requires more than legal skill – it requires political dexterity and instinct.[76] Courts must be 'tacticians' and must avoid decisions that will 'erode its reservoir of authority and legitimacy' for the sake of institutional survival.[77]

It is important to note that, when referring to 'political considerations' underpinning judicial decisions, I do not have in mind personal political preferences, of the kind that would fall within the recognised ambit of judicial bias. In such a scenario, the primary problem is the fact of bias, rather than its disguise by use of esoteric decision-making. Rather, I am referring to the *realpolitik* inherent in certain judicial decisions – decisions that have consequences for the relative power of the judiciary vis-à-vis the other branches of government; and for the distribution of political power generally. Inevitably, many of the decisions that the Constitution empowers the Constitutional Court to make are imbued with political considerations, as the discussion in section two above explains. To acknowledge that these decisions are 'political' is to be realistic.

47, 49). For further accounts that argue that judges are required to offer public reasons for their decisions, see J Rawls *Political Liberalism* (1996) 230–235; R Dworkin *Law's Empire* (1986) 380; and Jeremy Waldron 'Theoretical foundations of liberalism' (1987) 37 *Philosophical Quarterly* 127.

70 Mendes (note 9 above) 39.

71 Ibid 38–40.

72 Ibid 39.

73 P Singer & K Lazari-Radek 'Secrecy in consequentialism: A defence of esoteric morality' (2010) 23 *Ratio* 37.

74 Klug (note 7 above) 32.

75 The executive's apparent election to ignore the Gauteng High Court's order interdicting Omar Al Bashir from leaving South Africa is a case in point. See S Musker 'Government guilt: Al-Bashir and South Africa's culpability' (2016) *Daily Maverick* 16 March <https://www.dailymaverick.co.za/opinionista/2016-03-16-government-guilt-al-bashir-and-south-africas-culpabiity/>

76 Mendes (note 9 above) 39.

77 Ibid.

A jurist committed to protecting and upholding the Constitution, and the role that it carves for accountability-enforcing institutions, is likely to favour, for example, a decision that holds the party deliberately seeking to erode such institutions to account. Such a decision may be constitutionally sound, but this does not mean that it is not political.

Some scholars reject esoteric decision-making as a justifiable technique of adjudication, owing to its departure from the usual norms of political morality applicable to adjudication, referred to above.[78] Political calculations should be openly expressed, as this promotes judicial responsibility and accountability. For Dennis Thompson, if the judge finds she cannot make the reasons for her decision public, then this indicates that she ought to reconsider the decision.[79] Thompson's preferred approach might be plausible in a jurisdiction where legal tradition is not steeped in a strict distinction between law and politics.[80] However, in South African legal culture, this approach is flawed for the same reasons as Choudhry's: articulating substantive political theorisations in response to a politically charged case would place the Constitutional Court in jeopardy and earn it the censure of both legal scholars and political elites. In any case, it is precisely the secrecy of esotericism that makes it successful: for a Court to say openly that it is not making a certain decision because it lacks the institutional power to enforce it (or to survive the political reaction it might elicit) would be 'an unwise way of managing its public reputation'.[81]

If we accept the descriptive claim that esoteric decision-making is employed by our Constitutional Court in some cases; and if we are prepared to consider the normative claim that its use is justified in at least some instances to protect the Court from institutional attack; then we are also forced to confront the unique risks that this practice of strategic decision-making introduces. As the analysis of the divergent reactions to *Democratic Alliance* and *Glenister* demonstrates, the Court's adoption of esoteric decision-making is not always successful. Clearly, the Court's use of esoteric decision-making is more effective in some cases than others.

Thus arises the question of what is meant by 'effective' esoteric decision-making. To answer this question, we must remind ourselves of what esoteric decision-making should be trying to achieve: reducing the threat of a political attack on the Court and its independence; while nevertheless allowing the Court to hand down outcomes that best accord with democratic principles and the protection of South Africa's constitutional project. Effective esoteric decision-making, at the very least, should leave the Court less, and not more, exposed to potential accusations that it has been 'playing politics'.

This is where the chief risk of esoteric decision-making presents itself. Necessarily, when the Court uses esoteric decision-making, not all of the reasons underpinning its judgment are expressed. But, in keeping some of its reasons hidden, the Court opens up the possibility for conjecture as to the motivations behind its judgment. In the face of this 'reasoning vacuum', competing hypotheses are likely to emerge. One potential

[78] D Thompson *Restoring Responsibility: Ethics in Government, Business, and Healthcare* (2004) at 80.
[79] Ibid; Mendes (note 9 above) 40.
[80] Roux (note 64 above) 13.
[81] Mendes (note 9 above) 40.

hypothesis is that the Court's sensitivity to the political constraints under which it operates, and its concern for its long-term institutional security, preclude it from openly disclosing all of the reasons underpinning its judgment. Another potential hypothesis, which is far more susceptible to being politically weaponised, is the hypothesis that the Court is intentionally frustrating executive power and attempting to influence certain political outcomes that ordinarily would not fall within its adjudicative terrain. Where the Court engages in esoteric decision-making while avoiding the popular proliferation of this second hypothesis, it uses esoteric decision-making effectively.

The most effective way for the Court to pre-empt and limit the proliferation of this second hypothesis is, unsurprisingly, through the careful and diligent application of legal reasoning, of the kind permitted by, and persuasive for, the legal-professional and broader political community. The more convincing the Court's expressed reasons and the lesser the reasoning vacuum, the less opportunity there will be for accusations of political interference and judicial overreach to take root. The differing reactions – from both the political elite and legal scholars – to *Democratic Alliance* and *Glenister* illustrates this point well. As mentioned, the core condition on which the Court has been handed its power is that it will hand down legally legitimate decisions. Esoteric decision-making, by its very nature, risks compromising the perception that the Court is meeting this condition. This risk is only increased when it is deployed without the requisite discipline. It is with this background in mind that I turn to consider the Court's decision in *EFF II*, which analysis aims to develop this argument further.

5. Esoteric decision-making and *EFF II*

EFF II was decided in the dying days of a tumultuous political year primarily characterised by Jacob Zuma's steady political decline. In March, a second Cabinet re-shuffle[82] by the President prompted nationwide protests.[83] In August, President Zuma narrowly survived a vote of no confidence held by secret ballot following the Constitutional Court's declaratory order[84] in *United Democratic Movement v Speaker of the National Assembly*.[85] Throughout the year, the GuptaLeaks scandal further implicated President Zuma and members of his family in corruption.[86] In court, Zuma repeatedly lost several key cases.[87] Then, a mere 11 days before the Constitutional Court handed down *EFF II*, Zuma's favoured successor, Nkosasana Dlamini-Zuma, lost the position of

82 This reshuffle notably saw the sacking of respected Finance Minister Pravin Gordhan.

83 News24 (no author) '2017: News24's year in review' 31 December 2018 <https://www.news24.com/SouthAfrica/News/2017-news24s-year-in-review-20171231>.

84 The Court ordered that the Speaker of the National Assembly had the powers to order a secret ballot be held for the purposes of the vote.

85 2017 (5) SA 300 (CC).

86 *The Sunday Times* initially broke the GuptaLeaks story, but the *Daily Maverick* also covered it in partnership with the amaBhungane Centre for Investigative Journalism.

87 In October, the Supreme Court of Appeal dismissed Zuma's application to appeal a High Court ruling that had found that the NPA's 2009 decision to drop hundreds of corruption charges against him was irrational (see *Zuma v Democratic Alliance; Acting National Director of Public Prosecutions v Democratic Alliance* 2018 (1) SA 200 (SCA)); in the *Corruption Watch* case, Zuma was found to have been conflicted in his appointment of the NDPP, and was heavily criticised by the court for his unlawful behaviour (see *Corruption Watch (RF) NPC v President of the Republic of South Africa; Council for the Advancement of the South African Constitution v President of the Republic of South Africa* 2018 (1) SACR 317 (GP)).

party president to then-Deputy President Cyril Ramaphosa in the ANC Elective Conference leadership battle. In all, the odds were clearly stacked against Zuma by the time the Court handed down its judgment.

The case was brought to the Court by the two largest opposition parties: the Economic Freedom Fighters (EFF)[88] and the Democratic Alliance (DA),[89] against the Speaker of the National Assembly (NA) in her capacity as representative of the NA. The case concerned the NA's alleged failure to hold President Zuma to account for his conduct in relation to state-funded upgrades of his private residence, which the Court had declared unconstitutional in 2016 in *EFF I*.[90] The applicants[91] essentially sought an order (i) declaring that the NA had failed to 'put all appropriate mechanisms and processes in place to hold [President Zuma] accountable for violating the Constitution'[92] and (ii) instructing the NA to convene a committee 'to conduct an investigation into the conduct of the President [with a view to implementing the s 89[93] impeachment provisions]'.[94]

It is important to acknowledge at this juncture that *EFF II* falls squarely within the category of cases most illustrative of judicialisation in South Africa. It concerned the 'how' and 'when' of presidential impeachment, which is the 'ultimate form of constitutional censure [arising] in extreme situations of political crises'.[95] Opposition parties were calling on the Court to intervene directly in a core legislative prerogative and to propel the political demise of a corrupt, albeit democratically elected, President. Whatever the outcome of the case, it was clear it would have significant consequences for the executive and legislative branches of state, and the political landscape in South Africa more broadly. Moreover, it touched directly on the Court's own power as an institutional actor, concerned as it was with the legislature's inaction in respect of the Court's findings in *EFF I*.

5.1 The majority and minority judgments in EFF II

The Court produced four judgments, three of which contributed substantively to the resolution of the dispute.[96] Zondo DCJ authored the minority judgment, Jafta J the majority judgment, and Mogoeng CJ concurred in Zondo DCJ's minority in a separate dissent. The first issue was whether the mechanism of an ad hoc committee[97] was an

[88] As first applicant.
[89] As an intervening party.
[90] *Economic Freedom Fighters v Speaker of the National Assembly; Democratic Alliance v Speaker of the National Assembly* 2016 (3) SA 580 (CC).
[91] Henceforth I will refer to the EFF, DA, UDM and other parties as 'the applicants'.
[92] Note 1 above 24 (the violation was that President Zuma had failed to implement the remedial action prescribed by the Public Protector for using state money to effect upgrades to his private residence). Although the EFF later abandoned this claim, the intervening party, the DA, did not, so the issue was still considered.
[93] Section 89 (1) of the Constitution of the Republic of South Africa, 1996 states that the National Assembly, 'by a resolution adopted with a supporting vote of at least two thirds of its members, may remove the President from office only on the grounds of—(a) a serious violation of the Constitution or the law; (b) serious misconduct; or (c) inability to perform the functions of office'.
[94] Note 1 above 27.
[95] F Cachalia, 'Precautionary Constitutionalism, Representative Democracy and Political Corruption' (2019) 9 *Constitutional Court Review* 45 at 73.
[96] The fourth was a remark by Froneman J on the tone of the Chief Justice's dissent.
[97] A motion for the establishment of which can be tabled by any member of Parliament.

adequate mechanism by which an investigation into the President's conduct for the purposes of s 89(1) impeachment proceedings could be instituted.[98] The minority found that such a mechanism was sufficient, and relied on the fact that all the applicants themselves, with the exception of the DA, had acknowledged this in supplementary affidavits.[99] The majority found that s 89 imposed objective requirements to be satisfied before an impeachment motion could be considered.[100] Thus, any impeachment inquiry had to be preceded by a determination of whether a listed ground exists.[101] The majority went so far as to find that s 89(1) was, in its current form 'impossible to implement'.[102] However, the majority paid little attention to the ad hoc committee mechanism.[103] When it did address this mechanism, it found that it entitled parties to be represented in the same proportion as they were represented in the National Assembly. Interestingly, the majority explicitly argued that this would raise 'the risk of an impeachment complaint not reaching the Assembly [...] members of the majority party in the ad hoc Committee may prevent an impeachment process from proceeding beyond the committee, to shield a President who is their party leader'.[104]

The majority concluded that Parliament had failed to enact adequate rules for determining the existence of impeachment grounds. As a result, it ordered the NA to 'make rules regulating the removal of a President in terms of section 89(1) of the Constitution'.[105] However, the majority neglected to acknowledge that the Assembly's failure to make rules for the impeachment process was directly attributable to the applicants' own failure to return to the rules sub-committee.[106] This was a factual issue that the minority judgment, in contrast, had emphasised heavily. Zondo DCJ had criticised the applicants, who had all been members of a 2015 subcommittee established to develop rules for the s 89 impeachment procedure, for failing to return to the subcommittee and instead instituting proceedings in court.[107] Yet, the majority held that 'the Constitution does not impose the obligation to make rules for impeachment upon political parties. That duty falls squarely on the shoulders of the Assembly'.[108] In the context, the distinction drawn by the majority between the NA and the political parties that constitute it is contrived. This is especially so when one considers the strict party discipline that characterises most MPs' engagement in the NA, and the majority's own comment that members of an ad hoc parliamentary committee might block efforts to remove their party leader.

A related issue was whether the NA had held the President to account for his violations of the Constitution, as pronounced upon by the Court in *EFF I*. The minority found that the NA had held the President to account: he had been subjected to two

[98] Note 1 above 39, 78.
[99] Ibid 48.
[100] Ibid 177.
[101] Ibid 180.
[102] Ibid 182.
[103] Ibid 184.
[104] Ibid 191–192.
[105] Ibid 222 point 8 of the order.
[106] Ibid 196.
[107] Ibid 59, 81–82.
[108] Ibid 213.

motions of no confidence and one impeachment motion since the release of the Public Protector's report.[109] The fact that such motions had been brought, regardless of their outcomes, was sufficient for the discharge of Parliament's oversight obligations.[110] Conversely, the majority found that the Assembly had failed to hold the President accountable since no 'actions [had been] taken in terms of section 89(1)'.[111] The majority went so far as to hold that the impeachment motion heard in March 2016 had not amounted to a s 89(1) procedure proper since there had been no prior enquiry into whether the s 89(1) grounds existed – had the motion been successful, it would have been unconstitutional and liable to be judicially reviewed.[112] After remarking upon the wide and flexible powers of the Court to grant any just and equitable remedy, even one that goes beyond the applicant's prayers, the majority ordered the National Assembly to fulfil its obligation to determine whether President Zuma had breached s 89(1)(a) or (b) of the Constitution without delay.[113]

In contrast, the minority provided useful critiques of the majority reasoning, which highlighted the over-zealousness on the part of the majority to intervene in the exercise of legislative authority. For example, it noted that it would be inappropriate for a court to order that an ad hoc committee (for investigating whether impeachment grounds existed) be established, as this would assist the applicants to bypass democratic process.[114] The minority also remarked that it was not appropriate that the Court order the NA to establish a strict procedure[115] to be followed for every impeachment motion.[116] The argument that a committee was needed to establish whether the said violation was 'serious' was without merit, since 'serious' was a value judgment that would have to be made by the National Assembly in the course of voting.[117] Mogoeng CJ found that the majority judgment's poorly-substantiated[118] conclusion that the NA would always have to hold an enquiry to establish the existence of impeachment grounds, and its order that rules be made to provide permanently for such a mechanism; clearly contradicted the separation of powers and encroached on the constitutionally-ordained domain of Parliament.[119] Further, it was unacceptable that the majority had ordered the NA to initiate an impeachment process against President Zuma, given that none of the applicants had asked for such relief, that the applicants had never been refused such relief by the Speaker, and that they had in fact failed to make use of the existing ad hoc committee mechanism.[120]

---

109 Note 1 above 89.
110 Ibid 93.
111 Ibid 200. Notably, this order deviated from the applicants' prayer, which was that the Assembly had failed to hold the President to account (not that it had failed to initiate s 89(1) proceedings).
112 Ibid 205–206.
113 Note 1 above 211 and 222, orders 10 and 11. (Note that the order's paragraphs are incorrectly numbered 7–12 instead of 1–6.)
114 Ibid 73. There was nothing stopping the applicants from tabling a motion to establish such a committee themselves, and no indication that they had been frustrated from doing so.
115 For example, in this particular case, the Court had already found in *EFF I* that the President had violated the Constitution.
116 Note 1 above 106.
117 Ibid 113.
118 See, in particular, Mogoeng CJ's comments at 246.
119 Note 1 above 224.
120 Ibid 237.

5.2 Criticisms of the majority judgment

In its final substantive paragraph, the majority asserts that all it has done 'is to interpret section 89 of the Constitution and apply it to the present facts'.[121] Yet, it failed to take key factual considerations into account. It ignored the fact that it was the DA and EFF's representatives on the sub-committee who had stalled the process of drafting rules for a s 89 procedure. Instead of rejecting the application and ordering the applicants to return to the rules drafting committee, the majority drew a superficial distinction between the responsibilities of the NA and of political parties. The majority also failed to address the minority argument that, on the facts of the case, it would be inappropriate for the NA to begin investigations into the impeachment grounds, since the Court had already held that President Zuma's conduct constituted a violation of the Constitution. However, one factual element that the Court did seem to take into account was the ANC's electoral dominance in the NA.

Concern for the majority party's dominance in the legislature was the subtle driving force behind the majority judgment; it was the main reason why the suggested ad hoc committee mechanism was found to be insufficient. Yet, s 53(1)(c) of the Constitution requires that 'all questions before the Assembly are decided by a majority of the votes cast'. In terms of the constitutional framework, the actions of the NA should reflect the will of the majority, as this is the basis of the NA's power. The majority judgment's endorsement of an approach whereby the EFF, DA and other parties are entitled to be disproportionately represented in a parliamentary committee mandated to evaluate the misconduct of the President contradicts s 57(1)(b)[122] of the Constitution, and is at odds with founding constitutional principles.[123] Though not always explicit, concern for the ANC's political dominance in the legislature clearly featured in the majority's reasoning, yet it failed to provide adequate justification for its departure from the fundamental constitutional principles of representative democracy and majoritarianism.[124] It also allowed this concern to obscure the fact that all of the opposition parties to the case, barring the DA, had agreed that the ad hoc committee mechanism was sufficient for the impeachment proceedings.[125]

The applicants' prayers were for a *declaratory* order that the NA had failed to hold the President to account.[126] They did not pray for an order that the NA had failed to hold a s 89(1) impeachment process. Yet, this is how the majority construed the applicants' prayers, ignoring the fact that two no confidence motions had already been voted upon (not to mention one impeachment motion). The majority's order that the NA fulfil its obligation 'to determine whether the President has breached section 89(1)(a) or (b) of the Constitution' went beyond the order requested by the

---

121 Ibid 220.

122 This section requires that the Assembly's rules must be made with due regard for representative democracy.

123 For a helpful discussion of this point, see Cachalia (note 95 above) 61, 63–64.

124 Ibid; Cachalia similarly criticises the majority's departure from s 53(1) and 57(1) of the Constitution, arguing that 'the majority's justifications for its circumvention of majority-rule with respect to decision-making procedures appear somewhat opaque'.

125 Note 1 above 51.

126 Ibid 18, prayers 2 and 3.

applicants.[127] An order to investigate whether there are grounds to use the s 89(1) powers, is different from an order *to* exercise the s 89(1) powers. Given the case's proximity to core legislative prerogatives, it was bold for the majority to so easily depart from the relief explicitly sought by the applicants.

What the analysis of the weaknesses in the majority's judgment does is illustrate that the majority took certain political considerations into account, but failed to offer a legally legitimate basis – particularly of the kind expected by South Africa's formalist legal culture – for doing so. There was 'little textual basis' for the intrusive outcome that interfered directly with internal parliamentary processes.[128] The departure from the applicants' prayers in such a highly politicised case was not adequately justified by the Court's reasoning. It is plausible to conclude, as Mogoeng CJ did, that 'the language of section 89 is […] being overly strained to divine from it an elusive justification for a particular conclusion'.[129] It is possible that the majority read the political context, characterised as it was by the declining support for Zuma's presidency,[130] and took the opportunity to hand down a judgment that would hasten the termination of a presidency that had overseen the systematic erosion of democratic institutions and the abuse of public resources – even though the express provisions of the Constitution arguably did not entitle it to do so on the facts of the case before it. The extraordinary nature of the remedy ordered by the majority, its departure from the applicants' prayers, its strained interpretation of s 89(1), and its decision to ignore key factual elements of the case, makes this interpretation of the judgment worthy of serious consideration. Indeed, Froneman J's brief concurring judgment explained that the Court had done nothing more than 'provide the National Assembly with guidance on the tools necessary to […] *hold the President to account in the direst of situations*' (emphasis added).[131] Froneman J's comments 'left unexplained the considerations which led him to reach this assessment'.[132] Yet their making suggests that unexpressed political factors featured in the majority's reasoning, and drove it to the bold outcome that it reached. Ultimately, the quality of the public reasons provided for the Court's conclusion give the lie that it had other, private reasons for deciding as it did.

6. *EFF II*: A lesson for esoteric decision-making

Cases such as *EFF II* are precisely why we need to critically consider the Constitutional Court's use of esoteric decision-making as a response to judicialisation. From the work of Roux, Mendes and Issacharoff, it becomes clear that esoteric decision-making is

127 The applicants prayed for the convening of a committee to determine whether the President's conduct warranted the exercise of Parliament's s 89(1) powers – see para 222 orders 7 and 8; contrast with para 18 prayer 6.

128 Cachalia (note 95 above) 61.

129 Note 1 above 269.

130 Indeed, Stephen Gardbaum, in his discussion of the judgment, notes that over the course of the past two decades, 'the political constraints on the Court have loosened […] as the dominance of the ANC has seemingly declined' and comments further that 'in 2002, or even 2012, the Court did not have the political space to act as it did in 2017' (see S Gardbaum 'Pushing the boundaries: Judicial review of legislative procedures in South Africa' (2019) 9 *Constitutional Court Review* 1, 12).

131 Note 1 above 285.

132 Cachalia (note 95 above) 64.

a necessary ingredient to the Constitutional Court's institutional survival, particularly in light of South Africa's dominant-party democracy. This is especially so given that judicialisation has drawn the Court into political controversies and pitted it against the other branches of government. Esoteric decision-making is a defence mechanism; it may be used to protect the Court from confrontation with the executive, or to avoid being drawn into controversial political decisions for fear that they will be ignored or will lead to attacks on the judiciary. It must be recognised that when the Court is acting to protect its institutional power and longevity, the Court is also acting in the interests of constitutional supremacy itself. Without an independent, respected and institutionally powerful Constitutional Court, the constitutional project will suffer significant damage.

The use of esoteric decision-making may be a justified response to judicialisation. Yet, used too bluntly, it becomes a reckless and ineffective approach, and its very essence and advantage – its discretion – is lost. The core problem with the majority judgment in *EFF II* is that the majority's public reasons for its judgment are insufficient to explain the case's outcome.[133] It handed down a judgment that intruded on the ambit of the legislature's authority and intervened in the highly political impeachment process; without having carefully set out legally legitimate reasons for doing so. The majority's expressed reasons failed to substantiate the outcome at which it arrived, leaving a 'reasoning vacuum' waiting to be filled by competing hypotheses. One potential hypothesis gives the Court the benefit of the doubt: the majority, though handing down a 'troubling' decision 'not justifiable from a 'traditional' separation of powers perspective', was ultimately acting to reinforce the democratic process, in acknowledgement that Parliament had egregiously failed in its duty, as representative of the people, to hold political elites to account.[134] Similarly, Stephen Gardbaum, in an effort 'to understand the Court's intervention as promoting, rather than […] trenching on the separation of powers', suggests that the Court's intervention in *EFF II* may be justifiable when read as an attempt to 'open up blockages' in political accountability when Parliament has become 'captive', thus 'loosening party control and boosting the independence of opposition voices to help secure [the legislature's] key separation of powers function'.[135] However, alternative hypotheses – put forward by those seeking to exploit the vacuum as part of a political campaign against judicial power – might be less favourable. The problem with a reasoning vacuum is that it is capable of being exploited by anyone: whatever hypothesis is put forward to explain the judgment competes equally with other hypotheses, some of which may have worrying consequences for public perceptions of the judiciary.

The courts certainly have a role to play in addressing the pathologies arising out of the ANC's legislative dominance. *Democratic Alliance* represents an example of how this was achieved skilfully and discreetly. In the *Democratic Alliance* case, the Court

---

133 Cachalia observes that the majority's concern for 'the utter failure of the democratic process […] operates as *the unmistakeable background to EFF II*' (note 95 above) 78 (emphasis added).

134 See Cachalia (note 95 above) 72, 78–79. This interpretation is sympathetic to the invidious position in which the Court found itself, and acknowledges that the Court's intervention, legally inelegant as it was, was nevertheless motivated by founding constitutional principles and the desire to defend democracy.

135 Gardbaum (note 130 above) 11, 16–17.

needed to rely on the esoteric approach to deliver an outcome that had the effect of blocking ANC attempts to undermine accountability mechanisms. This outcome was nevertheless legally legitimate and was borne out by the Court's reasoning. The Court knew it needed to be careful in how it framed its decision for the sake of protecting its institutional security, and it was. The carefully reasoned and incremental expansion of the rationality test built naturally on previous decisions, and allowed the Court to deliver a politically necessary judgment without engaging directly with the anti-democratic threat before it. Crucially, the public reasons provided by the Court were sufficient to wholly support the judgment. As such, the Court minimised the risk of speculation that its judgment was 'politically motivated', and was able to reduce its exposure to institutional attacks.

The circumstances of *Glenister* similarly called for the strategic use of esoteric decision-making. Yet the Court's dependence on non-binding international treaties and its strained reliance on sections 39(1)(b) and 7(2) resulted in a controversial and at times unpersuasive judgment, which, critically, attracted the attention of political elites who then exploited the judgment's weaknesses to score political points. The Court's attempt to disguise its motivations – which, once again, were likely constitutionally sound –ultimately resulted in the censure that it had been trying to avoid.

In *EFF II*, one finds a particularly troubling example of the undisciplined and ineffective use of esoteric decision-making. The majority delivered a thinly substantiated and unpersuasive judgment on the politically vexed issue of the impeachment of a sitting President, an issue 'only likely to arise [...] in extreme situations of political crises, fraught with risk to the body politic and the judiciary itself'.[136] The majority's publicly expressed reasons lacked legal legitimacy and were inadequate for the task of supporting the bold outcome that it delivered. The outcome reached by the majority in *EFF II* was simply not borne out by its reasoning or the facts of the case. The Court's use of the esoteric approach in *EFF II* was reckless. It put the Court's institutional security at significant risk, which is exactly the outcome esoteric decision-making seeks to avoid.

Cachalia, while sympathetic to the Court's intervention in the face of gross political dysfunction, argues that if the majority was so concerned with protecting the basic structures of the country's democratic institutions, it 'had an obligation to state this basis for [its] counter-majoritarian intrusion crystalline clear'.[137] Yet, as the discussion above has illustrated, it is unlikely that the Court could afford to address this democratic threat so directly. Such an approach would have been too risky in the political circumstances, and the Court may well have attracted institutional attacks on its legitimacy and independence.[138] Clearly, esoteric decision-making was a justified response to the Court's precarious position in *EFF II*. The problem with *EFF II* is rather that the Court's use of esoteric decision-making was undisciplined, legally unpersuasive (particularly in the sense understood in South Africa's formalist legal culture) and ultimately ineffective given the goals this decision-making technique tries to achieve.

---

[136] Cachalia (note 95 above) 73.
[137] Cachalia (note 95 above) 65.
[138] This is especially so given that the subject matter of the judgment drew the Court directly into the question of whether President Zuma ought to be removed from power.

Gardbaum's discussion of *EFF II* suggests that 'where sufficient institutional independence has survived' to 'make possible' judicial interventions aimed at bolstering Parliament's accountability function in the face of abusive party dominance, such interventions 'are justified and proportionate as a means to the goal of saving constitutional democracy'.[139] Yet, had the political outcomes following *EFF II* been different, the Court's institutional independence may well have been under threat, hampering the Court's ability to deliver such interventions in the future. This is precisely why esoteric decision-making is a valuable adjudicative approach: it aims to protect the Court's institutional position in the long-term, which in turn bolsters its ability to hand down judgments necessary for the protection of constitutional democracy, in a manner that preserves the Court's reservoir of legitimacy and shields it from allegations of 'playing into the political space'. The Court's use of esoteric decision-making in *EFF II* was short-sighted and paid insufficient attention to this important goal.

There is a further, more fundamental problem that decisions like *Glenister* and *EFF II* present. The more often the Court uses esoteric decision-making poorly, the more likely it is that political elites who would otherwise be unaware of the Court's use of this approach become alive thereto. The very success of esoteric decision-making lies in its discretion: if the Court shows its hand too many times, the value of esoteric decision-making, and the contribution that it makes to the institutional stability of the judiciary, will be diluted. This point links to a broader point about the importance of protecting and strengthening public perceptions of the Court as being legally legitimate. As Gardbaum recently noted, in his discussion of the Constitutional Court's increasingly bold interventions in parliamentary processes, 'in almost every case […] the leading opinion was able to cite a relevant section of the text [such that] the Court could reasonably claim – and be seen – to be doing "lawyer's work"'.[140] Yet it is difficult to apply this statement to *EFF II*, given the majority's circumvention of the key constitutional principles of majoritarianism and representative democracy. The Court needs to be mindful of the fact that, with every poor application of esoteric decision-making, it risks eroding the belief that the Court's decisions are the product of 'lawyer's work', which in turn will compromise the very basis of the Court's legitimacy. In so doing, the very institutional power of the Court – so crucial for the defence of democracy in the face of abusive political party dominance – may decline, an outcome that South Africa's constitutional project cannot afford.

The analysis of *EFF II* reveals a simple, perhaps trite, point: esoteric decision-making is most successful when it is used undetected. Conversely, poor esoteric decision-making gives itself away easily. Good esoteric decision-making occurs when the Court's publicly expressed reasons are sufficient to support the outcome delivered, such that its additional, private reasons for its decisions are rendered unnecessary to explain the Court's judgment, and the opportunity for speculation as to the Court's motivations is limited. Poor esoteric decision-making occurs when the Court's publicly

[139] Gardbaum (note 130 above) 17.

[140] Gardbaum (note 130 above) 11–12. Gardbaum's use of the phrase 'lawyer's work' is a reference to the late US Justice Scalia's critique of the popular legitimacy of the Supreme Court's work product when its decisions make little or no reference to the constitutional text. A Scalia 'Originalism: The lesser evil' (1989) 57 *University of Cincinnati Law Review* 849, 854.

expressed reasons are inadequate for explaining the outcome delivered by the Court; and this absence of explanatory power creates a reasoning vacuum that may be filled by competing hypotheses about the Court's other, private reasons for its judgment. Some of these hypotheses may be sympathetic to the Court's position and the outcome that it was trying to achieve; others may be less favourable and may paint the Court as attempting to enter the political arena.

The phenomenon of the judicialisation of politics is unlikely to subside. The Constitutional Court needs a strategic approach to adjudicating the cases that it presents. Esoteric decision-making allows the Court to deliver outcomes that are in the best long-term interests of the constitutional project, but that are nevertheless substantiated in the instant case by reasoning that is legally legitimate, and most importantly, unlikely to expose it to the accusation that it is playing politics, despite the political sensitivity of the case before it. It should be the priority of the Constitutional Court to act in the long-term interests of the constitutional project by ensuring that it guards itself against attacks on its independence, and by protecting itself as the only institution ultimately capable of enforcing and upholding the Constitution. However, the Court puts this long-term interest at great risk when it hands down doctrinally suspect decisions to achieve a particular outcome (even if it believes this outcome to be in the interests of protecting democracy), leaving a reasoning vacuum that may be exploited by those seeking to undermine the judiciary. Clearly, esoteric decision-making is used most effectively when it is coupled with legally legitimate and cogent reasoning, which itself is able to fully support the outcome delivered.

With the analysis above in mind, perhaps Mogoeng CJ's interruption may be viewed in a different light. Perhaps the Chief Justice appreciated precisely how much the majority judgment had exposed the Court to accusations of political interference. Possibly, his bold interruption was an attempt to pre-emptively capture the narrative that would likely emerge from ANC quarters about *EFF II*: that it was an offensive example of judicial overreach. In so doing, the Chief Justice may well have limited the extent to which the reasoning vacuum left by the majority judgment was able to be politically weaponised.

7. Conclusion

This paper provides an academic account of the phenomenon of the judicialisation of politics as it has manifested in South Africa. It has argued that the Constitutional Court tends to use esoteric decision-making in order to minimise the chances of attracting threats to its independence and institutional security when it hands down decisions in cases symptomatic of judicialisation. It shows that, while esoteric decision-making may be justified in certain circumstances, it presents particular risks when it is poorly executed. Given that the judicialisation of politics is a phenomenon that is unlikely to cease in the near future, the Court needs to employ greater discipline in its use of esoteric decision-making to achieve the goal of preserving its legal legitimacy in the face of judicialisation. Ultimately, the Court's institutional survival and success will depend on whether it is able to respond to judicialisation in a strategic, disciplined and justified manner in the years to come.

Acknowledgements

This article relies in part on research completed in 2018 during the final year of my LLB degree at the University of Cape Town. I would like to thank Professor Pierre De Vos for his comments on the 2018 version of this paper, and Lyle Aspeling for comments on a more recent draft. I am further hugely indebted to two anonymous reviewers for their detailed insights, suggestions and critiques. All errors are my own.

Disclosure statement

No conflict of interest was declared by the author.

Are judicial monitoring institutions a legitimate remedy for addressing systemic socioeconomic rights violations?

Ropafadzo Maphosa

ABSTRACT
Sections 26(2) and 27(2) of the Constitution of the Republic of South Africa, 1996 provide that the state must take reasonable legislative and other measures to ensure the progressive realisation of socio-economic rights including, housing and social security. The executive is generally responsible for the implementation of these rights. However, a core challenge in South Africa is that the executive is beset by chronic incapacity, especially at provincial and local government levels, which has hindered the realisation of socio-economic rights. This article investigates the increasingly intrusive orders by the judiciary to address this problem; these orders include, specifically, appointing bodies to manage service delivery by the executive. I will situate these mechanisms within the broader powers of the judiciary and provide a justification for them, under particular conditions, against criticisms of judicial overreach. In engaging with their legal justifiability, I will analyse recent South African case law as well as examples from India and Colombia so as to highlight that the South Africa judiciary is not unique in developing such mechanisms. In concluding, I identify the conditions under which the deployment of these mechanisms may be considered justifiable as well as their value in advancing the realisation of socio-economic rights in South Africa.

The Constitution of the Republic of South Africa, 1996 places an obligation on the judiciary to provide effective relief where a constitutional right has been violated. This applies not only in the case of civil and political rights, but also in relation to socio-economic rights. In light of the close relationship between the executive and the legislative branch, citizens rely on the judiciary to ensure executive accountability and the protection of their basic interests and fundamental rights. However, the role of courts in enforcing these rights is undermined where other branches of government fail to comply with court orders issued in this regard.[1]

---

[1] C Mbazira 'You are the "weakest link" in realising socio-economic rights, goodbye: Strategies for effective implementation of court orders in South Africa' (2008) Socio-Economic Rights Project Research Series 3 Community Law Centre University of the Western Cape <http://repository.uwc.ac.za/bitstream/handle/10566/4871/Mbazira,_Weakest_Link_in_Realising_Socio-Economic_Rights.pdf?sequence=1&isAllowed=y>

Often, failures by the executive to give effect to court orders arise from systemic problems that cannot be easily resolved. In several cases, successful litigants – including both communities and individuals – have been left stranded and unable to benefit from the orders arising from their victories in court. What is more, various commentators maintain that South Africa's apex courts have been averse to using the structural interdict as a remedy in socio-economic rights cases,[2] and have attributed the failure of adjudication on socio-economic rights to make a significant impact in the lives of the poor, to the reluctance of the courts to follow up on the enforcement of its orders.[3]

As a result, the South African Constitutional Court has articulated the need to shape innovative remedies to ensure that when the legal process establishes an infringement of rights, they can be effectively vindicated.[4] This was highlighted in *Pheko v Ekurhuleni Metropolitan Municipality* where the Constitutional Court held that in the case of a human rights violation, including the violation of a socio-economic right, a court is under a duty to ensure that effective relief is granted and, where necessary, this may require both a mandamus and the exercise of the court's supervisory jurisdiction.[5] The court drew its authority from s 172(1)(b) of the Constitution, which provides that in constitutional matters, courts may grant 'any order that is just and equitable'. This provision empowers courts to order structural interdicts.

Although previously reluctant, our apex courts are becoming increasingly open to exercising supervisory jurisdiction, and the use of the structural interdict can be seen as a recent development moulded by 'a new and transformative constitutional order'.[6]

This article will examine the use of a particular model of structural interdict that courts have recently adopted to ensure the effective enforcement of socio-economic rights. This model involves the appointment of monitoring institutions or experts to oversee the implementation of court orders, otherwise known as the 'expert remedial formulation model'. I will begin with an examination of whether the use of structural interdicts is compatible with the dictates of the Constitution. It will be argued that structural interdicts are justified as they are often necessary in order for courts to enforce their orders effectively. Thus, structural interdicts requiring the court to exercise its supervisory jurisdiction do not constitute judicial overreach as they buttress the judiciary's constitutional obligation to ensure the realisation of socio-economic rights.

In the second event, I will consider the different types of structural interdicts that exist as well as their advantages and disadvantages. I will proceed to focus on a particular form of supervisory interdict, namely, the appointment of experts to monitor compliance with court orders or the creation of a plan that ensures the implementation of a court order. This approach is relatively new in South Africa. Given its strong

---

2 C Mbazira 'From ambivalence to certainty: Norms and principles for the structural interdict in socio-economic rights litigation in South Africa' (2008) 24 *South African Journal on Human Rights* 1.

3 D Bilchitz 'Giving socio-economic rights teeth: The minimum core and its importance' (2002) 3 *South African Law Journal* 501.

4 *Fose v Minister of Safety and Security* 1997 (3) SA 786 (CC) para 69.

5 *Pheko v Ekurhuleni Metropolitan Municipality* 2015 (5) SA 600 (CC) para 106.

6 K Roach & G Budlender 'Mandatory relief and supervisory jurisdiction: When is it appropriate, just and equitable?' (2005) 122 *South African Law Journal* 328.

interventionist approach to the functioning of the executive, this remedy has been met with stern concerns of judicial overreach by academic critics. However, I will argue that the appointment of monitoring institutions and experts is consistent with the separation of powers given that it can help address *structural* or *systemic* challenges that impede the realisation of rights, such as a lack of resources or inadequate staffing. In section 3, I provide an analysis of foreign and domestic cases wherein the courts have appointed monitoring mechanisms. Ultimately, this article aims to demonstrate that the appointment of experts in the context of widespread executive malfunction is consistent with the courts' judicial mandate to ensure the fulfilment of socio-economic rights and is not an instance of judicial overreach.

1. Application of structural interdicts in South Africa

Where state policy is challenged for alleged inconsistency with the Constitution, the courts have to consider whether, in formulating and implementing such a policy, the state has given effect to its constitutional obligations. Section 172(1) of the Constitution provides that:

When deciding a constitutional matter within its power, a court—

a. must declare that any law or conduct that is inconsistent with the Constitution is invalid to the extent of its inconsistency; and
b. may make any order that is just and equitable, including—
c. an order limiting the retrospective effect of the declaration of invalidity; and
d. an order suspending the declaration of invalidity for any period and on any conditions, to allow the competent authority to correct the defect.

The implication of this provision on the remedial powers of the courts was previously unclear and had to be clarified by the courts. For the purpose of this discussion, the most important case is *Minister of Health v Treatment Action Campaign* (*TAC*).[7] The government's contention in that case was that the separation of powers doctrine prevents courts from making orders that would encroach on the executive's policy terrain. This argument was based on the premise that policy is the prerogative of the executive rather than the judiciary.[8] Therefore, it was further argued that a declaratory order is the only competent order that a court can make upon a finding that the government's policies fall short of constitutional requirements.[9] The Court rejected this argument stating that South African courts have a wide range of powers, including mandatory and structural interdicts, which allow them to ensure that the Constitution is upheld. Therefore, when it is appropriate to do so, courts should use their powers to make orders that affect policy as well as legislation.[10]

The Court here established that while the principle of separation of powers is an important principle in a constitutional democracy, it cannot provide the basis for the

[7] *Minister of Health v Treatment Action Campaign* 2002 (5) SA 721 (CC) (*TAC*).
[8] Ibid para 97.
[9] Ibid para 106.
[10] Ibid para 113.

judiciary to avoid its obligation to provide appropriate relief that is just and equitable. The Court reasoned that although there are no bright lines that separate the spheres of the legislature, the executive and the judiciary from one another, there are certain matters that are pre-eminently within the domain of one arm of government rather than another. However, this does not mean that the judiciary cannot make orders that have an impact on policy.[11] The Court in *TAC* also held that the power to grant relief in terms of s 172(1) (b) includes the power to mandate the government to perform certain tasks.

There is a spectrum of possibilities for declaratory orders by courts. These vary from weak orders where the court simply declares the legal position, to stronger forms of intervention. Courts, sometimes, suspend a declaration of invalidity in order to allow the executive branch more time to work out the most appropriate remedial solution, thus inviting more collaboration and input from the other branches.[12] Sandra Liebenberg supports this approach and argues that the separation of powers should be understood as 'a relationship of mutual accountability, responsiveness and openness between the three branches'.[13] However, this represents what Mark Tushnet terms 'weak-form' review.[14] To some extent, this form of judicial review might be viewed as deferential as the development of the final remedy is left to the elected branches of government. This differs from 'strong-form' review.

According to Tushnet, 'strong-form review is a system in which judicial interpretations of the Constitution are final and unrevisable by ordinary legislative majorities'.[15] Although there are different types of strong-form review, the common feature across the board is that the judiciary has 'normative finality' over other branches on questions of rights.[16] Supervisory jurisdiction is usually regarded as a strong form of intervention, not a weak one. Where it is appropriate, the court retains supervisory jurisdiction to ensure that the order is implemented by other branches.[17] This remedy counters the potential defects of weak-form review by ensuring that the executive fulfils its constitutional obligations.

1.1 The significance of structural interdicts in socio-economic rights cases

Kent Roach and Geoff Budlender describe the structural interdict as a recent development introduced by a new transformative constitutional order.[18] This remedy is distinct in that it involves the continued participation of the court in the implementation of its orders. Once the court has handed down its judgment and made an order, it does not relinquish the case. Thus, a structural interdict is not a 'one-shot and one-way approach to providing judicial remedies'; instead, 'it creates a complex ongoing regime

[11] Ibid para 98.
[12] A Kavanagh 'What's so weak about "weak form review"? The case of UK Human Rights Act, 1998' (2015) 13 *International Journal of Constitutional Law* 1019.
[13] S Liebenberg *Socio-Economic Rights: Adjudication Under a Transformative Constitution* (2010) 67.
[14] M Tushnet 'Weak-form judicial review and "core" civil liberties' (2006) 41 *Harvard Civil Rights-Civil Liberties Law Review* 10.
[15] M Tushnet *Weak Courts, Strong Rights* (2008) 33.
[16] Ibid 34.
[17] *TAC* (note 7 above) 104.
[18] Roach & Budlender (note 6 above) 328.

of performance'.[19] The objective of the structural interdict is performance, not solely deterrence, or compensation as is the case with traditional remedies such as ordinary interdicts. Certain forms of the structural interdict also aim to eliminate structural violations by focussing on changes that need to be effected in institutional design and functioning.[20]

Traditional remedies often fail to address systemic violations, namely, human rights violations that are likely to result in structural poverty and inequality. Such infringements affect a large number of people due to prevalent public policy failures by governmental agencies. The design of structural interdicts can attempt to ensure the development of lasting capacities and institutional reform that is essential to the fulfilment of fundamental rights.[21] The structural interdict, therefore, 'seeks to adjust future behaviour and is deliberately fashioned rather than logically deduced from the nature of the legal harm suffered'.[22] As alluded to earlier, what sets the structural interdict apart from traditional remedies is the retention of supervision by the court.[23] However, the Constitutional Court in South Africa has been reluctant to supervise its court orders. The High Court, on the other hand, has been more open to crafting novel judicial remedies. In fact, structural remedies became routinely used in housing/eviction cases. In *Blue Moonlight Properties 039 (Pty) Ltd v the Occupiers of Saratoga Avenue*,[24] the High Court confirmed that municipalities have a duty to report to courts in circumstances where an eviction might lead to homelessness. The State was ordered to produce a further report within four weeks setting out the steps it had taken and would subsequently take to provide emergency shelter or other housing for the occupiers in the event of an eviction.[25]

Over the years, the jurisprudence of the High Court has included structural interdicts imposing reporting mechanisms, internal audits, the appointment of independent bodies to verify needs and to administer claims and court supervision to secure effective remedies for socio-economic rights violations.[26] By retaining supervisory jurisdiction, a court can secure a response from another branch of government in the form of a report and thereby assists in preventing failure to comply with the positive obligations imposed by its order.[27] It thus engages other branches in a form of continuing dialogical relationship situation.[28] Dialogue refers to a judicial review technique in which the judiciary engages with other branches in shaping and implementing the obligations that flow from rights.[29]

---

[19] Mbazira (note 2 above) 4.

[20] C Mbazira *Litigating Socio-Economic Rights in South Africa: A Choice between Corrective and Distributive Justice* (2009) 176.

[21] S van der Berg 'A capabilities approach to remedies for systemic resource-related socio-economic rights violations in South Africa ' (2019) 19 *African Human Rights Law Journal* 292.

[22] Mbazira (note 20 above) 176.

[23] Ibid 181.

[24] *Blue Moonlight Properties 039 (Pty) Ltd v the Occupiers of Saratoga Avenue* 2009 (1) SA470 (W).

[25] Ibid para 78.

[26] J Brickhill & Y van Leeve 'From the classroom to the courtroom: Litigating education rights in South Africa' in S Fredman, M Campbell & H Taylor (eds) *Human Rights and Equality in Education* (2018) 165.

[27] Ibid.

[28] *Meadow Glen Home Owners Association v City of Tshwane Metropolitan Municipality* 2015 (2) SA 413 (SCA) para 35.

[29] K Young 'A typology of economic and social rights adjudication: Exploring the catalytic function of judicial review' (2010) 8 *International Journal of Constitutional Law* 395.

Although it is questionable whether any real dialogue can take place between the judiciary and other branches that are obligated to obey the former, it is indeed possible for meaningful dialogue to take place especially where judgments are left open to reversal, modification or avoidance by other branches.[30] Depending on the circumstances, this may lead to either strong-form review or weak-form review. The dialogue theory advanced by Rosalind Dixon argues for 'an intermediate approach to the judicial enforcement of constitutional rights, which allows courts both to define rights in relatively broad terms and to adopt strong remedies, provided they defer to legislative sequels that evidence clear and considered disagreement with their rulings'.[31]

1.2 Models of the structural interdict

The inherently flexible nature of structural interdicts has led courts to develop variations or models in order to satisfy the demands of remedial efficacy as well as to realise key features of legitimate judicial decision-making, including the promotion of dialogue between government branches.[32] The objective of this discussion is to provide a brief analysis of the different models in order to reach an understanding of the particular circumstances in which judicial monitoring mechanisms can be appropriately employed.

The different models of the structural interdict include the bargaining model, the legislative/administrative hearing model, the report back to court model, and the expert remedial formulation model. Courts in South Africa generally apply the 'report back to court model' and the expert remedial formulation model as will become evident in the case references made below. However, all the models of the structural interdict have positive merits and deficiencies that I will now discuss below (as distilled from literature).

1.2.1 The 'report back to court' model

Extensively built up in *Brown v Board of Education of Topeka*,[33] the 'report back to court' model has since been considered in the jurisprudence of other courts, and it has become the most commonly used model in South Africa. This model is effectively the one described above where a number of stages must be procedurally complied with until the court is satisfied that the violation of the socio-economic rights has been remedied.[34] After the court has issued orders compelling the government to comply with its constitutional obligations, it requires them to report back to the court with a plan on how they propose to remedy the violation or continuously mitigate the harm.[35] Usually a fixed date is set for the filing of the plan, and the other party is given an

---

[30] P Hogg & AI Bushnell 'The Charter dialogue between courts and legislatures (or perhaps The Charter of Rights isn't such a bad thing after all)' (1997) 35 *Osgoode Hall Law Journal* 79.

[31] R Dixon 'Creating dialogue about socio-economic rights: Strong-form versus weak-form judicial review revisited' (2007) 5 *International Journal of Constitutional Law* 393.

[32] S Liebenberg 'Remedial principles and meaningful engagement in education rights disputes' (2016) 19 *Potchefstroom Electronic Law Journal* 11.

[33] *Brown v Board of Education of Topeka* 347 US 483.

[34] Strathmore Law Clinic 'Structural interdicts for socio-economic rights: What the Kenyan jurisprudence has missed' (2019) 4 *Strathmore Law Review* 141.

[35] Mbazira (note 2 above) 7.

opportunity to provide commentary. Finally, the court evaluates whether the proposed plan sufficiently remedies the harm caused by the constitutional infringement and whether the government is complying with its obligations.[36] When the court is satisfied with the defendant's proposal, it will concretise it as part of its final order. As a result of this particular step, any failure to adhere to this plan amounts to contempt of court.[37] Where the court is not satisfied, it can order a further report and modifications to reach this final stage.

The High Court has frequently employed this model when adjudicating on socio-economic rights. In *Section 27 v Minister of Education,* the court ordered the Limpopo Department of Education to consult with schools, educators, parents and learners in order to formulate an effective 'catch-up' plan that would address the gaps in teaching that arose from the failure to deliver textbooks during the first half of the year.[38] A deadline was given for such a report to be submitted to the court and the court prescribed that the report had to address 'the gaps in the curriculum, gaps in quality, the nature of the remedial measures, the timeframes, the role of various roleplayers'.[39]

The report back model is favoured by the High Court because it seeks to respect the doctrine of separation of powers as the court defers to the executive or legislature on matters that lie within their competence when addressing the violation. This shields the judiciary from accusations that it has encroached impermissibly into the sphere of the legislature or executive. Also, it allows for the remedy to be developed by the defendant as the court leaves the relevant branch of government with the discretion to decide on how to respect and promote socio-economic rights through the means and resources that are available to them. This has the benefit of making the implementation of the remedy practical as it is highly unlikely that defendants will propose a plan that they cannot carry out.[40]

Such a remedy will also allow for the government to tailor a solution within its budgetary needs and ensure it has buy-in from the relevant players as seen from *Madzodzo v Minister of Basic Education.*[41] In that case, the Department of education suggested the formulation of a comprehensive plan to address the shortage of school furniture in numerous Eastern Cape schools.[42] Therefore, once the court had established a violation of the right to basic education, the department was ordered to file a copy of a completed Independent Development Trust audit of all learner furniture needs at Eastern Cape public schools. A possible drawback of the model is that the process of implementation can be left entirely to the defendant thereby limiting engagement with other litigants. Therefore, it is important both that the court and the other party should be afforded an opportunity to scrutinise the plan and make amendments or reject the plan if it is considered inadequate.[43]

---

36 Ibid.
37 Strathmore Law Clinic (note 34 above) 141.
38 *Section 27 v Minister of Education* 2013 2 SA 40 (GNP) para 43.4.
39 Ibid.
40 Strathmore Law Clinic (note 34 above) 141.
41 *Madzodzo v Minister of Basic Education* 2014 (3)SA 441 (ECM).
42 Ibid para 7.
43 Strathmore Law Clinic (note 34 above) 141.

1.2.2 The bargaining model

The judiciary usually employs this model to address the limitations of the traditional adversarial process through a bargaining procedure, between the lawyers for the parties, aimed towards an agreement on the terms of the remedy.[44] In other cases, the parties may be ordered to undergo a mediation process in order to achieve a solution that is mutually acceptable to all parties.[45] In *Lingwood v Occupiers of R/E ERF 9 Highlands,* the court ordered the parties, including the municipality, to engage in a mediation process that would allow an exploration of all reasonable possibilities of securing suitable alternative accommodation in a manner that suited the parties involved.[46] The case law of the High Court indicates that when there is no genuine attempt at negotiating an alternative to an eviction that would lead to homelessness, the court is unlikely to grant an eviction order.[47]

The court may order the parties to submit proposals as to how the infringement of the specific right can be remedied.[48] The submission of proposals is generally enforced by penalising one or more parties with an unfavourable order if no agreement is reached.[49] The biggest benefit of this model is that it produces a remedy that is satisfactory to all litigating parties, thereby easing implementation. It also highlights issues that may have been ignored by the court yet are relevant to having an effective remedy.[50] Therefore, this model is likely to promote a meaningful engagement between all the stakeholders.

However, the bargaining model does not adequately address concerns relating to institutional capacity or administrative malfunction to implement any agreed order. The objective is often to reach consensus and this may not always be equivalent to remedying the root cause of the infringement.[51] Furthermore, issues of power relations between the parties often emerge during bargaining and this can act to the detriment of vulnerable individuals and groups.[52]

1.2.3 The legislative or administrative hearing model

Similar to a legislative committee process that provides the opportunity for direct and informal participation by a broad range of interested actors,[53] in the legislative or administrative hearing model, the court conducts a series of informal hearings that allow persons not originally party to the litigation to participate in the informal hearings.[54] It is especially effective in ameliorating the information deficit that courts often face in cases of systemic rights violations.[55] The objective of the informal hearings is to

---

[44] SP Sturm 'A normative theory of public law remedies' (1990) 79 *Georgetown Law Journal* 1368.
[45] *Cashbuild (South Africa) (Pty) Ltd v Scott* 2007 (1) SA332 (T).
[46] *Lingwood v Occupiers of R/E ERF 9 Highlands* 2008 (3) BCLR 325 (W) para 28.
[47] S Wilson 'Breaking the tie: Evictions, homelessness and the new normality' (2009) 126 *South African Law Journal* 288.
[48] A variant of this model is the consensual remedial formulation model, which is beyond the scope of this article.
[49] M Bishop 'Remedies' in S Woolman, T Roux & M Bishop (eds) *Constitutional Law of South Africa* (2014) 9.
[50] P Swanepoel 'The potential of structural interdicts to constitute effective relief in socio-economic rights cases' (2017) LLM Dissertation, Stellenbosch University 151.
[51] Sturm (note 44 above) 1355.
[52] Ibid.
[53] Sturm (note 44 above) 1370.
[54] Mbazira (note 2 above) 6
[55] Mbazira (note 20 above) 188.

allow a different set of interests to enter the enquiry in order to determine what the most appropriate and effective remedy will be.

A major pitfall of this model is that although it allows for diverse participation, such participation comes at a cost.[56] According to Susan Sturm, participation under this model may result in a process of 'airing differences' rather than 'developing solutions'.[57] The focus of the court is on acquiring information and understanding the reasoning underpinning diverse points of view. The remedy is thus not focussed on remedying the systemic incapacity of government. If a decision is not reached, the court may have to impose a court-ordered remedy or to compel the parties into an agreement. Either way, the court's conduct would then entail a stronger and less deferential role to other branches of government.[58]

1.2.4 Expert remedial formulation model

This model involves the appointment of experts by a court with a mandate to design and develop a remedial plan.[59] Sometimes these experts are designated as court officials and possess judicial powers. In some instances, the expert can be 'designated as an administrator with a mandate to take over and manage the institution under scrutiny for the purpose of effecting reforms'.[60] The court can alternatively order the appointment of an individual – sometimes known as a master of the court – who bears the responsibility of coordinating the panel of experts and their operations.[61] The expert model is particularly appropriate in cases where specialised and technical skill is a necessity in order to formulate an appropriate remedy and where the court may not have the expertise to establish the social facts. Nonetheless, the experts are usually required to involve the litigants in the remedy-finding process and may be obliged to consult with the parties in formulating the remedial plans.[62] This contributes to the legitimacy of this model. By including the rights-bearers, the expert remedial model makes it possible to draw remedial plans that are informed by experts but also take into consideration the interests of the persons whose rights have been violated.

Unlike the other models, a key advantage of the expert remedial model is that it actually allows experts to be involved in the creation of the agenda, framing of the issues, and proposing solutions.[63] This means that it can also address the systemic incapacity or blockages in government directly. Furthermore, the appointed expert or experts can easily consult affected stakeholders meaning that diverse participation is possible.[64] A potential pitfall of the model, in this regard, is that participation under this model might be limited since the experts decide who is allowed to participate.

---

56 Sturm (note 44 above) 1418.
57 Ibid.
58 Ibid.
59 Mbazira (note 20 above) 7.
60 Swanepoel (note 50 above) 153.
61 Mbazira (note 20 above) 7.
62 Ibid.
63 Sturm (note 44 above) 1419.
64 Ibid.

The expert remedial model is perhaps the most interventionist of the models as it grants power to an expert to directly intervene in the activities of another branch of government. It is clear from the above discussion that, in situations of systemic incapacity of another branch of government, the expert remedial model can be effective in allowing direct intervention to ensure the realisation of fundamental rights. A number of criticisms are launched against this model. It is argued that courts lack the competency and the legitimacy for economic and social rights adjudication.[65] However, the court does not directly contribute to the formulation of the remedy. Instead, the experts are tasked with the development of the remedy in consultation with the parties involved and other branches of government are not excluded from the process. Thus, the expert remedial model ensures that the judiciary still demonstrates a degree of deference to other branches in developing the final remedy.

2. The development of the expert remedial model in the Constitutional Court

The South African Constitutional Court has been generally reluctant to adopt supervisory models as seen in *Government of the Republic of South Africa v Grootboom* and *Mazibuko v City of Johannesburg*.[66] Instead, the Court has often opted for the employment of meaningful engagement through the bargaining and report-back model. The Constitutional Court has also condoned the 'managerial role' of the judiciary in exceptional cases.[67] However, the degree to which the expert remedial has been employed by the court is inconsistent. This model and the others discussed above are not mutually exclusive, and as the case law analysis will show, sometimes they are employed together and can complement one another. This section offers a detailed discussion of the expert remedial model by juxtaposing an analysis of *Black Sash Trust v Minister of Social Development* with similar developments in *Mwelase v Director-General for the Department of Rural Development and Land Reform*.[68]

2.1 Case discussion: Black Sash Trust v Minister of Social Development

In 2017, the Constitutional Court handed down a landmark judgment that prevented an imminent crisis that threatened to disrupt monthly social grant payments to millions of poor and vulnerable South Africans in the *Black Sash Trust v Minister of Social Development* (*Black Sash I*).[69] Forging ahead along the innovative pathway of previous judgments, *Black Sash I* broke new ground in our remedial jurisprudence through its response to persistent non-compliance.[70]

---

[65] Young (note 29 above) 385.

[66] *Government of the Republic of South Africa v Grootboom* 2000 (11) BCLR 1169 (CC); *Mazibuko v City of Johannesburg* 2010 (4) SA 1 (CC).

[67] *Port Elizabeth Municipality v Various Occupiers* 2005 (1) SA 217 (CC) para 39.

[68] *The Black Sash Trust v Minister of Social Development* 2018 (12) BCLR 1472 (CC); *Mwelase v Director-General for the Department of Rural Development and Land Reform* 2019 (6) SA 597 (CC).

[69] Ibid.

[70] H Taylor 'Forcing the court's remedial hand: Non-compliance as a catalyst for remedial innovation' (2019) 9 *Constitutional Court Review* 248.

The case was brought before the court by two non-governmental organisations namely, Black Sash Trust and Freedom under Law against several respondents, including the South African Social Security Agency (SASSA), a government organ tasked with the dispensing of social grants and a private company, Cash Paymaster Services (CPS). *Black Sash I* is a sequel to the *Allpay* cases.[71] The case began in 2012 when SASSA entered into a contract with CPS to pay out social grants on its behalf. In an earlier decision handed down in *Allpay I*, the Constitutional Court declared that the procurement process leading to the award of this contract was invalid.[72] In *Allpay II*,[73] the declaration of invalidity was suspended. CPS was required to continue paying grants in the interim on the premise that either SASSA would take over the duty of paying grants when the contract with CPS was due to expire on 31 March 2017 or conduct a new procurement process under s 217 of the Constitution.[74] The Court retained supervisory jurisdiction over social grant payments and ordered SASSA to submit a report to it on any future tender process and its outcome. Therefore, the 'report back to court' model was employed initially in this case.

In a report provided to the court, SASSA indicated that instead of awarding a tender to a new service provider, it was going to take over the payment of social grants itself from 1 April 2017.[75] The Constitutional Court subsequently withdrew its supervisory jurisdiction over the social grant payments system. On the eve of this deadline, various reports from civil society organisations made it apparent that SASSA was not well positioned to take over disbursement of the grants as it had previously indicated.[76] It also came to light that the responsible functionaries of SASSA had been aware for a year that it would not be able to comply with its undertaking to the Court.[77] By February 2017, when a formal communication was made to the Court, there was no formal agreement between CPS and SASSA pertaining to the party responsible for the payment of social grants after 31 March 2017. However, the Minister and SASSA informed the Constitutional Court that CPS was the only entity capable of paying grants for the foreseeable future after 31 March 2017.[78]

The Court was faced with the challenge of practically avoiding a systemic breach of the right to access to social assistance as prescribed by s 27 of the Constitution through the exercise of its discretionary remedial powers.[79] In light of SASSA's failure to comply with the order set out in *AllPay II*, the applicant petitioned the Court to reinstate its supervisory jurisdiction over the disbursement of social grants. The applicant asked the court for an order that SASSA must submit a report setting out how it intended to handle the interim contract with CPS. Furthermore, it was requested that under the

---

71 *AllPay Consolidated Investment Holdings (Pty) Ltd v Chief Executive Officer, South African Social Security Agency* 2014 (1) SA 604 (CC) [*Allpay I*] ; *AllPay Consolidated Investment Holdings (Pty) Ltd v Chief Executive Officer, South African Social Security Agency (No 2)* 2014 (4) SA 179 (CC) [*Allpay II*].

72 *AllPay Consolidated Investment Holdings (Pty) Ltd v Chief Executive Officer, South African Social Security Agency* 2014 (1) SA 604 (CC) para 63.

73 *AllPay II* (note 71 above)para 78.

74 *Black Sash* (note 68 above) para 16.

75 Ibid para 11.

76 Ibid para 21.

77 Ibid paras 5–6.

78 Ibid para 7.

79 Ibid para 15.

court order, SASSA and the Minister of Social Development ('Minister') report continually to the Court on the measures to be adopted to forestall disruption of grant payment from 1 April 2017.

The Court began its judgment with a reflection on the nature and significance of the government's non-compliance as the direct cause of the remedial predicament that confronted the Court.[80] The court reasoned that the Minister and SASSA's inability to comply with the court order compromised the continued protection of access to the right to social assistance for grant recipients. Froneman J's analysis of the evidence identified the 'demonstrated inability of SASSA to get its own affairs in order' as the underlying reason for non-compliance.[81] Furthermore, the Court highlighted that SASSA and the Minister of Social Development showed 'no reciprocal comity' towards the judicial branch and did not even 'deign to inform the Court' of its inability to meet the April 2017 deadline.[82] This formed the basis for the Court's decision to retain its supervision.[83]

Having determined this breach of socio-economic rights, the order featured a range of remedial mechanisms to enhance accountability for SASSA's compliance with its constitutional obligations. Court supervision was complemented by extensive reporting requirements, with both the Minister and SASSA being mandated to file regular progress reports with the Court detailing compliance with a timetable of deliverables.[84] As none of the parties opposed the appointment of independent monitoring mechanisms, the remedial order made provision for the appointment of the Auditor-General and suitably qualified independent legal practitioners and technical experts.[85] These court-appointed monitoring mechanisms were jointly tasked with evaluating the implementation of the payment of social grants; assessing the steps envisaged or taken by SASSA for any competitive bidding processes aimed at the appointment of a new contractor for the payment of social grants; and evaluating the steps envisaged or taken by SASSA aimed at administering and paying the grants in the future.

To ensure payment of grants to recipients, the Court continued the suspension of its declaration of invalidity of the contract between SASSA and CPS for a period of 12 months starting from 1 April 2017. The Court order also made provision for the involvement of the Auditor-General in reviewing the operationalisation of the interim contract. The Auditor-General was tasked further with evaluating the implementation of payment of social grants and the steps envisaged by SASSA aimed at administering and paying the grants in the future.[86]

The court recognised that the country is confronted with the predicament that the executive arm of government is not able to fulfil its constitutional and statutory obligations to fulfil the right to social assistance of its people.[87] In this particular case, the Court could not accept the assurance that SASSA under the guidance of the responsible

---

[80] Ibid para 9.
[81] Ibid para 57.
[82] Ibid para 13.
[83] Ibid para 62.
[84] Ibid para 76.
[85] Ibid.
[86] Ibid order 12.
[87] Ibid para 8.

Minister would be able to fulfil its executive and administrative functions. As a result, the court had a legitimate reason to retain its jurisdiction over the matter as there was a need to address government recalcitrance and incapacity.

The decision by the court to appoint independent monitoring mechanisms, therefore, demonstrates institutional responsiveness to the reasons underlying SASSA's non-compliance. The court sought to address the issue of accountability of governmental agencies and the employment of the expert remedial model required SASSA to account for its behaviour to other experts and institutions. The Constitutional Court held that CPS qualified as an organ of state in terms of s 239 of the Constitution as it exercised a public function.[88] Therefore, it was subject to the principles of public administration in s 195, which include the provision of services in an impartial, fair and equitable manner. Furthermore, the Constitution highlights the importance of accountability in cases of outsourcing to ensure the 'efficient, economic and effective use of resources'.[89]

The management of resources was one of the focal points of this case, and thus the technical and legal expertise of the experts compensated for the institutional incapacity that had thus far prevented SASSA from being able to pay social grants itself.[90] The use of the expert remedial formulation model was also warranted as a number of technical aspects such as financial records needed to be assessed and large amounts of information had to be amassed. Furthermore, the court could not oversee any bidding processes conducted by SASSA aimed at appointing a new contractor for the payment of social grants as this is the duty of the organ of state and beyond the scope of the court.

As indicated earlier, the executive was not opposed to the appointment of an independent monitoring mechanism.[91] This makes it clear that none of the parties had concerns that they would be substituted by the experts. The outline of the duties of the Auditor-General and other experts in the court order shows that they were not appointed to assume executive functions that are reserved for SASSA. Rather, the move from the report back model to a model aimed at incentivising executive action was due to the lack of success of a weaker model. The executive had previously failed to comply with court orders and the movement to a stronger form of intervention is often required when a weak-form remedy is ordered.[92] There is thus often a need for the judiciary to develop remedies that are more effective in spurring action from other branches of the government.[93]

2.2 Mwelase v Director-General for the Department of Rural Development and Land Reform

The Land Reform (Labour Tenants) Act 3 of 1996 (LTA) was enacted to enable labour tenants to gain security of tenure as promised in s 25(6) of the Constitution. A labour tenant is a person 'who provides labour on a farm as a type of payment-kind for the

---

[88] *Allpay* II (n 71 above) para 52.
[89] Section 195(1)(b) of the Constitution of the Republic of South Africa, 1996.
[90] Taylor (note 70 above) 260.
[91] *Black Sash* (note 68 above) para 66.
[92] Dixon (note 31 above) 401–403.
[93] D Landau 'Aggressive weak-form remedies' (2013) 5 *Constitutional Court Review* 249.

right to live there and work a portion of the farm for his or her own benefit'.[94] Labour tenancy has deep roots in South Africa's malevolent racial past as patterns of racial subordination meant that labour tenants were overwhelmingly black, and the landowners on whose favour they depended were overwhelmingly white.[95] The LTA was therefore aimed at ensuring that those with legally insecure land tenure resulting from past racist policies received security of tenure or comparable redress.[96] In terms of s 16(1)(a)-(d) of the LTA, a labour tenant may apply for specified property rights.

The Department of Rural Development and Land Reform failed to process applications made in accordance with this provision, thus effectively preventing labour tenants from having their tenure rendered more secure.[97] The Department admitted that it had ceased the processing of claims due to heavy backlogs. As a result, the Legal Resources Centre launched litigation on behalf of the applicants in the Land Claims Court (LCC) challenging the Department's enduring and systemic failure to process LTA applications. Amongst other things, the Legal Resources Centre sought a structural interdict directing the Department to provide statistics detailing the status of all labour tenant claims and an order for the Department to report regularly on its progress to the LCC until all outstanding claims had been settled.[98] The Department repeatedly failed to provide the relevant statistics, in spite of having agreed to an order that it would collate and present the statistics to the court by March 2015.[99]

It estimated to the LCC that it would require at least two years to capture the details of the outstanding applications. However, the Department was not able to ascertain the nature and scale of the backlog challenge, thus precluding progress from being made in addressing it. In 2015, the parties came to an agreement on a detailed plan of court supervision that would enable the LCC to monitor the Department's compliance. The Court's involvement would require regular reports through which it would evaluate the targets set by the Department and assess its progress in reaching them.[100] The report back model was therefore employed as the Department had to report back to the LCC with a plan on how it proposed to remedy the backlog of applications. Nevertheless, the Department did not comply with the implementation plan agreed to, failed to meet the deadlines set for filing its progress reports, and never responded to the concerns raised by the applicants in relation to the reports.[101] The reporting requirements ordered by the LCC assisted in diagnosing non-compliance and prompting the Department to acknowledge its obligations to implement the LTA.[102] Therefore, the 'report back to court' model was initially utilised by the court before the extent of the institutional incapacity became clearer.

After two years of failed court supervision and multiple settlement agreements that were met with non-compliance, the applicants returned to the LCC to push ahead with

94 *Mwelase* Con Court (note 68 above) para 5.
95 Ibid.
96 Section 25 (6) of the Constitution.
97 Land Reform Act 3 of 1996.
98 *Mwelase* Con Court (note 68 above) para 21.
99 Ibid.
100 Ibid para 23.
101 Ibid para 24.
102 Ibid para 17.

their request for the appointment of a special master. The rationale for a special master put forward was that this remedy would be the most effective means of supervision to co-ordinate the efforts of all parties in achieving the common goal of implementing the LTA.[103] The special master is an independent person who is appointed by, and reports to the court.[104] His or her duty is to assist the court according to the mandate set by the court. Special masters generally have expertise in specialist areas of government and they assist with either devising a remedial plan or implementing it. They may help the court with a range of matters including complex electronic discovery, undertaking fact-finding investigations, or formulating remedies and monitoring compliance.[105] The LCC found that it was not only desirable but also urgent to enlist the aid of a 'Special Master of Labour Tenants'.[106] In reaching this conclusion, Ncube AJ found that ordinary court supervision had been undermined by the Department's failure to set accurate implementation targets or provide proper plans for reaching those targets.[107] Ncube AJ held that a special master would significantly ameliorate the disadvantages that result from the capacity constraints experienced by the LCC.[108] The order was appealed to the Supreme Court of Appeal (SCA) and then the Constitutional Court.

The SCA overturned the LCC decision and held that appropriate relief cannot licence the appointment of a special master to implement legislation.[109] The SCA invoked the words of Chief Justice Mogoeng in his dissenting judgment in the *Economic Freedom Fighters v Speaker of the National Assembly case,*[110] and labelled the court order by the LCC as a 'gross intrusion by a court into the domain of the executive' and a 'textbook case of judicial overreach'.[111] The basis for the SCA's decision was that, in granting the powers of the special master to draw up budgets and plans, the LCC allowed the special master to usurp the functions of the department.

The majority of the Constitutional Court disagreed with the SCA and re-instated the order of the LCC to appoint a special master. The majority judgment pointed out that courts are very aware of the perils of overreach and therefore, they intervene only when the evidence and arguments compel them to conclude that the executive or the legislature has done wrong, or has not done enough.[112] The court explained, for instance, how, in *Black Sash I*, the circumstances were unique and warranted the appointment of a panel of experts. The court further explained that during the implementation of a remedy, the main task of a special master is to oversee and monitor instead of usurping the performance of executive functions.[113]

---

[103] Ibid para 22.
[104] *Mwelase v Director-General for the Department of Rural Development and Land Reform* 2017 (4) SA 422 (LCC) para 19.
[105] *Mwelase* Con Court (note 68 above) para 58.
[106] Taylor (note 70 above) 269.
[107] Ibid 270.
[108] *Mwelase* LCC (note 104 above) para 28.
[109] Ibid para 35.
[110] *Economic Freedom Fighters v Speaker of the National Assembly* 2018 (2) SA 571 (CC).
[111] *Mwelase* Con Court (note 68 above) para 35.
[112] Ibid para 53.
[113] Ibid para 58.

The Constitutional Court made it clear, following the LCC, that the special master remains an agent of the Court and acts in extension of the Court's supervisory jurisdiction.[114] As such, 'the independence of the special master is not merely the detached neutrality of a third-party expert unaffiliated with the parties. It is, rather, an extension of judicial independence, because it derives from appointment as an agent of the court, continuingly subject to court control and authority'.[115] The Constitutional Court thus did not authorise an outside, unaccountable body to intrude into the executive domain; instead, the Court appointed a mechanism to ensure that nationally critical land reform and restitution processes become effective.

In concluding, the Court held that the facts showed failing institutional dysfunctionality of an extensive and sustained degree that cried out for an effective remedy. In understanding the LCC's exercise of its discretionary powers, it is important to note that it identified the fundamental issues as institutional: the LCC's order was 'directed at remedying institutional dysfunction and other blockages that imperil rights at a systemic level'.[116]

Despite the justifications offered by the majority, Jafta J found that parts of the majority order extended beyond a constitutionally permissible intervention by a court in the performance of administrative functions.[117] He further ruled that although the LCC has the competence to grant a supervisory order and appoint a special master, some of the functions the order authorised the special master to perform fall beyond the Court's supervisory jurisdiction.[118] He highlighted that the LCC's order differed from orders previously granted by the courts as it required the special master to prepare a plan that entails the determination of a budget.[119] This raised the question of whether supervisory jurisdiction extends to cover the performance of departmental functions, including the preparation of budgets. In answering this question, Jafta J reached the conclusion that a court may not make a decision that encroaches into the heart of the competences of executive branch of the state. If a court exceeds the limits of judicial authority, it merits a charge of judicial overreach.[120]

It is noteworthy that according to Jafta J, 'no matter how egregious the breaches of the Constitution by the other arm are and how loud the facts of a particular case call for justice, a court may not step in and exercise powers or perform functions entrusted to other arms of the state'.[121] This statement reflects a formal view of the separation of powers that assigns particular functions to specific branches of government. Jafta J's judgment also displays a preference for a weak form of review as he views the executive as better placed to make final decisions pertaining policy.[122]

As indicated earlier, the Constitutional Court's precedent has generally adopted weak-form review and discouraged the judiciary's involvement in the executive's

---

114 Ibid para 61.
115 Ibid.
116 Ibid para 69.
117 Ibid para 85.
118 Ibid para 93.
119 Ibid para 97.
120 Ibid para 106.
121 Ibid para 108
122 Tushnet (note 14 above) 1.

budgetary matters. However, this has never been explicitly prohibited.[123] The Constitutional Court acknowledges that 'the evaluation of measures taken by the state may have budgetary implications, but such an evaluation should not be directed at rearranging budgets'.[124] The role of the special master in the *Mwelase* case was never intended to include the allocation or rearrangement of the budget. The court order made it clear that the special master would act in collaboration with the Director-General of the Department. Therefore, the court did not intend to take over the functions of the Department.

The duty of the special master was simply to supervise the performance of the Director-General and other officials, and to assist with the implementation of plan. The supervisory role of the special master was not to ensure the actual implementation of the budget but rather to exercise oversight over such implementation. Thus, the court order, in this case to appoint such a master was not *aimed* at rearranging the Department's budget, but rather incentivising and ensuring that the executive comply with its constitutional obligations.

3. The employment of monitoring mechanisms in foreign jurisdictions

The utilisation of monitoring institutions to ensure compliance with remedies to vindicate fundamental rights is part of an emerging trend in Latin America and Asia.[125] The jurisprudence of the Colombian Constitutional Court, for instance, shows its positive stance towards judicial intervention in structural cases when addressing the widespread violations of socio-economic rights.[126] The Colombian Constitutional Court is an ideal point of comparison as it has employed a more interventionist set of remedies compared to the South African Constitutional Court within a constitutional context that is not so different from South Africa.[127]

3.1 The appointment of monitoring institutions in Colombia

The *tutela* is a protection writ that can be filed in an informal way before a judge for immediate protection of fundamental constitutional rights in the case of an action or omission by a public authority (and, in some instances, private actors).[128] This is based on Article 86 of the Colombian Constitution, which further provides that the law must determine 'the cases in which the order of protection should apply to individuals entrusted with providing a public service or whose conduct may seriously and directly

---

[123] In *City of Johannesburg Metropolitan Municipality v Blue Moonlight Properties 39 (Pty) Ltd* 2012 (2) SA 104 (CC) para 74, the court held that a 'determination of the reasonableness of measures within available resources cannot be restricted by budgetary and other decisions that may well have resulted from a mistaken understanding of constitutional or statutory obligations. In other words, it is not good enough for the City to state that it has not budgeted for something, if it should indeed have planned and budgeted for it in the fulfilment of its obligations'.

[124] *TAC* (note 7 above) para 38.

[125] C Rodríguez-Garavito 'Beyond the courtroom: The impact of judicial activism on socioeconomic rights in Latin America' (2011) 89 *Texas Law Review* 1671.

[126] Ibid 1672.

[127] Landau (note 93 above) 254.

[128] K Merhof 'Building a bridge between reality and the Constitution: The establishment and development of the Colombian Constitutional Court' (2015) 3 *International Journal of Constitutional Law* 719.

affect the collective interest'.[129] In most of the *tutelas* brought before the Colombian Constitutional Court, the court has had to deal with the issue of political inaction either through a deficient legislative framework, institutional incapacity or simply the unwillingness of the executive to implement an extant legal framework.

The Colombian Court has become innovative in finding ways to spur political action in such contexts. The appointment of institutions to monitor measures taken by the state has proven to be quite effective. In the *T-760* judgment, the Colombian Constitutional Court issued an order that combined 22 *tutelas* that sought the protection of the right to health, specifically, access to primary health services.[130] The issue before the Court was whether the regulatory failures presented through the joined cases represented a violation of the constitutional obligations of the competent authorities to respect, protect, and fulfil the right to health and its effective enjoyment.

In its judgment, the Colombian Constitutional Court pointed out that the *tutela* action was a tool aimed at ensuring the effective enjoyment of fundamental rights like the right to life and healthcare.[131] As a result, the constitutional obligations derived from a fundamental right, are violated when the entity responsible for guaranteeing the enjoyment of a right does not provide a program or a public policy that would permit the progressive advancement in the fulfilment of its corresponding obligations.[132] In crafting a remedy, the Court acknowledged the need for a more intense approach that required the exercise of powers of monitoring and oversight to prevent constant violations of the right to health to continue.[133] Nonetheless, the judges enjoined the government to adopt deliberate measures to progressively realise universal health coverage and where this is not possible, the reasons for this failure should be provided and a new goal set and duly justified.[134]

Consequently, the Court issued a set of structural injunctive remedies including the employment of the expert remedial formulation model. The court ordered the Ministry of Social Protection and the National Superintendence of Health to fulfil their obligations by identifying the Health Promoting Entities and Health Care Providing Institutions that frequently refuse to allow timely health services included in the Obligatory National Health Plan.[135] The Court further ordered national authorities to clarify the lists of covered benefits and to equalise benefits between the 'contributory system', which includes formal sector workers, and the 'subsidised system', which caters to the unemployed and those in the informal sector.[136] This was necessary as the contributory system offered a larger package of benefits compared to the subsidised system. To this end, the court appointed the Ombudsman and the Attorney General of the Nation to monitor the Ministry and the Superintendent.

[129] Article 86 of the Colombian Constitution of 1991.

[130] *T-760/2008* July 31, 2008 (transl International Network for Economic, Social and Cultural Rights) <http://www.escr-net.org/usr_doc/English_summary_T-760.pdf>

[131] Ibid para 2.3.

[132] Ibid para 3.3.13.

[133] Ibid para 6.1.4.1.2.

[134] Ibid 29th Order.

[135] Ibid 20th Order.

[136] Ibid.

These actions were taken in order to 'nudge the government to address long-standing administrative and legislative bottlenecks that crippled the health-care system and overwhelmed courts with thousands of patients' petitions for basic medications and treatment'.[137] This according to Katharine G. Young, represents the 'catalysing role' of the judiciary that seeks to unblock dormant areas of socio-economic policy.[138] In this way, the judiciary still ensures that politicians have room to take part in the development of remedies.

Following the *T-760* case, the number of *tutelas* claiming remedies in terms of the right to health significantly decreased for the first time between 2008 and 2010 due to the newly implemented measures and subsequent transformation of the Colombian health sector.[139] Despite the effectiveness of this remedy, the classic objection against judicial activism and the use of managerial institutions in Colombia surfaced, claiming an apparent lack of democratic legitimacy and the violation of the doctrine of separation of powers.[140] In response to the critics, César Rodríguez-Garavito points out the benefits of the order, which not only helps to ensure the efficient realisation of the right but also that it elicits collaboration among the different branches of government and promotes deliberation on public issues.[141] Furthermore, such 'intrusive' remedies are employed as a measure of last resort.

There is an evident pattern in the Colombian Constitutional Court's judgments where the Court begins with relatively open-ended orders, both in terms of substance and the timeframe given for compliance. It is only when these orders prove to be ineffective that the court adopts more innovative remedies and gives detailed orders that may include monitoring mechanisms. Tushnet points out that this sequence is of some importance when designing effective remedies in this area.[142] Courts may for example want to begin with broader solutions, moving towards firmer remedies as they gauge both the political reaction to their orders and as they learn more about how to respond in a complex area of policy.[143]

Therefore, the approach employed by the Colombian Constitutional Court in its structural cases is not subject strongly to competency and legitimacy critiques surrounding court interventions as the Court leaves the crux of policymaking in the hands of the bureaucracy, while ordering monitoring institutions in order to impel steady progress.[144] David Landau explains that the Court's efforts in structural cases lies 'somewhere on an intermediate point in between weak-form and strong-form review, oscillating depending on the particular issue and the prior resistance faced by the Court'. This approach is similar to the one taken in the *Black Sash* and *Mwelase* cases where the court only made use of the expert remedial model following several instances of non-compliance.

---

137 Rodríguez-Garavito (note 125) 1675.
138 Young (note 29) 172.
139 Merhof (note 128) 725.
140 Rodríguez-Garavito (note 125) 1688.
141 Ibid 1672.
142 Tushnet 'A response to David Landau' (2012) 53 *Harvard International Law Journal Online* 163.
143 Landau (note 93) 250.
144 Ibid 258.

3.2 The employment of supervisory jurisdiction in India

In Asia, India is often hailed as the first jurisdiction to develop a relatively mature socio-economic rights jurisprudence.[145] According to Justice Prafullachandra Natwarlal Bhagwati, it was imperative, in the Indian context, to evolve a methodology that would secure the implementation of court orders in public interest litigation. Therefore, courts started appointing monitoring agencies.[146]

In *Sheela Barse v State of Maharashtra*,[147] a journalist brought a case before the Supreme Court concerning custodial violence among women in police custody. The Supreme Court tasked a female judicial officer to periodically visit the police holding cells and to report to the High Court on whether the directives ordered by the court were being implemented. This strategy has been employed by the Supreme Court in several cases. The jurisprudence of the Supreme Court of India provides one of the most well-known examples of judicial activism. The landmark decision in *People's Union for Civil Liberties v Union of India* (*Right to Food* case),[148] is a good example of the innovative remedial approach taken by the Court to ensure compliance with orders in socio-economic right cases. This case was initially brought by the People's Union for Civil Liberties (PUCL) petition of 16 April 2001 against the Government of India, the Food Corporation of India (FCI), and six State Governments.

The FCI operated 'godowns' (reserves) for storing grains. By 2001, the godowns had about 60 million tonnes, whereas the required buffer stocks were supposed to be about 20 million tonnes. Hence, the government had about 40 million tonnes above the required buffer stock.[149] As the grains were kept outside the godowns, they started rotting due to the rainfall. Yet, in a village in Rajasthan State, situated about 5 kilometres from some of the reserves, people were experiencing drought and thus, facing starvation. At the time, the people in the village were reportedly eating in rotation, whereby certain members of a family could eat only one day and the remaining members could eat on the other day.[150] Therefore, despite having the reserves overflowing with stocks with about 40 million tonnes above the required buffer stocks, people were dying of starvation.

It was argued that the Central and State Governments had violated the right to food by failing to respond to the above-mentioned drought situation and, in particular, by amassing immense food stocks while people were dying due to starvation. The primary objective of the petition was based on the premise that, since food is essential for survival, the right to food is an implication of the fundamental 'right to life' contained in article 21 of the Indian Constitution.[151] The petition therefore posed two major questions for determination by the Indian Supreme Court. Firstly, whether the right to life under the Constitution's article 21 includes the right to food and, secondly, whether

[145] M Langford 'Domestic adjudication and economic, social and cultural: A socio-legal review' (2009) 11 *International Journal on Human Rights* 92.
[146] PN Bhagwati 'Judicial activism and public interest litigation' (1985) 23 *Columbia Journal of Transnational Law* 577.
[147] *Sheela Barse v State of Maharashtra* 1983 AIR 378 (SC) (Supreme Court of India decision).
[148] *PUCL v Union of India* WP (C) 196 of 2001 (Supreme Court of India decision).
[149] E Durojaye & EM Chilemba 'Accountability and the *Right to Food*: A comparative study of India and South Africa' (2018) 3 *Food Security SA Working Paper Series* 20.
[150] Ibid 20.
[151] Ibid 21.

the right to food as upheld by the highest court implies the state's duty to provide food, especially in situations of drought to people affected by the drought and who were not in a position to buy food.[152]

PUCL relied on the Supreme Court's precedent defining the right to life as 'the right to live with human dignity and all that goes with it, namely, the bare necessaries of life such as adequate nutrition'.[153] This formed the basis of the Court's interpretation to affirmatively incorporate the right to food into Art 21 (the right to life); thereby transforming the former into a justiciable and enforceable fundamental right. Over the last ten years, the Supreme Court has taken steps to protect the right to food through a series of interim orders that comprehensively set out minimum allocations of food grains for India's poor and identify the public officials who are to be held accountable in the event of non-compliance.[154]

While early interim orders in the litigation were focussed on the public distribution of food grains to families and persons falling below the poverty line, in 2001, the Supreme Court went one step further and made an order that identified the food schemes that were to be considered legal entitlements under the constitutional right to food, and detailed how those government schemes were to be implemented.[155] In 2002, the Court subsequently appointed a commission[156] to monitor the effect of the interim orders on the lives of the affected people, proposing changes and reporting to the court.[157]

The commissioners are also empowered to carry out investigations into any violations of the interim orders and to demand redress with the full support of the Court.[158] In addition, the commissioners take part in the negotiation and mediation of changes to laws, policies, and programs together with the state and central governments to ensure the improved implementation of the feeding schemes and to address any elements of state action that exclude marginalised groups.[159]

The jurisprudence of the court shows its willingness to adopt monitoring mechanisms if broader constitutional rights are affected by the incessant non-adherence of the state. In various cases, the Supreme Court and High Courts have appointed social activists, researchers, government and judicial officers as commissioners to monitor certain locations for fact-finding and to submit a detailed reports setting out their findings, suggestions and recommendations.[160] This approach was also evident in the South African and Colombian case discussions as the decisive factor in all of these cases seems to be the unwillingness or incapacity by the executive to comply with its

[152] G Kent 'The human right to food in India' (12 March 2002) University of Hawai'i <http://www.earthwindow.com/grc2/foodrights/HumanRightToFoodinIndia.pdf>.

[153] *Francis Coralie Mullin v The Administrator, Union* (1981) 2 SCR 516, 518 (Supreme Court of India decision).

[154] *People's Union for Civil Liberties v Union of India,* Writ Petition (Civil) No. 196 of 2001 (India) (Nov. 28, 2001 interim order).

[155] L Birchfield & J Corsi 'Between starvation and globalisation: Realising the right to food in India' (2010) 31 *Michigan Journal of International Law* 722

[156] *People's Union for Civil Liberties v Union of India,* Writ Petition (Civil) No. 196 of 2001 (May 8, 2002 interim order).

[157] Birchfield & Corsi (note 155) 722.

[158] S Hassan 'Rights, activism and the poor in India: Supreme Court and the "*Right to Food*" case' paper presented at international conference on 'Social protection for social justice' Institute of Development Studies, UK (13–15 April 2011) 4.

[159] Birchfield & Corsi (note 155) 728.

[160] Bhagwati (note 146) 574.

constitutional obligations. The similarities between the South African cases, the right to food case and the *T-760* case are striking and highlight the approach used by courts to determine when structural interventions are likely to be successful.

In *PUCL v Union of India*, the Supreme Court's orders became more interventionist following its initial orders, which were simply aimed at remedying the government's failure to identify 'below poverty line' households. The court's subsequent orders grew stronger over time as discussed earlier (from ordering the implementation of feeding schemes to the appointment of the commission). The Supreme Court therefore followed the same sequence as the Colombian and South African Constitutional Courts, which adopted the expert remedial model following a series of weak-form remedies. However, Sue-Mari Viljoen and Saul Makama argue that the employment of monitoring institutions in India is an example of an intrusive form of structural relief, as 'the courts overtake the decision-making powers of bureaucratic institutions over extended periods of time to restructure such institutions'.[161] These contentions made against the use of supervisory jurisdiction are generally couched around legitimacy.[162]

The legitimacy argument also stems from the view that the right to food involves the allocation of resources and decision-making that should be left to the executive and the legislature.[163] However, the right to food like any other human right is a justiciable right under the concept of rule of law. Therefore, its realisation cannot be left exclusively to politically elected authorities. Although the state enjoys a large discretionary power in adopting legislation and policies for the realisation of the right to food, it is the duty of the judiciary to determine the reasonableness of the measures and ensure that they are being implemented. Therefore, the appointment of commissioners or experts should not be viewed as an encroachment on the sphere of the executive but a necessary response to systemic failure aimed at assisting the executive in its functions.

4. Conclusion

The question posed at the beginning of this article is whether judicial monitoring institutions constitute a legitimate remedy for systemic socio-economic rights violations. The Constitutional Court has neither given a principled basis for its rejection and use of the remedy nor laid down any norms and principles for determining when the remedy is appropriate, just and equitable. However, in all the jurisdictions discussed above, there exists a common denominator: the political systems are characterised by the incapacity of state institutions to effectively resolve serious systemic challenges related to the realisation of socio-economic rights. This has been illustrated with examples such as the state of health care in Colombia and land reform in South Africa. The appointment of experts to supervise the implementation of court orders is thus a strong response to the reluctance or inability of governmental authorities to act on court orders.

---

161 SM Viljoen & SP Makama 'Structural relief: A context-sensitive approach' (2018) 34 *South African Journal of Human Rights* 228.

162 J Cassels 'Judicial activism and public interest litigation in India: Attempting the impossible?' (1989) 37 *The American Journal of Comparative Law* 513.

163 Ibid 509.

The innovative remedies employed by the courts discussed in this article represent a stronger form of remedial relief that still retains respect for the functions of other branches. The apex courts are moving away from generalised deference towards the more specific goal of ensuring that the executive takes action to fulfil its constitutional obligations. The Colombian and Indian experiences highlight that unconventional remedial strategies can effectively induce important changes in the bureaucracy. However, the argument in this article is not that the expert remedial model is the only solution to social rights problems, rather other models can complement the creation of monitoring mechanisms. The expert remedial model arises from the need to develop better and more effective remedies if socio-economic rights are to live up to their transformative promise. These courts have undeniably responded to the need to ensure the enforcement of socio-economic rights by spurring political action using the pressure of monitoring institutions.

A number of factors contribute to the legitimacy of the expert remedial model. Beyond its ability to comply with the separation of powers, this model allows for the formulation of remedies that benefit both the litigants and other rights-bearers. In most cases, the litigants propose the type of remedial plan that they feel is necessary and this is included in the court order. The expert remedial model makes for meaningful participation as experts must first gather evidence before designing a remedy. During this phase, the appointed experts can consult with affected stakeholders. Therefore, the parties can play an active role in finding a suitable remedy while the court remains neutral and impartial.

The judicial decisions discussed in this article are aimed not only at combatting non-compliance by the executive, but at ensuring that the very root of systemic failures is addressed. It is noteworthy that the judiciary often begins with weaker remedies so as to minimise the impact on the separation of powers. Stronger remedies such as the appointment of monitoring mechanisms follow where these measures fail. To this end, the use of monitoring institutions under certain conditions such as consistent non-compliance and institutional incapacity should be seen as a collaborative effort on the part of the judiciary to promote dialogue and ensure the realisation and protection of socio-economic rights. It is difficult to predict whether executive officials will be responsive to courts' use of structural orders and act in a good faith to meet their obligations.

While it is uncertain what trajectory the use of structural interdicts will follow, it is clear that the success of the remedy will ultimately be determined by the executive's willingness to respect court orders. There is a real danger that when the executive fails to comply, the authority of the judiciary is undermined and the rule of law is thus weakened. Structural interdicts do not necessarily fix executive incompetence or recalcitrance. The courts can look to using different models of the structural remedy to add further measures of accountability and engagement.

Holding officials and political office bearers personally liable for legal costs in cases occasioned by their actions (or lack of action), is another means of executive accountability that has the potential to be highly effective in compelling officials to adopt more responsible attitudes. Most of all, however, it falls to officials to be responsive to the courts and use structural orders as a framework to aid their decision making, in a good faith attempt to meet their obligations.

Acknowledgements

I am grateful to Professor David Bilchitz for meticulously editing earlier versions of this article. Many thanks to the anonymous reviewers and editors of the *South African Journal on Human Rights* for their helpful comments and suggestions.

Disclosure statement

No conflict of interest was declared by the author.

OPEN ACCESS

Designing remedies for a recalcitrant administration

Gaurav Mukherjee and Juha Tuovinen

ABSTRACT
This article concerns remedial design by courts in cases where constitutional rights are jeopardised by a recalcitrant administration. We focus on the recent judgment of the South African Constitutional Court in *Bhekindlela Mwelase v Director-General for the Department of Rural Development and Land Reform* – in particular its doctrinal innovation in appointing a Special Master to oversee the processing of labour tenant claims by the Department of Rural Affairs and Land Reform. We argue that the case raises both conceptual and practical questions about the relationship between rights and remedies, substantive law, and the separation of powers. We approach these questions after considering the judgment in its socio-political context through a consideration of the factors underlying the granting of the remedy, from both a theoretical and comparative perspective. The paper identifies a set factors that underpinned the Court's decision that will be likely to influence the granting of invasive remedies in future cases. We then apply these factors to the judgment of the Supreme Court of India in the Right to Food Case to better understand the ways they play out in a different jurisdictional context. These factors can provide doctrinal and normative guidance for courts – especially in the so-called Global South – that often operate under conditions of chronic recalcitrance, inattentiveness, inaction, or incompetence of the coordinate branches of government.

The longstanding jurisprudence of the Constitutional Court of South Africa requires that constitutional remedies be 'effective'. A recent line of cases has forced the Court to consider what this means in the context of a constitutional system that is beset by a range of failures to institutionally deliver on its constitutional obligations. The latest of these decisions was handed down on 19 August 2019 by the Constitutional Court of South Africa in *Bhekindlela Mwelase v Director-General for the Department of Rural Development and Land Reform*.[1] The case was brought by a group of petitioners who claimed that the Department had violated their constitutional rights by failing to

[1] *Bhekindlela Mwelase v Director-General for the Department of Rural Development and Land Reform* [2019] ZACC 30 (*Mwelase* Con Court).

process their claims as labour tenants to certain property rights under the provisions of the Land Reform (Labour Tenants) Act 3 of 1996. These actions came in the backdrop of the long-running failure by successive ANC-led governments to restore land to those who were deprived of it during apartheid and the increasing public anger and political mobilisation in response to that anger.[2]

The majority judgment was authored by Justice Edwin Cameron on his last day in office and was hailed as 'poetry in social justice'.[3] The case is of significant import not only for the process of land reform in South Africa, but also for providing nuance to a distinctly South African understanding of the separation of powers and the principles that govern appropriate relief in constitutional litigation. In the case, three courts, the Land Claims Court (LCC), the Supreme Court of Appeal (SCA), and the Constitutional Court split on whether the adoption of a novel remedy – the appointment of a Special Master – overstepped the powers accorded to courts. With the majority of the Constitutional Court ultimately upholding the decision of the LCC to appoint a Special Master, the case raises both conceptual as well as practical questions about (1) the relationship between rights and remedies, (2) substantive law and (3) separation of powers.

In this article we put some of these questions into context and ask how we are to understand the outcome in *Mwelase*: We start by contemplating neglected questions about where remedies fit in the general framework on the separation of powers in the Constitution of the Republic of South Africa, 1996. Moving on, we consider whether the case provides a sufficient account of the conditions under which courts will be willing to forge innovative remedies. Does it provide judicially manageable thresholds that, if triggered, would estop an appellate court from interfering with a remedy granted by a lower court that potentially impinges upon the constitutional separation of powers? We situate the case in the current political climate surrounding land reform and constitutionalism in South Africa and ask: Was the outcome in the case so heavily contingent on a set of extra-textual factors, which can be gleaned by a close reading of the judgment, and as a consequence, unlikely to be replicated in the near future? The answer is a tentative yes. We test our hypothesis by applying the conditions identified to the invasive remedies developed by a similarly powerful apex court with a proclivity towards strong judicial interventions: the appointment of external commissioners to oversee its orders by the Supreme Court of India (SC) in the *Right to Food* (*RTF*) litigation in 2001.

The article proceeds in five sections. Part 2 discusses the *Mwelase* Constitutional Court judgment in detail, including its factual and procedural background, and the evolution of the case and order from the LCC, its overturning in the SCA, and its eventual reinstatement in the Constitutional Court. Part 3 answers the central questions identified in the second paragraph of this introduction by considering nine factors that guided the remedy granted in the *Mwelase* Constitutional Court judgment, including the thresholds for each. Part 4 applies the factors in the previous section to the case of

---

[2] T Roux 'Constitutional populism in South Africa' in M Krygier, W Sadurski & A Czarnota (eds) *Constitutional Populism* (forthcoming 2021) <https://papers.ssrn.com/sol3/papers.cfm?abstract_id=3583270>.

[3] M Heywood 'Poetry in the air during Judge Edwin Cameron's send-off' (22 August 2019) *Daily Maverick* <https://www.dailymaverick.co.za/article/2019-08-22-poetry-in-the-air-during-judge-edwin-camerons-send-off/>.

the *RTF* litigation in India, which was relied on by Cameron J and Ncube J in the *Mwelase* Constitutional Court and LCC judgments respectively in order to derive authority for the judicial appointment of a Special Master to devise, oversee and implement a plan for solving a polycentric problem pursuant to a court order. Part 5 concludes by discussing the convergences and divergences between the *RTF* case and *Mwelase*, while also considering the possible institutional and interpretive risks of the path chosen by the Constitutional Court in the case.

1. *Mwelase*: the judgment

The 2019 judgment of the Constitutional Court in *Mwelase* concerned a matter that originated in a set of labour tenants' (the named claimant being already deceased) claims to acquire property rights that had not been processed by the Department of Land Reform, an issue that dovetailed with a nationwide discussion on the issue of land reform and captured the public imagination.

1.1 The Land Claims Court

The case originated in the LCC, which had delivered a judgment[4] appointing a Special Master of labour tenants to help the Department of Rural Development and Land Reform (DLR) process labour tenants' land claims.[5] The judgment in this case is one in a very long line of litigation between the applicant and the Department in an effort by a set of claimants to acquire ownership rights over a parcel of land known as the Hilton College in KwaZulu-Natal. According to the terms of the Land Reform Act, labour tenants' right to acquire certain ownership rights over the land can be realised only through the detailed mechanisms set out in the Act, all of which are critically contingent on timely departmental action and processes.[6]

The applicants had lodged their claim in June 2000; however, the claim was never referred to the LCC in order to resolve the dispute between the applicants and the Hiltonian Society, the trust in charge of administering the land.[7] In July 2013 the applicants approached the LCC to settle their dispute while arguing that their case was emblematic of the wider problems in the department and asking for structural relief. The LCC noted that the processing of claims had been neglected and the related statistics were not properly maintained or incapable of being furnished. In some cases, applicants had died or moved away due to the inordinate delay, and files had been lost, requiring the claims process to commence anew, and subjecting the applicants to needless hardship.[8]

The applicants approached the LCC a number of times, each time acceding to an agreement with the DLR that included supervision by the LCC but did not include the

[4] *Mwelase v Director-General for the Department of Rural Development and Land Reform* 2017 (4) SA 422 (LCC) (per Ncube AJ) (*Mwelase* LCC).
[5] *Mwelase* Con Court (note 1 above) para 3 (per Cameron J).
[6] Ibid para 10.
[7] The facts appear at paras 14–36 of the Constitutional Court's judgment (note 1 above).
[8] *Mwelase* LCC (note 4 above) paras 5–7.

institution of a Special Master. These measures did not yield results and the parties found themselves in the LCC again. Only this time, the applicants persisted in their claim for a Special Master. The LCC, considering the nature and scale of the problem,[9] and noting its 'ancillary powers necessary or reasonably incidental to the performance of its functions, including the power to grant interlocutory orders and interdicts' (derived from s 29 of the Land Reform (Labour Tenants) Act), validated the appointment of a Special Master of Labour Tenants. Ncube AJ reasoned that the mandate of the Special Master would be circumscribed, and the Special Master would act as an *agent of the court* to aid the Department in processing and adjudication of land claims brought under the Act. The Special Master would be tasked with devising an implementation plan that would have a number of clearly demarcated elements.[10] The rationale behind appointing a Special Master would be to ensure effectiveness, continuity, and the provision of expertise – all while being independent of the Department to a certain extent.

1.2 Overturning by the SCA

On appeal, the SCA promptly overturned the decision[11] on seven grounds: first, it held that the appointment of the Special Master was a 'textbook case of judicial overreach'[12] and that it was a violation of the doctrine of separation of powers. Second, it stated that it would require a massive increase in the Department's budget and drastic reallocations between budget items.[13] Third, it stated that there were no rules governing the appointment of a Special Master or its equivalent in South African law. Fourth, it stated that s 32(3)(b) of the Restitution of Land Rights Act 22 of 1994 (the law under which the LCC was set up) only permitted the LCC to 'conduct any part of any proceedings on an informal or inquisitorial basis', and did not constitute adequate authority for the appointment of a Special Master. Fifth, it stated that the LCC had not

---

[9] The LCC also found violations of various provisions of the Constitution, including s 195 on certain principles of public administration, s 33 on the right to administrative action that is lawful, reasonable and procedurally fair, as well as s 237, which requires that all constitutional obligations must be performed diligently and without delay.

[10] The elements of the plan, which would then be approved by the LCC, were (*Mwelase* LCC (note 4 above) para 38, emphasis added):

(a) an assessment of total number of claims lodged to date, and the number which have not yet been processed and finalized,

(b) an assessment of the skill pool and other infrastructure required for processing labour tenant claims, and to what extent such skill pool and infrastructure is available within the Department of Rural Development and Land Reform,

(c) devising of targets, on a year-to-year basis, for the resolution of pending labour tenant claims, either by agreement or by referring the claim to the Court,

(d) a *determination of the budget* necessary during each financial year for carrying out the Implementation Plan, including both the Department's operating costs for processing claims and the amounts required to fund awards made pursuant to applications in terms of s 16 of the LTA,

(e) plans for co-ordination with the Land Claims Court to ensure the rapid adjudication or arbitration of unresolved claims referred to the Court in terms of s 18(7) read with s 19 to s 25 of the [Labour Tenants Act]; and

(f) any other matters which the Special Master may consider relevant.

[11] *Mwelase v Director-General for the Department of Rural Development and Land Reform* 2019 (2) SA 81 (SCA) (Schippers JA; Leach JA, Seriti JA and Willis JA concurring; Mocumie JA dissenting) (*Mwelase* SCA).

[12] Ibid para 51, borrowing the phrase from Mogoeng CJ in *Economic Freedom Fighters v Speaker of the National Assembly* 2018 (2) SA 571 (CC) para 223.

[13] Ibid para 6.

enquired as to why the Senior Manager (who had been appointed by way of a Negotiation Order in the interim stages of the case) could not adequately deal with the inefficiencies and how the Special Master would accelerate or improve the settlement of claims.[14] Sixth, it held that the Special Master would take over existing functions of the Department, which would incur an extra cost incurred as well as an uncertainty about what would happen in cases of disagreement on budgetary priorities.[15] Seventh, it sought to distinguish the legal position of referee[16] (which the applicants had contended was a position analogous to the Special Master) from that of the Special Master, since the referees' powers under South African law is strictly circumscribed and consented to by both parties. The Court also distinguished the Special Master's mandate from that of the independent panel of experts appointed to oversee remedy implementation in *Black Sash Trust v Minister of Social Development* (*Black Sash I*),[17] where the Constitutional Court had set up independent oversight of SASSA, the government agency responsible for social grant payments.

Importantly, however, there was a dissent from Justice Mocumie, who stated that the considerations that were taken into account by the majority did not: 'tilt favourably on the scales to justice and equity'[18] and that 'the social circumstances, historical reality of labour tenants, scope of powers of the LCC, specificity of our judicial methods to interpret transforming legislations and our courts' ever available oversight powers would shape the institution of a Special Master in a way that makes it compatible, specific and appropriate (in) this context'.[19]

The judge also cautioned against interference with orders of the LCC, which is granted special powers and has expertise and experience.

1.3 Constitutional Court overturns the SCA judgment

In a judgment delivered by Justice Edwin Cameron, who had once written that 'litigation is not the solution to all problems of social justice',[20] the Constitutional Court reinstated the order of the LCC, placing great emphasis on the specialist nature of the Court, its broad remedial powers, and the fact that there was clear systemic failure on the part of the Department to engage in processing of land claims in any meaningful way.[21] It also stated that the LCC had at all times set the scope of the Special Master's mandate itself and retained control over its role in formulating the remedy.[22] At all times, the Court took pains to establish the culpability of the Department in precipitating the kind of action the LCC took.[23] The salience of the issue in the national

---

[14] Ibid paras 44–45.

[15] Ibid paras 48–49.

[16] See s 38 of the Superior Courts Act 10 of 2013, and ss 21 and 28C of the Restitution of Land Rights Act.

[17] *Black Sash Trust v Minister of Social Development* 2017 (3) SA 335 (CC) (*Black Sash I*).

[18] *Mwelase* SCA (note 11 above) para 74.

[19] Ibid para 79.

[20] E Cameron 'A South African perspective on the judicial development of socio-economic rights' in L Lazarus, C McCrudden & N Bowles (eds) *Reasoning Rights: Comparative Judicial Engagement* (2014) 319, 338.

[21] The judgment in *Mwelase* Con Court (note 1 above) para 69 noted that the Department 'showed failing institutional functionality of an extensive and sustained degree. That cried out for remedy'.

[22] Ibid para 59.

[23] Ibid para 40: 'The Department has manifested and sustained what has seemed to be obstinate misapprehension of its statutory duties.'

imagination also played a key role in the reasoning of the Court.[24] Given the care with which the Court has in the past treated the question of remedy, the brevity of the majority's reasoning is quite striking. The emphasis on the LCC's discretion is especially curious, given how frequently the Constitutional Court has overturned lower court orders that were much less intrusive than the appointment of the Special Master.

Justice Jafta seised upon these points in his dissent. In a detailed discussion of the powers of the Special Master, Jafta pointed to the budgetary powers granted to the Special Master – which were notably absent from the powers of the independent committee of experts constituted in *Black Sash I*.[25] Drawing on the classic case law on the limits of judicial power in budgetary decisions – *Doctors for Life, Soobramoney, Treatment Action Campaign* – Jafta J stated that he would have rejected the appeal.[26]

There is much to note in these brief judgments by the majority and minority that makes the reasoning in *Mwelase* susceptible to criticism. In particular, the cursory manner in which the majority addressed the question of remedy and its strong emphasis on lower court discretion are worthy of critique. The minority's reasoning is more substantive, but also raises questions about the structure of the judgment. Heretofore, the appropriateness of the intervention has been dealt with at the stage of interpreting the right. Indeed, all the quotations from Jafta J's judgments that are included here were made in the course of interpreting rights, rather than determining the appropriate relief.

In some sense, then, the Constitutional Court's judgment failed to clarify the relationship between right and remedy and to offer an account of how these two should co-exist in the structure of constitutional argument.

2. Does *Mwelase* provide judicially manageable standards for the grant of an invasive remedy?

Having discussed the grounds for reinstatement of the LCC order by the Constitutional Court in its majority judgment, in this section we assess the factors that can be distilled from the judgment to illustrate when remedial innovations like the appointment of a Special Master might be ordered in subsequent cases by the judiciary. We also recount the Court's previous holdings on invasive remedies, since *Mwelase* builds on these existing criteria. Such a reconstruction of the existing case law crucially lays the groundwork for the development of factors and conditions that help overcome traditional separation of powers issues in the grant of remedies.

- Likelihood of government non-compliance with order – Invasive remedies are likely to be granted in cases where there is a likelihood of non-compliance with the court's order. This is seen in the early cases of the Constitutional Court. In

---

[24] Ibid para 41: 'South Africans have been waiting for more than 25 years for equitable land reform. More accurately, they have been waiting for centuries before.' *Doctors for Life International v Speaker of the National Assembly* 2006 (6) SA 416 (CC); *Soobramoney v Minister of Health, KwaZulu-Natal* 1998 (1) SA 765 (CC); *Minister of Health v Treatment Action Campaign (No 2)* 2002 (5) SA 721 (*TAC*).

[25] Ibid para 97.

[26] *Mwelase* Con Court (note 1 above) paras 99–104.

Sibiya v Director of Public Prosecutions: Johannesburg High Court,[27] the Court exercised a supervisory role in ensuring that the government's non-compliance with its judgment in *Makwanyane*[28] was remedied. The likelihood (or lack thereof) of governmental non-compliance was also a key factor behind the choice not to impose supervisory jurisdiction in *TAC.*[29] Therefore, the conduct of government authorities is determinative for this criterion to kick into operation. In constitutions that have a textual judicial remedial mandate[30] that is as broad as that in South Africa, and guided by the principles of creativity, innovation and effective vindication of constitutional rights,[31] it may be useful to consider whether the principle of institutional comity can provide a benchmark.[32] Certain principles of institutional morality flow from the separation of powers and frame and shape the interaction between the branches of government. Where there are departures from adherence to the principle, courts would be likely to intervene in a more concerted way. While Froneman J repeatedly invoked SASSA's extraordinary intransigence in justifying the invasive remedy in *Black Sash I,*[33] Cameron J in the majority judgment in *Mwelase* notes the repeated failure of the Department to comply in good faith with previous negotiation orders from the LCC, which assumes greater significance in the backdrop of the salience of land reform in the project of transformative constitutionalism.

- Degree of harm by non-grant/consequentialism – It is almost trite to state that the graver the likelihood of harm, the likelier the Court will be to impose an invasive remedy. This does have some more concrete elements, such as the importance of the right at issue as well as practical concerns such as 'how many people will be affected by the order and whether the result of delay will be discomfort or death or something in between.'[34] It is also important whether a delay will result in irreparable harm, as was the case with death row inmates in *Sibiya*. Take for example, the supervisory order issued by the Court in *Black Sash I*[35] where the Court was concerned with the consequences of non-compliance with its orders relating to the redoing of the tender process for appointing an external agency to handle social grant payments. The Court had reasoned that this was not only important for maintaining the rule of law and legality in the tender procurement processes, but also key to ensuring the uninterrupted payment of social grants on which millions depended. This line of reasoning also undergirded its decision, in

---

27 *Sibiya v Director of Public Prosecutions: Johannesburg High Court* [2005] ZACC 6. The release of supervisory jurisdiction was done in *Sibiya v Director of Public Prosecutions* [2006] ZACC 22 after the Constitutional Court was satisfied that adequate steps were taken to comply with its orders in *S v Makwanyane* 1995 (3) SA 391.

28 Ibid.

29 *TAC* (note 24 above) paras 116–118.

30 See the Constitution s 38, 172.

31 *Fose v Minister of Safety and Security* 1997 (3) SA 786 para 69.

32 See for example *Black Sash I* (note 17 above) para 13: 'Until the forced reply to this Court's directions there has certainly been no reciprocal comity from the Minister and SASSA in respect of the remedial order and withdrawal of the supervisory order, towards the judicial branch of government'.

33 Ibid para 10.

34 K Roach & G Budlender 'Mandatory relief and supervisory jurisdiction: when is it appropriate, just and equitable' (2005) 122 *South African Law Journal* 325, 333.

35 *Black Sash I* (note 17 above).

AllPay I,[36] to suspend its order of invalidity conditional upon the successful reconduct of the tender process in which certain procedural flaws were alleged by the unsuccessful bidder. In *Mwelase*, the Court is concerned about the abject and varied failures of the Department, as well as the centrality of the process of granting ownership rights to labour tenants to the 'project of land reform and restitution that our country promised to fulfil when first the interim Constitution came into effect, in 1994, and after it the Constitution, in 1997'.[37] Therefore, a line of consequentialist reasoning that considers the consequences of not granting an invasive remedy appears to guide the Court. This may not necessarily be a bad thing. It is our view that in disputes that have an impact on the fulfilment of a socioeconomic right, courts should be guided by the effect that a refusal of remedy grant would have upon the most vulnerable constituencies.

- Clarity of remedial steps – The clarity of steps to be taken to remedy the problem is a relevant factor while granting a remedy that possibly impinges on the separation of powers. Here it is important to restate that since the purpose of complex remedies like that of the Special Master are 1) to determine future steps to be taken to remedy a problem, and 2) to ensure compliance, it would depend on the specific context to see how these two factors play out. With respect to its early cases, the South African canon of social rights case law indicates that this was the reason for the reporting requirement (and an unstated retention of supervisory jurisdiction) in the High Court order in *Grootboom*.[38] In the more recent cases, the need for greater clarity on possible remedial steps (which can be achieved by greater stakeholder consultation) led the Court to order meaningful engagement in eviction cases. In contrast, while the steps needed to remedy the problem in *Black Sash*[39] were clear; at each stage, newer considerations (a classic polycentric problem) could be introduced. In addition, there was also the spectre of non-compliance, and so the Court opted for the retention of supervisory jurisdiction. In *Mwelase*, the Court is largely agnostic about the exact line of action that the Department should pursue in order to remedy its failure to process the labour tenants' claims, and opts to defer to the expertise of the LCC in the appointment of an external agent as the best way forward. Courts adjudicating issues arising out of complex polycentric social problems routinely face issues of democratic legitimacy and a lack of information and expertise. The appointment of external experts helps alleviate some of these problems. Therefore, depending on the clarity of the way forward to address the underlying problem, as well as the likelihood of governmental compliance identified above, the Court is likely to fashion an invasive remedy of the kind seen in *Mwelase*.
- Underlying issue salience and systemicity – The salience of the underlying issue in the public imagination appears to be a motivating factor in the degree of

---

[36] See *AllPay Consolidated Investment Holdings (Pty) Ltd v Chief Executive Officer of the South African Social Security Agency* 2014 (1) SA 604 (CC) (*AllPay I*) para 56: 'Here it will be the imperative interests of grant beneficiaries and particularly child grant recipients in an uninterrupted grant system that will play a major role (in the approach to the remedy.'

[37] *Mwelase* Con Court (note 1 above) para 2.

[38] *Grootboom v Oostenberg Municipality* 2001 (1) SA 46 (*Grootboom*).

[39] *Black Sash I* (note 17 above).

invasiveness of the remedy, and consequently whether the court will retain supervisory jurisdiction. While it is true that the Constitutional Court has retained supervisory jurisdiction even in cases where an issue as 'everyday'[40] as evictions are concerned,[41] when supervisory orders are combined with more invasive steps such as the appointment of external agents, the salience of the underlying is very relevant. The Court takes great pains in *Mwelase*,[42] *Black Sash*[43] and *AllPay*[44] to establish, in addition to the endemic government ineptitude and intransigence on display in both the cases, the systemicity of these cases, as well as their importance to the public. Here, we use *systemicity* in a very particular sense – as the characteristic of an individual case to be representative of an underlying systemic problem of governmental incompetence, inattentiveness, intransigence, or persistent non-compliance with a judicial order, which has a knock-on effect on the realisation of a socioeconomic right. In these cases, the problem was not with the usual quandaries courts face while adjudicating socioeconomic rights issues – those of democratic legitimacy in giving content to a right, or of lack of institutional fit in determining steps to realise it. Rather, they were issues of (mis)governance. In *Mwelase*, the Court could point to the inertia of the DLR and its responsible Minister (against whom contempt proceedings were brought), and order an invasive remedy to attempt to engage with the problem of land reform – an issue that has immense currency in public discourses around the Constitution today.[45] Similarly, with the invasive remedy in *Black Sash*, it is critical to appreciate that over 15 million people rely on social assistance in South Africa, a number that has only increased following the global Covid-19 pandemic. What remains constant is SASSA's incompetence in handling payments and the kinds of deleterious effects such ineptitude has had.[46] This shows how salience is a factor in determining if courts are willing to expend their institutional capital on invasive remedies.

---

[40] The reality of everyday violence experienced by South Africa's public at the hands of state authorities, especially in respect of evictions and demolition of homes, has also been noted by supranational organisations. See for example, the United Nations Committee on Economic, Social and Cultural Rights 'Concluding Observations on the Initial Report of South Africa' (2018) UN doc. E/C.12/ZAF/CO/1 11: 'The Committee is also concerned at reports of illegal evictions and the excessive use of force during evictions, as well as evictions taking place without municipalities offering suitable alternative accommodation.'

[41] Take for example its orders in *Pheko v Ekurhuleni Metropolitan Municipality* 2012 (2) SA 598 (*Pheko*).

[42] *Mwelase* Con Court (note 1 above) para 3 per Cameron J: 'At issue is the extent of the Land Claims Court's power to fashion and implement remedies to secure practical justice for claimants who, 25 years into our democracy, still have no secure tenure – even though a statute promised them this more than 20 years ago.'

[43] Note 17 above para 1 per Froneman J: 'One of the signature achievements of our constitutional democracy is the establishment of an inclusive and effective programme of social assistance. It has had a material impact in reducing poverty and inequality and in mitigating the consequences of high levels of unemployment. In so doing it has given some content to the core constitutional values of dignity, equality and freedom. This judgment is, however, not an occasion to celebrate this achievement. To the contrary, it is necessitated by the extraordinary conduct of the Minister of Social Development (Minister) and of the South African Social Security Agency (SASSA) that have placed that achievement in jeopardy.'

[44] Note 36 above.

[45] See H Klug 'Book review: *Land Reform and the Future of Land Ownership in South Africa*' (1992) 109 *South African Law Journal* 373 and H Klug 'Decolonisation, compensation and constitutionalism: Land, wealth and the sustainability of constitutionalism in post-apartheid South Africa' (2018) 34 *South African Journal of Human Rights* 469.

[46] See J Maromo 'DA to report SASSA to Human Rights Commission over social grants payment "ineptitude"' 5 June 2020 *IOL* <https://www.iol.co.za/news/politics/da-to-report-sassa-to-human-rights-commission-over-social-grants-payment-ineptitude-48966076?fbclid=IwAR0yMjHXwznJGMy1SYq4hXUTpycGd16da-tdB8HxTayKC2FDv2KRDpAIGnY>

- Political and electoral salience of issue – Land reform has posed a particularly difficult and multifaceted challenge to constitutionalism in South Africa.[47] The sharp question in *Mwelase* related to the failure to process claims from labour tenants by the Department of Land Reform. This in itself is a crucial question affecting the lives of millions of South Africans, many of whom live in precarious conditions. However, as Justice Cameron's opening paragraph reminds us, land reform provides both a 'promise for structural change' and also a possibility for the improvement to the lives of labour tenants, one of the most pressing and explosive political issues facing the country. It is probably not an understatement that the survival of the constitutional project in South Africa will depend to a great extent on the success of land reform and restitution. In this sense it is also important to note that the government has had a weak record in other areas of land reform apart from labour tenants' rights.[48] While the government has made some strides in the redistribution of land, the ownership of arable land still rests with in the hands of the few, land invasions and attendant evictions run rampant, and the pace of government land reform is not nearly adequate to quell public anger and resentment.[49] The Economic Freedom Fighters (EFF) have also taken up the cause of land reform, reframing the shortcomings in this area as a direct challenge to the moral legitimacy of the mandate of the African National Congress (ANC) and the broader constitutional project – all the while increasing the party's electoral support. As such the subject matter of the case could not be more pressing and as the political and administrative branches have failed to perform their duties, judicial intervention seems warranted in this particularly crucial domain for the future of the South African constitutional project.
- Personal conduct of government officials – One of the central factors that guided the development of the Special Master remedy by the Court in *Mwelase* is the *systemic*, rather than personal failure, that lay at the heart of the Department's failure to process labour tenants' claims. Cameron J articulated what appears to be a coherent standard that has the capacity to guide future claimants in showing 'failing institutional functionality of an extensive and sustained degree' that 'cried out for remedy'.[50] He went on to state that the LCC's exercise of its discretionary powers is tempered by the fundamental issue at hand being *institutional, not personal.*[51] It is

[47] JL Gibson *Overcoming Historical injustices: Land reconciliation in South Africa* (2009) 1; J Tuovinen 'Land reform in the time of populism: The law and politics of land reform in South Africa' in A Sajó & R Uitz (eds) *Critical Essays on Human Rights Criticism* (2020) 157. Land reform was already a challenging topic during the negotiation for the new Constitution: L Segal & S Cort *One Law, One Nation: The Making of the South African Constitution* (2012). On the drafting of the property clause, see: M Chaskalson, 'The property clause: Section 28 of the Constitution' (1994) 10 *South African Journal of Human Rights* 131. For two high-level government panels analysing the success of land reform, see: High Level Panel on the Assessment on Key Legislation and the Acceleration Of Fundamental Change *Report of the High Level Panel on the Assessment on Key Legislation and the Acceleration Of Fundamental Change* (25 November 2017) <https://www.parliament.gov.za/press-releases/download-report-high-level-panel-assessment-key-legislation-and-acceleration-fundamental-change>; Final report of the presidential panel on land reformand agrarian reform for his excellency the President of So>.

[48] A Akinola 'Land reform in South Africa: An appraisal' (2018) 10 *Africa Review* 108.

[49] H Wissink 'The struggle for land restitution and reform in post-apartheid South Africa' in A Akinola & H Wissink (eds) *Trajectory of Land Reform in Post-Colonial African States: Advances in African Economic, Social and Political Development* (2019) 67.

[50] *Mwelase* Con Court (note 1 above) para 69.

[51] Ibid.

also important to note here that the SCA's dismissal of the contempt of court[52] claim against the Minister of DLR was upheld in appeal in *Mwelase.*[53] *Mwelase* therefore departs from a recent development in case law of ordering personal costs against public officials, as seen in *Black Sash* against the Minister of Social Development and the attachment of state assets censure that is seen in *Linkside.*[54] It remains to be seen how this standard will play out in future litigation, but it is quite likely that the impleading of public officials as parties to suits in cases of systemic failure will continue and will have to be determined on a case-by-case basis.

- Extent of diffusion of powers in cooperative government – One of the persistent challenges in diffused systems of cooperative government like that in South Africa is pinpointing the authority responsible for a particular act.[55] While the government is constituted as national, provincial and local spheres that are 'distinctive, interdependent and interrelated',[56] there is 'a clear hierarchy which runs from national government down to provincial government down to local government.'[57] One of the many implications of such a structure is the allocation of responsibility for public service provisioning like housing or sanitation to be determined primarily at the local level with auxiliary inputs from the provincial and national governments.[58] Conversely, areas like land reform as well as the provision of social grants are administered by a central authority. This results in a heightened allocation of responsibility, power and competence to a national authority, and lower levels of diffusion. We believe this to be a predictor of the Court's willingness to use invasive remedies. In *Black Sash*, it was the inertia, incompetence and 'extraordinary conduct'[59] of a single federal government agency, SASSA, which precipitated a 'national crisis'[60], that led the Court to order its intrusive remedy. This was also the case in *Mwelase* and *Madzodzo*, where self-standing government departments and their ministers were called to task for their delicts. Therefore, the more clearly identifiable the government department or the source of a delict, the greater the likelihood of an order that is invasive in nature. A guiding principle of this nature may comport with our intuitions about higher courts' deference to local institutions of governance. Yet it risks privileging certain categories as meriting strong judicial intervention into disputes whose origin can be traced back to federal, rather than provincial, government departments.

---

52 In *Meadow Glen Home Owners Association v City of Tshwane Metropolitan Municipality* [2014] ZASCA 209 para 35, this is described as a 'blunt instrument [. . .] to address and resolve complex social problems [. . .] and courts should look to orders that secure on-going oversight of the implementation of the order'.

53 *Mwelase* Con Court (note 1 above) para 77.

54 *Linkside v Minister for Basic Education* [2015] ZAECGHC 36.

55 S Woolman & T Roux 'Co-operative government & intergovernmental relations' in S Woolman & M Bishop (eds) *Constitutional Law of South Africa* (2013).

56 Section 40 of the Constitution.

57 *Cape Metropolitan Council v Minister for Provincial Affairs and Constitutional Development* 1999 (11) BCLR 1229 (T) para 2. Woolman & Roux (note 55 above) 14–10 note that the 'apparent autonomy and independence' of the local government sphere is 'relative and limited by unequivocally expressed constitutional restraints. Its status is, to a large extent, that of a junior partner in the trilogy of spheres that make up the government of the country'.

58 *Grootboom* (note 38 above) paras 39–40, quoted in Woolman & Roux (note 55 above).

59 *Black Sash I* (note 17 above) para 1.

60 Ibid para 51.

- Institutional fit and epistemic superiority – A persistent refrain about the adjudication of questions that involve an element of expertise is that of epistemic uncertainty that inheres in complex social problems. This manifests itself in two ways. The first is the usual practice of superior appellate judicial fora like the Constitutional Court not engaging in fact-finding and leaving such matters to lower courts. The second is the way in which epistemic uncertainty serves to constrain expansive judicial orders due to courts' lack of expertise in technical matters.[61] Both of these factors operate parallelly in the affirmation of the LCC's holding in *Mwelase*. By locating the power granted to the LCC to 'make any order that is just and equitable' and analogising it with its power to strike down a statute on the ground of constitutional invalidity, Cameron J likely sought to limit future application of a remedy that is as invasive as that of the Special Master. The judge insisted that the power 'is no invitation to judicial hubris' but rather 'an injunction to do practical justice, as best and humbly, as the circumstances demand, and that it would be wrong to understate the breadth of these remedial powers'. It is curious that the remedial power of the LCC is located by Cameron J in terms of the provision permitting it to 'conduct any part of any proceedings on an informal or inquisitorial basis',[62] rather than relating it either s 172 of the Constitution, or to the alleged governmental delict of the failure to take a decision as contemplated in terms of s 6(2)(g) of the Promotion of Administrative Justice Act, 2000. We believe this nod to the epistemic superiority of the LCC should be seen as a *diagonal separation of judicial competence*, which serves to both respect the relative expertise of some specialist courts in remedying complex problems, as well as to limit the possible future application of an invasive remedy – unless it is specifically ordered by a specialist court that is set up to deal exclusively with a particular issue (whether or not arising from South Africa's apartheid history).
- Nature and functions of the invasive remedy – The LCC, while granting the remedy of the Special Master, granted it the power to draw up a plan. Such a plan would contain an assessment of claims lodged to date and how many were yet to be processed; available human resources to process such claims; the devising of labour tenant claim-resolution targets; a determination of the budget necessary during each financial year for carrying out the plan; coordination plans to ensure rapid adjudication or arbitration of unresolved claims; as well as a residual power to decide on any other matters that the Special Master may consider relevant.[63] These powers are clearly extensive and fairly unprecedented in South African public law jurisprudence. What is important is that the Special Master would act as an agent of the LCC. Cameron J does not fully engage with the LCC's perfunctory dismissal of the Senior Manager as a possible option for solving the problem of departmental inertia (as averred by the SCA), and it is clear that he believed that there was a breach of the obligation to negotiate in good faith that could have possibly made an internal candidate from within the Department a viable choice. All of this indicates a remedial power that is far greater, including the drawing of budgets, than what the Court was willing to do in *Black Sash*. The panel of experts

---

[61] J King *Judging Social Rights* (2012) 107.
[62] See Restitution of Land Rights Act s 32(3)(b).
[63] *Mwelase* Con Court (note 1 above) para 26.

in *Black Sash* included the Auditor General and suitably qualified independent legal practitioners and technical experts, who would jointly evaluate and report to the Court on SASSA's compliance with the terms of its orders. Similarly, the auditors in *Madzodzo* would evaluate compliance with the terms of the court's orders. The budgetary powers granted to the Special Master are wide-ranging and almost dispositive in nature. It remains to be seen whether future remedial jurisprudence will adhere to this position or whether the dissent by Jafta J in *Mwelase* will prove to be the controlling position.

3. The right to food litigation in India: an equilibrating approach

In the previous section, we identified certain factors that would attenuate the usual separation of powers concerns that accompany the provision of remedies in cases and thus provide nuance to our understanding of the kinds of remedies that the Constitutional Court can be expected to grant in future cases. In this section, we apply these factors to the instance of the *RTF* litigation in India – a case that pushed the envelope for the kinds of things that courts could or could not do. The primary motivation for this is to test the application of our factors, which can be normative in nature, to a case decided by a similar apex court, on an issue with similar underlying structural problems. A secondary motivation is to further extend the lively conversation about the judicial behaviour of apex courts relative to their respective positions in the constitutional scheme with respect to other political actors. This inquiry is methodologically justified to seek answers to the initial research question formulated at the outset of the article, as well as the lower hanging fruit of the *RTF* case having been used as a point of authority in the judgments of the LCC and the Constitutional Court.[64]

3.1 The Supreme Court of India and social rights: a primer

The social rights jurisprudence of the SC of India is somewhat puzzlingly celebrated in the academic literature.[65] This of course might have much to do with an apex court that is not doctrinally bound to any known legal limits in terms of its remedial powers, its feted position in the Indian middle class public imagination, and its pious pronouncements that straddle an incompetent, corrupt bureaucracy on one hand, and a dysfunctional, often gridlocked political system of parliamentary decision-making on the other.

The SC's interventions in the social rights arena have largely been on the basis of public interest litigation (PIL) by strategically placed NGOs,[66] but have been

---

[64] *Mwelase* LCC (note 4 above) para 22; *Mwelase* Con Court (ibid) para 35.

[65] For example, D Bonilla Maldonado 'Introduction: Toward a constitutionalism of the global' in D Bonilla Maldonado (ed) *Constitutionalism of the Global South: The Activist Tribunals of India, South Africa, and Colombia* (2013) 1.

[66] The concept of public interest standing, well known to South African public law in s 38(d) of the Constitution, was relatively alien to Indian litigation practice. It was a judicially led relaxation of standing requirements in *S.P. Gupta v Union of India* that was key to the surge of cases that sought to engage with social and economic deprivation: 'If public duties are to be enforced and social collective "diffused" rights and interests are to be protected, we have to utilise the initiative and zeal of public-minded persons and organisations by allowing them to move the court and act for a general or group interest, even though they may not be directly injured in their own rights.' See *S.P. Gupta v Union of India* AIR 1982 SC 149 para 19.

constrained (until recently) by the lack of judicially enforceable socio-economic rights constitutional provisions[67] or rights-based social welfare legislation.[68] The political environment within which the Court operates has been crucially relevant to its interventions. Previous generations of doctrinal scholars[69] and more recent empirically grounded work[70] have pointed to its early cases in the 1980s as being motivated by a need to 'bury its emergency past',[71] as well as trying to win the support of the 'huge underclass of people for whom the Constitution's promise of social and economic transformation had yet to be made real'. This phase ran between 1980 and 2000, with the court hearing cases involving the rights to work, shelter, health, education and food, while grappling with 'how much deference to grant to the executive and legislative authorities involved, especially on questions of budgetary allocation of funds for particular social rights.'[72] The *RTF* case, which was cited by the LCC in *Mwelase* to derive authority for the appointment of a Special Master, is part of the third phase, where the judiciary is characterised as being 'much more confident about its authority to rule on social rights issues' and being 'deeply immersed in politics'[73]. This consolidation of a democratic instrumentalist understanding of the Court's role has been facilitated through 'public and political acceptance of the Court's interventionist role'[74] and closer attention to 'questions of implementation and monitoring of its orders'.[75]

3.2 The Right to Food *case*

The *Right to Food* was inaugurated through PIL brought by the People's Union of Civil Liberties (PUCL) that had been built on the back of sustained grassroots activism by a number of organisations that had been working on the issue of rural hunger for a number of years.[76] Due to a shortage in rainfall in the 2001–2002 monsoon, there were drought-like conditions in a number of states in the north west of India, despite

[67] The social rights judgments of the Indian Supreme Court have thus far relied on an interpretation of the right to life, combined with a reading of the directive principles of state policy, which are textually unenforceable.

[68] In the period between 2004 and 2014, the Parliament enacted a number of rights-based legislation aimed at securing the rights to education, employment guarantee, food security and information. See generally, J Chiriyankandath, D Maiorano, J Manor & L Tillin (eds) *The Politics of Poverty Reduction in India: The UPA Government, 2004 to 2014* (2020); S Rupareli 'India's new rights agenda: Genesis, promises, risks' (2013) 86 *Pacific Affairs* 569; for an account of judicial treatment of cases brought on the basis of these laws, see G Mukherjee 'The Supreme Court of India and the inter-institutional dynamics of legislated social rights' (2021) 53 *Verfassung und Recht in Übersee* 411.

[69] U Baxi *The Indian Supreme Court and Politics* (1980) 122–123, 233–245; generally, SP Sathe *Judicial Activism in India* (2002); J Cassels 'Judicial activism and public interest litigation in India: Attempting the impossible' (1989) 37 *American Journal of Comparative Law* 495.

[70] T Roux *The Politico-Legal Dynamics of Judicial Review – A Comparative Analysis* (2018) 148–150.

[71] The Emergency was a period of social and political turmoil in Indian politics, with a large number of civil-political rights violations, which was aided by a supine judiciary.

[72] A Thiruvengadam 'Characterising and evaluating Indian social rights jurisprudence into the 21st century' unpublished paper based on a presentation at the Second APU Law and Development Conference held in August 2013 <https://azimpremjiuniversity.edu.in/SitePages/pdf/Characterising-and-evaluating-Indian-social-rights-jurisprudence-into-the-21st-century.pdf>

[73] Roux (note 70 above) 148.

[74] Ibid 149.

[75] Thiruvengadam (note 72 above) 17.

[76] L Birchfield & J Corsi 'Between starvation and globalization: Realizing the right to food in India' (2010) 31 *Michigan Journal of International Law* 691; P Chitalkar & V Gauri 'India: Compliance with Orders on the Right to Food' in M Langford et al (eds) *Social Rights Judgments and the Politics of Compliance: Making It Stick* (2017) 288.

which the state governments had desisted from an official declaration to that effect.[77] The SC of India delivered a judgment in response to a series of petitions[78] by the Peoples' Union of Civil Liberties seeking 'that the right to food should be recognised as a legal right of every person in the country, whether woman or man, girl or boy'.[79] What followed was a series of orders, which were not intended to be completely dispositive of the original petition and the relief sought. Since the Constitution of India does not contain a justiciable right to food, the Court interpreted the right to life[80] in light of the unenforceable, but morally and politically salient[81] directive principles of state policy. The interpretive gymnastics by the SC of India, in respect of the gradual expansion of Article 21 to include a panoply of rights, has not been accompanied by a strong remedial approach that is focussed on the implementation of their judgments, resulting in declarations without a concomitant remedy.[82]

The *RTF* case therefore marked a departure from this standard practice. These orders converted eight federal government-run schemes relating to food, livelihood and social security, into an entitlement. Moving beyond the scope of the original relief sought, one of the orders from the case in 2008 set up a commissionerate 'to track side-by-side hunger and the implementation of interim orders relevant to the *RTF* case across the country'.[83] A commentator, who had been appointed as one of the commissioners in the case, hails it as having 'paved the way for an enforceable right to food for the first time, preventing governments from removing or diluting these schemes, under pressures to reduce fiscal burdens'.[84] Additionally, the orders also set up a monitoring mechanism by appointing a commissioner to oversee the implementation and performance of a number of government schemes. This institutional form consisted of a separate commissionerate, which had its offices within the premises of the SC building, whose officers were tasked with reporting non-compliance with the court. They operated in close cooperation with allies – activists and civil society organisations through the right to food campaign.[85]

---

77 The legal consequences of the declaration of drought are manifold, including the kicking-in of a special emergency legal regime which includes the possibility of greater financial outlays from the Central government as well as dedicated funds from states in the realms of social provisioning. See Ministry of Agriculture, Government of India *Manual for Drought Management* (2009) <http://agricoop.nic.in/sites/default/files/DroughtManual.pdf>

78 *People's Union for Civil Liberties v Union of India* Writ Petition (Civil) No. 196 of 2001 (India).

79 H Mander 'Food from the courts: The Indian experience' (2012) 43 *IDS Bulletin* 17.

80 The Constitution of India, 1949 art 21: 'No person shall be deprived of his life or personal liberty except according to procedure established by law.'

81 T Khaitan 'Constitutional directives: Morally-committed political constitutionalism' (2019) 82 *Modern Law Review* 603, 605.

82 See generally M Tushnet *Weak Courts, Strong Rights: Judicial Review and Social Welfare Rights in Comparative Constitutional Law* (2008).

83 Chitalkar & Gauri (note 76 above) 288, 299: 'The commissioners are empowered to enquire into any violation of the court's orders and to demand compliance. They analyse central and state governments' data to monitor the implementation of various food and employment schemes, receive complaints of non-compliance from grassroots organisations and set up enquiry committees for verification purposes. They also work with governments to address obstacles to implementation.'

84 Mander (note 79 above) 18.

85 S Hertel 'Hungry for justice: Social mobilization on the right to food in India' (2014) 46 *Development and Change* 72.

Over time, the commissioners began to make a number of recommendations that the court sought to impose not only on the federal government, but also on a number of state governments who had been joined to the case. The SC ordered these states to identify 'vulnerable groups under their respective jurisdiction and ensure that these groups are informed as to the way in which their right to food may be satisfied.' Strategic litigation of this kind was only one limb of the organisational matrix of the social movements that coalesced around the case, along with the burgeoning use of a grammar of constitutional rights to articulate demands. The prevailing political climate helped advance the case, with members of opposition parties to the ruling Bharatiya Janata Party coalescing around civil society organisations in support of the cause of ending rural starvation deaths.

It has also been argued that the case 'increased the visibility of civil society groups and their leverage over the state', resulting in their presence becoming stronger and more organised in these sectors.[86] This eventually led to their emergence as a more cohesive force in national political discourse that culminated in their involvement in the framing of the food security law. In this case the Court was able to galvanise both political and civil society around a publicly salient issue, but one which often suffered due to bureaucratic inertia and a legislative blind spot.

This blind spot was addressed by way of the enactment of the National Food Security Act, 2013, which sought to crystallise what had become legal entitlements due to the *RTF* litigation discussed in the previous paragraph. In this way, the set of orders in the *RTF* case show how courts can sometimes be receptive to a popular outcry about crises of maladministration, corruption, or political stasis,[87] especially if the underlying issue has broad national salience.

The *RTF* case is now regarded as a high-water mark for social rights jurisprudence in India and has been a goldmine for the development of comparative law jurisprudence for courts across the world.[88] It has been used as authority for at least three propositions: first, that courts can mould their role conception[89] to that of a catalytic one[90] in certain categories of cases; second, that the *RTF* case exemplifies judicial role that is dynamic in nature, which looks to 'improve the performance of political institutions through time', while remaining unconcerned with the 'classic counter-majoritarian difficulty or the dilemma of courts imposing on democratic space and taking on legislative roles',[91] and third, that it is an example of the court engaged in an exercise

[86] D Landau 'Courts and support structures: Beyond the classic narrative' in EF Delaney & R Dixon (eds) *Comparative Judicial Review* (2018) 226.

[87] RA Kagan, D Kapiszewski & G Silverstein 'New judicial roles in governance' in Delaney & Dixon (ibid) 142; Delaney & Dixon *Research Handbooks in Comparative Constitutional Law* (2018) 144.

[88] See its use by Ncube J and Cameron J in the *Mwelase* judgments.

[89] Role conception places an emphasis of the 'understandings courts have of themselves', where they 'must contend with their own forms of legitimacy, in order to maintain the justification for their ongoing democratic role, adherence to their opinions, and execution of their orders.' K Young *Constituting Economic and Social Rights* (2012) 171, (but also chapter 6, providing examples of courts functioning in a catalytic manner in South Africa, India, and Colombia).

[90] Young (ibid) 173, conceptualises the role as one that tends to 'lower the political energy that is required to change the protection of economic and social rights, or at least the way in which the government responds to the protection of economic and social rights', by seeing itself as being 'in productive interaction with other political and legal actors'.

[91] D Landau 'A dynamic theory of judicial role' (2014) 55 *British Columbia Law Review* 1501.

of 'bounded deliberative democracy', which envisions a role for courts in human rights adjudication that 'strengthens the deliberative potential of democracy, displacing interest bargaining in the context of human rights'.[92]

This is all well and good, until courts that are considered catalytic, dynamic or engaged in bounded deliberative democracy, stop acting the way that they have done in past cases. It is trite to state that courts are not monolithic, they rarely ever speak in one voice,[93] and have almost distinct phases where their approaches to adjudication and the nature and volume of case-law on a given subject matter area vary widely.[94] There is adequate evidence to suggest that the legally unbounded nature of the SC's PIL has been overwhelmingly in favour of business interests over the rights of the poor for which it was originally envisaged,[95] as well as the fact that a large majority of the Court's interventions in the last ten years in the social rights domain had come from the bench of a single judge – Justice Madan Lokur, in a 31-member court.

Courts which look to cases like the *RTF* litigation in India for inspiration or authority for a certain remedial proposition on account of its effectiveness or similar social circumstances should exercise caution, since they often do not appreciate the background political circumstances and the critical mass of cross-class public salience that the issue held at the time when it is decided. This becomes crucial when asking why it is that the remedial innovation witnessed in the *RTF* case has never been replicated in subsequent cases at the Supreme Court of India, despite the persistence of the underlying issues it sought to address.

Therefore, we ask whether the structural and issue-specific factors we identified in the previous section can help us understand the conditions for the interventions of apex courts in a given case and assess convergences and divergences in *Mwelase* and the *RTF* cases. While all of the factors we identified were present in both of these cases, they vary widely. We find *similarities or relative convergences* in the likelihood of compliance, political and electoral salience of issue, the personal conduct of ministerial or government officials, and the systemicity of the problem, there are *dissimilarities or relative divergences* in the litigation history, the degree of harm by non-grant/consequentialism, the clarity of remedial steps, the extent of diffusion of powers/federalism that undergirded the problem, the approaches to the question of institutional fit or epistemic superiority of the courts, and the approaches to nature and functions of the invasive remedy.

3.3 Convergences between Mwelase *and* Right to Food

We have taken pains to establish how courts, beginning from the LCC, right up to the SCA, persistently invoked South Africa's apartheid history and how extensive and effective land reform was key to reconciling with this past. In the *RTF* litigation, the

[92] S Fredman *Comparative Human Rights Law* (2018) 91.

[93] This is especially true for courts like the Supreme Court of India, which does not sit en banc, and the record of which is heavily influenced by the Chief Justice at the time.

[94] See Roux (note 70 above).

[95] A Bhuwania *Courting the People: Public Interest Litigation in Post-Emergency India* (2016); A Bhuwania 'Courting the people: The rise of public interest litigation in post-Emergency India' (2014) 34 *Comparative Studies of South Asia, Africa and the Middle East* 314.

court was entertaining a PIL filed by the PUCL invoking the SC's jurisdiction under art 32 of the Constitution of India to pass orders to the Central and concerned State governments.

Hunger and malnutrition have always been a problem in India,[96] but had rarely been used as a political tool in this way prior to this case. The extensive coverage by the national and local media ensured that the issue became difficult to ignore and non-compliance with court orders was costly for the government. At the time, the political economic landscape of media coverage was also changing, with increased attention to starvation deaths proving to be an uncomfortable truth juxtaposed against international media coverage of India as an emerging economic power.[97] However, until the time when the Congress party (the political opposition) found that it could ally with members of civil society to press the issue of malnutrition deaths in a judicial forum, it was an issue that was relatively underutilised in political discourse. The Congress party, which was campaigning to be re-elected in the national elections in 2004, weaponised the rulings of the Court in the *RTF* case, and included a promise in its manifesto to enact a law on food security if elected.[98] This showed that the SC intervention opened up discursive spaces that could be used by strategically placed civil society and political actors to convert policy issues into a grammar of rights.

The orders of the SC in the *RTF* case display a marked reluctance by the Court to accept that government *compliance* with its orders were likely without the existence of an external monitoring mechanism.[99] This may be on account of systemic failures in the Indian system of public administration of the food distribution system, on account of which the bureaucratic heads of a number of states were joined to the litigation. There is also a marked culture of mistrust that exists between what is seen as an efficient court and a lackadaisical public administration. The likelihood of non-compliance however is not usually seen as being of a personal nature, much like what the Constitutional Court in *Mwelase* emphasises, but representative of a systemic malaise. This leads us to the final convergence between the *RTF* case and *Mwelase* – the question of systemicity, which was a factor in guiding the Court's decision.

3.4 Divergences between Mwelase *and* Right to Food

The consequentialist reasoning that the Constitutional Court in *Mwelase* uses was less on display in the reasoning of the SC of India in the *RTF* case. However, as already discussed, it needed a set of interpretive semantics in order to hold that the right to food was a part of the right to life, as well to convert existing government schemes aimed at alleviating food insecurity into justiciable entitlements. The Court was less clear about the way forward for the implementation of the remedy, after having designed it using a set of prayers advanced by the petitioners, who were themselves grassroots organisations with a sense of what would work. Therefore, unlike the Special Master in

[96] J Dreze 'Democracy and the right to food' (2004) 17 *Economic and Political Weekly* 1723–1731.
[97] Chitalkar & Gauri (note 76 above) 307.
[98] S Friedman & D Maiorano 'The limits of prescription: courts and social policy in India and South Africa' (2017) 55 *Commonwealth & Comparative Politics* 353, 357.
[99] Ibid.

Mwelase, the SC commissioners were not in charge of designing remedies and devising budgetary plans, but rather simply in charge of coordinating across a range of civil society actors and government institutions at the horizontal level in order to ensure compliance with a set of predetermined plans. The question of diffused responsibility in federal systems also assumes importance, since the lack of institutionalised coordinative mechanisms between national, state, and local governments is a persistent problem for welfare delivery systems in India. The Commissioners in the *RTF* litigation were tasked with also being nodal agencies for better coordination.[100] Finally, it is also important to stress that the Court was operating in uncharted waters, without the existence of a legislative framework to guide the question of food security, and was therefore playing a role that was more dialogic in nature and concerned primarily with the implementation of existing discretionary public distribution system entitlements parsed into the idiom of justiciable rights.

3.5 An emboldened court, a government on its back foot: contrasts and similarities

The interventions of an apex court in the remedial domain are heavily tempered by the surrounding social, political, economic circumstances, as well as the kinds of cases that are brought before it by parties, often depending upon their private interests. In the kinds of cases discussed, there is a classic dilemma on display: these individual cases being representative of a deeper underlying systemic problem that is capable of being engaged with through governmental action. In the *Mwelase* case, the occupants of the Hilton College Estate in KwaZulu-Natal sought to draw attention through their case to the larger problem of governmental intransigence in processing land restitution or property rights claims. In the *RTF* litigation, PUCL, which was the main petitioner, sought to draw attention to the feeble federal and state-wise response to the conditions of drought in parts of the country, with a combined focus on the dysfunctional public food distribution system and resultant starvation deaths. The administrative failures in the *RTF* case were addressed by not only an interpretation of the right to life to include a right to food, but also a remedial dimension that was facilitated by the sustained public discourse surrounding starvation deaths around the country.

The remedial oversight mechanism of the commissioners that the SC created as a response to state incapacity was greatly helped by its alliances with civil and political society. Therefore, the precise socio-political moment at which the *RTF* decision was delivered assumes monumental importance to understand why the Court felt comfortable in expending its institutional capital to engage with a cause that had broad public support, but could have opened it up to executive reprisals. At the time, the BJP government was in power as part of a coalition of a number of centre-right parties, and legislative attacks against the court would likely have found few cross-partisan takers.

---

[100] Y Aiyar & A Kapur 'The centralization vs decentralization tug of war and the emerging narrative of fiscal federalism for social policy in India' (2019) 29 *Regional & Federal Studies* 187.

3.6 The risks of unbounded judicial intervention

The *RTF* case represented the zenith of judicial intervention in the field of social rights. Such bold interventions were characterised by remedial innovation that have since disappeared from Indian social rights jurisprudence, despite the continued existence of the kinds of social problems that precipitated them. The SC's recent reticence in intervening into the massive social and economic displacement resulting from the strict lockdown due to the Covid-19 pandemic has been widely criticised.[101] So has its inexplicable zeal in causing a humanitarian crisis of unprecedented proportions with the citizenship registry exercise in the North Eastern Indian state of Assam, where the Court, using the same PIL jurisdiction, passed a number of orders requiring the subnational government to detain persons without identity papers.[102] Both of these actions have drawn widespread criticism, but are a symptom of the SC's telic jurisprudence that has often sacrificed process for outcome – outcomes that often disfavour the vulnerable, but usually prove to be popular among a large majority of Indians today. Perhaps it is best to view the Court's interventions, then, as now, as motivated by a desire to minimise 'confrontations with government, seeking instead to promote dialogues involving itself, government actors, and civil society organisations', while employing a shrewd political strategy of ensuring institutional longevity.[103]

4. Assessing the precedential value of *Mwelase*

4.1 A note on extra-textual factors in constitutional adjudication

Mwelase follows closely on the heels of *Black Sash II*, another major evolution in the Court's remedial jurisprudence. And while *Mwelase* represents no doubt the more intrusive remedy, the tone of the Court in *Black Sash II* was no doubt more cautious. Writing for a practically unanimous court (Madlanga J concurred in the order but reasoned in a somewhat dissenting manner), Froneman J stated that: 'It is necessary to be frank about this exercise of our just and equitable remedial power. That power is not limitless and the order we make today pushes at its limits. It is a remedy that must be used with caution and only in exceptional circumstances. But these are exceptional circumstances. Everyone stressed that what has happened has precipitated a national crisis.'[104]

Curiously in *Mwelase*, the majority downplayed the intrusiveness of its order, emphasising deference to the LCC's expertise in the matter. Yet *Mwelase* is arguably one of the most intrusive orders handed down by the Court to date. Upon the violation of one or more constitutional rights, a court has a range of remedial options available to it to redress such a violation. A separationist – rather than holistic – view of rights categories holds powerful explanatory appeal for the kinds of decisions that the

[101] R Mukherji 'Covid vs. democracy: India's illiberal remedy' (2020) 31 *Journal of Democracy* 91, 99–100.

[102] AP Kumar 'More executive-minded than the executive: The Supreme Court's role in the implementation of the NRC' (2019) 31 *National Law School of India Review* 203.

[103] PB Mehta 'The Indian Supreme Court and the art of democratic positioning' in M Khosla & M Tushnet (eds) *Unstable Constitutionalism: Law and Politics in South Asia* (2016) 234.

[104] *Black Sash I* (note 17 above) para 51.

Constitutional Court has taken to rights questions over the years.[105] Such an approach focuses our attention on *institutions* ('helpful in addressing the "regime" of governance, which ultimately works to realise the right'), the consideration of *bureaucracy and law* ('usually detailed as a regime'), *political leverage* ('the social support structures that buttress claim-making'), the existing *support structures* for rights-based claim making (social movements, cross-class support) and *judicial calculations* in light of fiscal and other pressures. A separationist approach also helps locate the factors we identify in the grant of a remedy within a coherent framework that is attentive to factors that are beyond the scope of legal hermeneutics or constitutional text. These theoretical approaches to the right-remedy gap are largely compatible with a range of theories on the actions of the Constitutional Court, including Theunis Roux's idea of the Court exploiting 'discretionary gaps'[106] in its decisions. There is good reason to believe that the Court engages in a set of calculations about the kind of decision that it takes – avoiding heading in directions that could potentially jeopardise its institutional position in a de-facto single party democracy, or a dominant party democracy.[107] It is also important to remember that the background political conditions within which Roux's theory holds true have been rapidly changing. Between 2004 and 2014, the ANC has witnessed a steady decline in support in both local and national elections.[108] The emergence of the EFF as well as the decline of the organised labour movements like the COSATU[109] has facilitated this process.[110] The behaviour of apex courts under conditions of endemic institutional failure in single party dominant regimes has been adequately, although not exhaustively, theorised.[111] It is generally argued that concerns about the separation of powers, democratic accountability, institutional fit, and popular legitimacy will influence outcomes in particular cases. This would generally imply deference to the coordinate branches of government in cases with an explicitly political nature, with a corollary adoption of a dialogic, cooperative approach to cases that implicate social goods like housing, healthcare, and education.[112] However, this

---

105 KG Young 'The right-remedy gap in economic and social rights adjudication: Holism versus separability' (2019) 69 *University of Toronto Law Journal* 124.

106 T Roux 'Legitimating transformation: Political resource allocation in the South African Constitutional Court' (2003) 10 *Democratization* (2003) 92, 93, where discretionary gaps are defined as 'fissures in the normative structure governing the decision that enabled the court to fashion an outcome in accordance with its sense of the degree of intrusion into politics appropriate to the case concerned'.

107 See generally H Giliomee & C Simkins *The Awkward Embrace: One-Party Domination and Democracy* (1999).

108 M Paret 'Beyond post-apartheid politics? Cleavages, protest and elections in South Africa' (2018) 56 *Journal of Modern African Studies* 471, 473.

109 L Gentle 'What about the workers? The demise of COSATU and the emergence of a new movement' (2015) 42 *Review of African Political Economy* 666.

110 For a recent account of the influence of economic populism on politics inflected with the idiom of constitutional rights, see Roux (note 2 above).

111 S Choudhry '"He had a mandate": The South African Constitutional Court and the African National Congress in a dominant party democracy' (2009) 2 *Constitutional Court Review* 1; R Dixon & S Issacharoff 'Living to fight another day: Judicial deferral in defense of democracy' (2016) *Wisconsin Law Review* 683; D Ma 'Explaining judicial authority in dominant-party democracies: The case of the Constitutional Court of South Africa' (2020) 52 *Comparative Politics* 1, 18.

112 D Landau 'Institutional failure and intertemporal theories of judicial role in the global south' in D Bilchitz & D Landau (eds) *The Evolution of the Separation of Powers Between the Global North and the Global South* (2018) 33; see also A Thiruvengadam 'Revisiting the role of the judiciary in plural societies: A quarter-century retrospective on public interest litigation in India and the global south' in S Khilnani, V Raghavan & AK Thiruvengadam (eds) *Comparative Constitutionalism in South Asia* (2009) 342, 363: 'typically, courts are required to confront the problem of sick, failing, or recalcitrant institutions in PIL cases.'

account does not map on neatly to the actions of the Constitutional Court. For one, disputes that have a political root have found its way into courts[113], replacing, as one commentator put it, 'political warfare' with 'lawfare'.[114] More recently, the Constitutional Court has ruled on the failure of the President to take action on the report of the Public Prosecutor.[115] It is impossible to not note that these judgments have come in the wake of an ANC that is not only electorally weakened, but also dealing with exogenous and endogenous competition with the emergence of the EFF as well as the presence of the 'radical economic transformation' faction within the party.[116] At the heart of these developments in the socio-political realm is the government's perceived failure to address rising inequality, disparities in an already creaking public service provision, as well as youth unemployment and absolute poverty.[117] The question of the slow pace of land reform has been one of the key reasons behind the deafening public discourse and political theatre on the issue of the expropriation without compensation.

How does the current social and political circumstance alter the way in which legal questions on land reform, which are directly linked to socioeconomic rights, are adjudicated? Does the change in circumstances signal a judicial willingness to consider and grant remedies to claimants who can secure their rights more effectively, but can also raise concerns about the separation of powers? We engage with these questions by assessing whether the Special Master remedy represents a natural culmination of the Court's recent remedial jurisprudence as well as its jurisprudence on land reform.

4.2 Subject matter jurisprudential convergence

As hinted at in section 2.1 above, *Mwelase* represents yet another case in which the Court is dealing with the fallout from the wide-ranging failure to enact land reform in a timely manner. Most of these cases deal with unlawful evictions,[118] an area of land law in which individuals enjoy strong judicial protections. Under the less stringent *Grootboom* approach the government enjoys significant leeway in the making of substantive policy choices and as such there has been relatively little litigation on these questions. However, with *Mwelase* we see a case in which the way in which the government implements policy is open to challenge. As such it opens a new chapter in land reform litigation, opening up avenues to enforce rights that were unprotected due to administrative incompetence.

---

[113] Illustratively, see *Glenister v President of the Republic of South Africa* 2011 (3) SA 347 (CC); *Justice Alliance of South Africa v President of the Republic of South Africa; Freedom Under Law v President of the Republic of South Africa* 2011 (5) SA 388 (CC); *Democratic Alliance v President of South Africa* 2013 (1) SA 248 (CC); *Mazibuko v Sisulu* 2013 (6) SA 249 (CC).

[114] DM Davis 'Separation of Powers: Juristocracy or Democracy' (2016) 133 *South African Law Journal* 258, 269.

[115] *Economic Freedom Fighters v Speaker, National Assembly* 2016 (3) SA 580 (CC).

[116] Roux (note 2 above) 6.

[117] Tuovinen (note 47 above) 157.

[118] *City of Johannesburg Metropolitan Municipality v Blue Moonlight Properties 39 (Pty) Ltd* (CC) 2012 (2) SA 104 (CC); *Pheko* (note 41 above).

4.3 Remedial jurisprudential convergence

The Constitutional Court has generally shied away from the use of external actors to oversee implementation of judgments. For instance, while the Court had initially indicated a role for the South African Human Rights Commission to oversee the compliance with its orders in *Grootboom*, it later demurred from entertaining a report by it on account of the doctrine of *functus officio.*[119] More recently, the Court has not shied away from the use of a panel of experts that included the Auditor General and suitably qualified independent legal practitioners and technical experts to jointly evaluate and report to the Court on SASSA's compliance with the terms of its orders to oversee implementation of its remedy in *Black Sash.* Authority for the constitution of such a panel was derived from the *Madzodzo* case,[120] which involved a litigation in the Eastern Cape High Court brought by the LRC against the Department of Education on the severe furniture shortages in public schools across the Eastern Cape. It has been argued that this represents a cross-fertilisation of remedial development across different tiers of the judicial system.[121] However, the remedy in *Mwelase* is markedly different – both in its nature and extent of powers, and should be seen as both a culmination of the Court's willingness to flex its remedial muscles, but also as a departure from its previous position on the judiciary being reluctant to dictate budgetary priorities to an executive authority.

5. Conclusion

In this paper, we pursued three lines of inquiry in answering whether the Court in *Mwelase* provides adequate guidance for a future grant of remedies that are as invasive and that raise as serious questions about the separation of powers as that of the Special Master. The *first* was the factors and conditions, articulated in existing case law and *Mwelase*, about the conditions under which remedial innovations might occur in the future. *Second*, we located the decision in *Mwelase* in a very particular social and political moment. This is a moment in which an assertive court has shaken off some of its doctrinal trappings in the face of an electorally weakened ANC that continues to operate in a dominant party democracy, but may be dependent on popular support for its decision in order to secure greater public legitimacy and safeguard its institutional capital. *Third*, we used the example of the *RTF* litigation in India to compare and contrast the actions of the SC of India and the Constitutional Court of South Africa, both of which use remedial innovations – which border on overreach – in order to address a discursively salient social issue.

Ultimately, we find that the Court is faced with only bad choices. If it does not act boldly, the rights of a great number of persons may go unenforced. And while the Court certainly has the power to craft innovative remedies as we have sought to show, its argumentation in this case was rather lacking. This raises the fear that by being too

---

119 K Pillay 'Implementation of *Grootboom*: Implications for the enforcement of socio-economic rights' (2002) 6 *Law, Democracy and Development* 255.

120 *Madzodzo v Minister of Basic Education* [2014] ZAECMHC 5.

121 See H Taylor 'Forcing the Court's remedial hand: Non-compliance as a catalyst for remedial innovation' (2019) 9 *Constitutional Court Review* 247.

bold the Court will undermine the proper functioning of the separation of powers in the South African state for the foreseeable future. Here we find that the comparison with the SC of India may be helpful. Like its South African counterpart, that court faced difficult cases at a time when other branches of the government were failing their duties. It also remains to be seen whether *Mwelase* might form the halting first steps in inaugurating an era with judicial remedies that are much less tethered to the legalism that has been the prevailing ideology behind judicial decision-making.[122] A recent supervisory order from the North Gauteng High Court[123], imposing a supervisory interdict to ensure the uninterrupted availability of a national school meal program during the COVID-19 pandemic, allays some of the separation of powers concerns associated with such a remedy by deriving authority from *Mwelase*. This could well be evidence of what Roux terms a judicial willingness and capability to drive transformation to new legitimating ideology[124] – a post-liberal South African understanding of separation of powers and the Court's own role in the constitutional scheme. However, this could also raise problems in the long term with judicial intervention compounding the pathologies besetting the administration, while also atrophying bureaucratic will and institutional capacity to be over-reliant on external prodding. In this article we have tried to stake out the two sides of the coin and to explore whether a court positioned like the South African Constitutional Court can walk the tightrope between fulfilling its duties without overstepping its mandate, and without ceding discursive space to those who seek to delegitimise the constitutional project from outside and within.[125]

Acknowledgements

The authors thank Joey Kok, Sanele Sibanda, Renáta Uitz, and the anonymous reviewers, whose comments and assistance were invaluable to this project. All errors remain the authors' own.

Disclosure statement

No conflict of interest was declared by the author(s).

[122] T Roux 'Losing faith in law's autonomy: a comparative analysis' in Delaney & Dixon (note 86 above) 204.
[123] *Equal Education v Minister of Basic Education* (22588/2020) [2020] ZAGPPHC 306.
[124] Roux (note 122 above) 207.
[125] F Venter 'The limits of transformation in South Africa's constitutional democracy' (2018) 34 *South African Journal on Human Rights* 143–166.

Index

Note: Endnotes are indicated by the page number followed by 'n' and the endnote number e.g., 20n1 refers to endnote 1 on page 20.

ad hoc committee 43, 44, 66–9
African National Congress (ANC) 1, 13–14, 58, 109
Albutt vs. Centre for the Study of Violence & Reconciliation 59
AllPay Consolidated Investment Holdings (Pty) Ltd vs. Chief Executive Officer, South African Social Security Agency 46, 86
AllPay I 106–8
anti-ANC 62
anti-democratic 62, 72
apartheid phase 33

Baloro vs. University of Bophuthatswana 35
Bato Star Fishing (Pty) Ltd vs. Minister of Environmental Affairs and Tourism 2004 48n121
Bernstein vs. Bester 1996 48n121
Bhagwati, Prafullachandra Natwarlal 95
Bharatiya Janata Party (BJP) 115, 118
Bhekindlela Mwelase vs. Director-General for the Department of Rural Development and Land Reform 100
Bickel, Alexander 27, 28, 41
Bill of Rights 13, 18, 25, 60
Black Sash II 119
Black Sash Trust vs. Minister of Social Development (Black Sash I) 5, 30, 47, 85–8, 90, 94, 104–6, 110, 111–12
Blue Moonlight Properties 039 (Pty) Ltd vs. the Occupiers of Saratoga Avenue 80
Brown vs. Board of Education of Topeka 81
Budlender, Geoff 79

Cameron, Justice Edwin 101–2, 104, 109, 111
Cash Paymaster Services (CPS) 46, 86
Chaskalson, Arthur 46
civil society organisations 114, 115
Colombia: monitoring institutions in 92–4
Congress party 117
constitutional adjudication 2, 3
Constitutional Court 8, 9, 26–30; *see also* institutional supremacy; democratic mandate 20–3; expert remedial model 85; guardianship of 19–20; judicialisation and 54–6; law-making mandate 25–6; and nascent democracy 57–8; political mandate 23–5; South Africa 10, 57n21, 100, 122; *sui generis* institution 12–16; superior constitutional functions, powers and authority 16–19; and Zuma presidency 59–61
constitutional guardian 19
Constitutional Principle XVIII 15
Constitution Seventeenth Amendment Act of 2012 16
contemporary constitutional theory 10
contributory system 93
cooperative government 110
COSATU 120
course of voting 68
court's supervisory jurisdiction 77
Covid-19 pandemic 1, 108, 123
Criminal Procedure Act 51 of 1977 25

decide controversial political disputes 56
declaratory 69
De Lange vs. Smuts 11–12, 29
democratic accountability 120
Democratic Alliance vs. President of the Republic of South Africa (Democratic Alliance) 59, 64–6, 71
democratic legitimacy 22
democratic phase 33
de Montesquieu, Baron 9–10
Department of Rural Development and Land Reform (DLR) 102
Dicey, A. V. 34
Dixon, Rosalind 81
Dlamini-Zuma, Nkosasana 65–6
Doctors for Life, Soobramoney, Treatment Action Campaign–Jafta J 105
doctrine of legality 36
doctrine of separation of powers 9–12

doctrine of transformative constitutionalism 47
Dube, Felix 2–3
Dugard, John 34
Du Plessis vs. De Klerk 1996 48n121

Eastern Cape High Court 122
Economic Freedom Fighters (EFF) 43, 49, 66, 109, 121; *EFF I* 44, 49, 66; *EFF II* 44, 45, 49, 53, 54, 65, 71–3
Economic Freedom Fighters vs. Public Protector vs. Gordhan 16
Economic Freedom Fighters (Democratic Alliance as Intervening Party) vs. Speaker of the National Assembly (EFF II) 4–5, 36, 52, 90
epistemic superiority 111
esoteric decision-making 5, 53, 54, 63; criticisms of majority judgment 69–70; EFF II 70–4; and EFF II 65–8; judicialisation 62–5
esoteric morality 63
Executive Council of the Western Cape Legislature vs. The President of South Africa 42
executive prerogative 34
expert remedial formulation model 5, 77, 84–5, 98; Constitutional Court 85

federal government-run schemes 114
5th National Policy Conference 53
Food Corporation of India (FCI) 95
Fose vs. Minister of Safety and Security 45–6, 46n106, 50n135
Freedom Charter in 1955 15
functus officio 122

Glenister vs. President of the Republic of South Africa 60–1, 64, 65, 72
Government of the Republic of South Africa vs. Grootboom and Mazibuko vs. City of Johannesburg 85
Grootboom 107, 121, 122

Hamilton, Alexander 28
High Court 17, 18, 80, 82, 83, 95, 96, 107
Hiltonian Society 102
Hirschl, Ran 54
hunger 113, 114, 117

India: convergences, *Mwelase* and *Right to Food* 116–17; divergences, *Mwelase* and *Right to Food* 117–18; KwaZulu-Natal 118; *Right to Food* case 6, 113–16; *Right to Food* litigation 112; risks of unbounded judicial intervention 119; socio-political moment 118; supervisory jurisdiction 95–7; Supreme Court of India and social rights 112–13
institutional fit 111, 120
institutional legitimacy 53n8
institutional security 58
institutional supremacy 8, 9, 30–1; Constitutional Court 26–30; democratic mandate 20–3; guardianship of the constitution 19–20; law-making mandate 25–6; political mandate 23–5; superior constitutional functions, powers and authority 16–19
Interim Constitution 47–8; Constitutional Principle VI 10, 11
Investigating Directorate: Serious Economic Offences vs. Hyundai Motor Distributors 2001 48n121
Issacharoff, Samuel 15, 53, 54, 70

Johannesburg Consolidated Investment Co vs. Johannesburg Town Council 34
judicial calculations 120
judicial dictatorship 20
judicialisation of politics 23, 36, 50, 55, 56; esoteric decision-making 62–5; notion of 36–9; political branches 42–5; politics 54; problematisation of 39–42; in South Africa 42, 54–6; structural interdicts 45–7; transformative constitutionalism theory 47–9
judicial overreach 3, 5, 6, 36, 44, 52, 53, 65, 74, 77, 78, 90, 91, 103
judicial review 2, 5, 12, 14, 15, 22, 28, 38, 39, 41, 42, 53, 54, 59, 79, 80
judicial supremacy 2–3, 9, 31, 37
judicial willingness 55

Kaunda vs. President of the Republic of South Africa 2005 58n27
Klug, Heinz 13, 53
Komape vs. Minister of Basic Education 50n136
KwaZulu-Natal 53, 102

Land Claims Court (LCC) 89, 91, 101, 109, 111, 112, 116, 119
land reform 91, 97, 101, 106–10, 116–17, 121
Land Reform (Labour Tenants) Act 3 of 1996 (LTA) 88–9, 100–1, 103
Lazari-Radek, Katrzyna 63
Lemieux, Scott 28
Liebenberg, Sandra 79
Limpopo Department of Education 82
Lingwood vs. Occupiers of R/E ERF 9 Highlands 83
Linkside 110
Locke, John 9–10

macro-political ramifications 4
Madzodzo vs. Minister of Basic Education 82, 110, 112
Makama, Saul 97
Makwanyane 28, 106
malnutrition 117
Maphosa, Ropafadzo 5
Mendes, Conrado Hubner 53
Mhango, Mtendeweka 47
Michelman, Frank 26
Minister of Health vs. Treatment Action Campaign (TAC) 57, 78–9
Motala, Ziyad 61
Mukherjee, Gaurav 5

Mwelase case 92, 94, 101–2, 109, 110, 113, 116–19, 121; extra-textual factors in constitutional adjudication 119–21; invasive remedies 105–12; jurisprudential convergence 121; Land Claims Court 102–3; remedial jurisprudential convergence 122; SCA 103–4; SCA judgment 104–5
Mwelase vs. Director-General for the Department of Rural Development and Land Reform 5, 85, 88–92

National Assembly (NA) 30, 43–5, 49–50, 66, 68
National Food Security Act, 2013 115
National Prosecuting Authority Amendment Act 60
Ndlwana vs. Hofmeyr 34–5
New National Party of South Africa vs. Government of the Republic of South Africa (NNP) 58, 62
non-grant/consequentialism 106
North Gauteng High Court 123
Nyane, Hoolo 3

Obligatory National Health Plan 93
Okpaluba, Chuks 47

Parliament 8, 26, 27, 30, 34, 36, 52
parliamentary sovereignty 34
People's Union for Civil Liberties vs. Union of India (Right to Food case) 95
People's Union of Civil Liberties (PUCL) 95, 96, 113, 114, 116–18
Pheko vs. Ekurhuleni Metropolitan Municipality 45, 77
political cases 54
political considerations 63
political leverage 120
political question doctrine 4
popular legitimacy 120
public administration 42
public interest litigation (PIL) 112–13, 115, 116–17, 119
Public Protector 43
PUCL vs. Union of India 97

radical economic transformation 121
recalcitrant administration 5
Restitution of Land Rights Act 22 of 1994 103
Right to Food (RTF) 101–2, 117; litigation 112
Roach, Kent 79
Roux, Theunis 53–4, 70

salience 107–8
Section 27 vs. Minister of Education 82
Seedorf, Sebastian 11
Sheela Barse vs. State of Maharashtra 95
Sibanda, Sanele 11
Sibiya vs. Director of Public Prosecutions: Johannesburg High Court 105–6
Singer, Peter 63
social grant payments system 86
socio-economic rights 36, 49, 76–8, 81, 82, 87, 95, 97, 98, 107, 112–13
South Africa 20, 21, 30, 31, 35, 36, 42, 46, 48, 49, 53, 54, 58, 77, 80, 81, 101, 106, 109; structural interdicts 78–9
(*see also* structural interdicts)
South African Social Security Agency (SASSA) 46, 47, 49, 86–8, 108, 110, 112, 122
Speaker of the Senate vs. Attorney General 3 48n123
Special Master 6, 90–2, 101–5, 107, 109, 111–13, 117–18, 121, 122
Special Master of Labour Tenants 90
structural interdicts 5, 18, 30, 36, 50, 77, 89, 98; enforcement of 45–7; models of 81–5; socio-economic rights cases 79–81; in socio-economic rights cases 79–81; in South Africa 78–9
Sturm, Susan 84
sui generis institution 2, 8, 19, 21
supervisory jurisdiction 5, 45, 77, 79–80, 86, 91, 107, 108; in India 95–7
supplementary affidavits 67
Supreme Court of Appeal (SCA) 90, 101, 111, 116
Supreme Court (SC) of India 95, 101, 116; and social rights 112–13
S vs. Makwanyane 25, 42
systemicity 107–8

T-760 case 93, 94
Thompson, Dennis 64
time-honoured principles 4
Tuovinen, Juha 5
Tushnet, Mark 79
tutelas 92–4

ultra vires (the doctrine that power *(vires)*) 34
United Democratic Movement vs. Speaker of the National Assembly 65

van der Schyff, Gerhard 14
Venter, Francois 14
Viljoen, Sue-Mari 97

Watkins, David 28

Zondo Commission 1–2
Zuma, Jacob 24, 65